Modern
English
Linguistics

A Structural and
Transformational
Grammar

Modern English Linguistics

A Structural and Transformational Grammar

John P. Broderick

University of South Florida

Thomas Y. Crowell
HARPER & ROW, PUBLISHERS
New York Philadelphia San Francisco London

For Carol and Julie

MODERN ENGLISH LINGUISTICS: A Structural and
Transformational Grammar

Copyright © 1975 by Harper & Row, Publishers, Inc.

Published simultaneously in Canada by
Fitzhenry & Whiteside, Ltd., Toronto.

Library of Congress Cataloging in Publication Data

BRODERICK, JOHN P.
    Modern English Linguistics.

    Bibliography: p.
    Includes index.
    1. English language—Grammar, Generative. I. Title.
PE1112.B716   1975   425   74-20928
ISBN 0-690-00067-7

Preface

TO THE STUDENT

This book contains no chapter attempting to persuade you that the study of the English language is interesting, or enjoyable, or even relevant. Such a chapter could have little effect on your decision to pick up the book in the first place and so would waste space. You probably have the book in hand because you are enrolled in a course which uses it. And you are enrolled because you have been required to or because the course has a good reputation. A course's reputation can derive from the course text, but it rarely does. Good reputations derive more often from good teachers. My hope, as the author of this book, is that good teachers can use it. My conviction is that, in the hands of a good teacher, the content itself will convince you in the doing that it merits your time and effort. Hopefully, you will find yourself fascinated by the material—perhaps scratching your head and wondering why, because on the surface the subject matter is dry. If it does interest you, this is because you are not really studying something out there—as you do in chemistry, or physics, or even biology (as fashionable as ecology is)—you are in fact studying and learning about yourself.

TO THE TEACHER

Chapters 2 through 10 are generally inductive: facts and examples precede generalizations and definitions where possible. When general concepts are presented, explicit discussion of theoretical controversies is avoided. But the price of the inductive orientation on the one hand and the polemical calm on the other is a relatively abstract and deductive first chapter. Few students will derive full benefit from one reading of the introductory chapter. You should probably emphasize this to them and recommend that they reread it occasionally as they learn their way through the other chapters. You may even choose to begin the course with the second chapter and assign the first one when you think sufficient groundwork has been laid. However, I recommend assigning and re-assigning the first chapter from the outset so that the conceptual framework it provides can lend added coherence to the details treated in later chapters, and these in turn can lend depth of insight to later readings of the introduction.

TO THOSE WHO HELPED

Each of the following persons has contributed in a special way to my work on this book: Michael Squires, Wilson Snipes, Edwin Robinson, Roger Cole, Robert O'Hara, Herbert J. Addison, Herman Makler, Coral Tysliava, Robert E. Callary, Brenda Griggs, and Sharon Broyles. I thank them all most sincerely. This is a better book because they helped, and would probably be even more improved if I had made full use of their kind assistance. What weaknesses remain are my own doing. Next I thank the nearly two dozen groups of students whose inquisitiveness, frustration, and even tears, but most especially whose patience helped me during a four-year period to adapt and relate highly abstract and sometimes diffuse materials to their needs. I wish also to thank David P. Harris, who over the years has been to me a model of the careful and thorough scholar. If these qualities are at all present in this book, they are there because he taught me them. Finally, and most importantly, I thank my wife, Carol. Only she can know how important a role she has played in bringing this work to completion.

J.P.B.

Contents

Chapter 1
Introduction

This book is about the English language. It devotes several chapters to word formation and sentence formation in contemporary American English and one chapter each to the meaning and sound systems of English. Sentence and word structure are emphasized not because they are more important than meaning or sound in English, but rather because they have traditionally been emphasized in the undergraduate English curriculum, where a one-term course usually studies "advanced grammar" or "modern grammar," treating word formation (**morphology**) and sentence formation (**syntax**) rather than meaning (**semantics**) or sound (**phonology**). Because of this tradition and because one term is barely adequate for significant work even with English syntax, there are seven chapters here devoted to morphology and syntax, and only one each for semantics and phonology. Nonetheless, the latter two chapters are substantive introductions to these areas of English linguistics.

Although the emphasis in this book derives from the tradition of grammar study, the method of presentation is taken from scientific linguistics, which provides dynamic procedures for investigating and organizing the facts of English. Linguistic methods can make the task of learning English grammar less trying, and perhaps even enjoyable. And since most active research in English grammar and language structure is the work of scientific linguists, this book will prepare you to read, understand, evaluate, and maybe even begin to contribute to this research.

I hope to present the facts of English clearly and coherently and may occasionally sacrifice some details on the altar of clarity, or come near to committing linguistic heresy in the name of coherence. But I never distort the facts. Whenever possible, you will observe and relate facts of English before you learn terms and definitions. When definitions need to be presented first, these appear in a context of practical analysis. My ultimate objective is to have you develop an ability, when you hear some grammatical term, to think of an example rather than a definition, and when you encounter an example word, or phrase, or sentence, to learn to relate it to other examples rather than label it or remember some definition of it.

Since my aim is to help you study English, using linguistics, I shall not, in the body of the book, explicitly discuss linguistic schools and theoretical controversies among linguists. However, it is appropriate to discuss them briefly here in the introduction, since this book draws on the findings of two conflicting schools of thought: American Structural Linguistics and Generative-Transformational Linguistics. To understand how we can base a coherent examination of the structure of English on theoretical systems considered by many linguists to be incompatible, we will first examine the nature of empirical scientific inquiry and then compare and evaluate the two schools.

EMPIRICAL SCIENTIFIC METHOD

In this book linguistics is taken to be an empirical science. But what does it mean to claim that an area of intellectual inquiry is an **empirical science?** At least four criteria apply: (1) the inquiry must treat *perceivable* phenomena; (2) it must result in *objective* statements about the phenomena; (3) these statements must be *systematically ordered;* (4) the statements must be *logical.*

Perceivable phenomena act upon the senses: they are seen, heard, touched, tasted, or smelled. They are by definition outside the mind, and by implication measurable in some way. But it is not enough for a scientist to see, hear, touch, taste, or smell for his labors to constitute part of an empirical inquiry; he must write down his perceptions or, in some other way, make *objective* statements to give them an independent existence. (Had Newton thought of but never communicated his observations about the physical universe, he could not have fathered classical physics.) But not just any statement based on sense perception qualifies as part of an empirical inquiry. Only statements of the following systematically ordered types qualify: (1) observations, (2) hypotheses, (3) laws, and (4) theoretical statements.

Observations describe specific facts. A chemist might write: "One cc from this bottle of blue liquid which I mixed today with one cc from this bottle of yellow liquid resulted in exactly these two ccs of green liquid." The words *this* and *these* refer to specific entities the chemist is looking at. He might also record the temperature in the room, the barometric pressure, even the elevation of his laboratory above sea level, or even use instruments to measure the spectral components of the light reflected from the liquids, just to be sure he perceived the colors accurately. A psychoanalyst's scientific observations might record the exact words a patient used at a specific time on a specific date to describe his dreams. An economist's empirical observations might include lists of food prices in a particular store on a given date, and copies of paycheck stubs issued at noted times and places.

An inquiry takes on the systematic order of an empirical science when an investigator, carefully examining and comparing his observations, formulates a different kind of statement: a **hypothesis**. Hypotheses do not directly describe specific facts; they are general statements expressing relationships among observed phenomena. The chemist, after making the observation described above, may mix two ccs of blue liquid with two of yellow and obtain four of green, and then three with three, obtaining six, and so on, until he is led to formulate a hypothesis like the following: "When equal parts of any amounts of certain types of blue and yellow liquid are mixed, the result is a green liquid exactly twice the volume." The psychoanalyst, having interviewed many patients, all of whom reported dreaming, might hypothesize that all humans can have dreams. The economist, having carefully compared his dated paycheck stubs and dated price lists, might formulate a hypothesis that as wages go up, prices go up.

In an empirical inquiry, hypotheses function as guiding principles for making further observations. That is, even though hypotheses logically follow observations in the practice of empirical science, they always give rise to further observations, which in turn may lead to revisions in the hypotheses, and so the cycle goes. For example, a chemist, having formulated the hypothesis quoted in the previous paragraph, might want to make further observations to test it. He may want to mix the blue and yellow liquids in different proportions to determine if a different color liquid results, or even to find out if the result will still be a liquid. Often enough a chemist will mix two liquids and produce a gas—or a solid. Thus most observations in an empirical inquiry are made for the purpose of testing hypotheses.

If, after a reasonable amount of investigation, a hypothesis is confirmed by all the scientist's observations and not falsified by any, then the hypothesis achieves the status of a **law**. Whereas observations and hypotheses differ in the way they are worded, hypotheses and laws are worded exactly alike: both are generalized statements which express relationships among observations. Hypotheses and laws differ in the relative amount of observation supporting them. Thus the chemist's claim that the green liquid will always result when equal parts of the blue and yellow liquids are mixed becomes a law if hundreds of observations using different amounts but equal proportions always produce the expected result, and if no observations contradict the hypothesis. If, however, even one observation contradicts a hypothesis, then the hypothesis cannot be a law. Suppose, for instance, even after years of observation, and even after the composition of the green liquid had long been considered a matter of empirical law, a chemist mixed 3,000 liters of the blue liquid and 3,000 of the yellow and the result was 5,000 liters (not the expected 6,000) of a turquoise liquid (not the expected green). He would first carefully check to be sure he had not made a procedural or observational mistake. But if the same result persisted in repeated experiments, the "law" would need revision. Additional experimentation might reveal that the previous ratio holds up to a certain volume, say 1,000 liters each of blue and yellow liquids, but not above it. This, then, is a new hypothesis, and extensive testing by further observation might establish it as a law.

Thus an empirical inquiry requires the formulation of statements which describe specific observed phenomena, but these observations are made with a view to formulating hypotheses, which in turn guide the investigator to make further observations aimed at verifying the hypotheses. And after a reasonable amount of verification, hypotheses achieve the status of empirical laws. This, in part, is what is meant by the third criterion of an empirical inquiry: that its statements are *systematically ordered.*

Notice that, even though hypotheses and laws are general statements, the terms used in them correspond to observed phenomena. The chemist's hypothesis, for example, while referring to "any amounts" and "a green liquid," remains a statement about the same perceived entities referred to in his observations. However a fourth type of statement is common in empirical science: the **theoretical statement.** But it differs from all three other types of statements. A theoretical statement is more than a descriptive generalization of observations. It does not *describe,* rather it attempts to *explain,* to give reasons for, observed phenomena and the relationships among them. The terms in theoretical propositions do not usually correspond to any observed phenomena. Thus the chemist, having formulated observations, hypotheses, and laws like those we have discussed, will then formulate statements for the purpose of explaining these observations, hypotheses, and laws. In this new type of statement he uses terms like *atom, atomic nucleus, proton, neutron, electron, electron ring, valence,* none of which he has observed. The same is true of the psychoanalyst: his observations, hypotheses, and laws all refer to statements he has heard his patients make about dreaming. But to explain such experiences, he uses terms like *subconscious mind, ego, id,* which do not, even as generalizations, correspond to anything he has observed about his patients. And the same is true of the economist. His observations, hypotheses, and laws mention prices and wages. But when he explains the interrelation of prices and wages by using a term like *inflation,* he is no longer simply generalizing about perceivable phenomena. He is attempting to explain these phenomena.

Theoretical statements can be viewed as hypotheses of a different sort. They usually introduce terms, like those in the previous paragraph, which name entities that are not observed to exist, but which, if they did exist, would explain what is observed. Theoretical statements are therefore, by definition, not verifiable in an experimental sense. Yet we call them empirical scientific statements because empirical science is as much rooted in *logic* as it is in experimentation. (This is the fourth criterion of science.) Empirical scientific method seems to be a function of the way the human mind works. If the investigator did not intuitively conceptualize (categorize), science would not exist. Science seems to presuppose a certain structure of mind. Flashes of insight in the initial stages of a scientific inquiry—where the first tentative hypotheses are drawn from the first few observations—happen because the mind of the investigator is disposed to notice and to categorize relationships. Theories are possible because the human mind functions logically. Science is possible because logical processes are seemingly invariable and inherent to all human intelligence. However, the logician's quest for definite knowledge about these processes is much like that of a dog chasing its tail. (How can human intelligence succeed in explaining the very processes used in exercising intelligence?) This paradox accounts for the great controversies in the history of every science and the constant competition among theories in the empirical sciences. Scientific theories are accepted only to the extent that they appeal to the mind of the investigator.

Since logic attempts to make explicit the processes of human thought and judgment, it is only by appeal to logical principles that scientific theories can be compared and evaluated. The following are three logical criteria often employed in evaluating theoretical statements: (1) **adequacy**, (2) **generality**, and (3) **simplicity**. A theoretical statement is *adequate* to the extent that it applies to all the known data which it is established to explain. It is *general* insofar as it posits entities beyond observed phenomena, and can therefore apply to the greatest amount of yet undiscovered data. Simplicity is an internal criterion: a set of theoretical terms and statements fulfilling the conditions of adequacy and generality but containing fewer terms and no internal contradictions is *simpler*.

Adequacy and generality are competing evaluative criteria. Adequacy requires a theory to be true to the facts as expressed in observations, hypotheses, and laws, but generality calls on a theory to be imaginative. If a theory is adequate but not general, it will do little more than paraphrase laws. If it is general but not adequate, it is fantasy. A chemical theory lacking some notion of valences and therefore ignoring the fact that elements combine with other elements would be grossly inadequate: it might explain the differences in size, weight, and shape of isolated elements, but it would ignore a major portion of the chemist's data—his observations, hypotheses, and laws describing chemical reactions. On the other hand, a chemical theory that explained both the structure of elements and the interaction of elements, but only in terms of weights and volumes of "solids," "liquids," and "gases," would not be very general because the terms are merely labels for observed phenomena. In fact, the history of atomic theory provides us with an excellent example of just what generality entails. When electrons were first posited as particles of matter they were inventions of scientific theoretical imagination—they contributed to· the generality of the formulation. Subsequent research, mainly through the use of refined equipment, has found observable evidence for electrons—that is, where atomic theory once predicted a certain number of electrons in a certain atom, the predicted number has been evidenced by such observable phenomena as markings on photographic plates.

For any given collection of observations, hypotheses, and laws, there are many alternative theoretical explanations of them that are both adequate and general. For this reason, the third evaluative criterion—simplicity—usually plays the decisive role in determining which of two competing theoretical explanations is preferred. Let us leave chemistry and look to astronomy for a classic example of the role of simplicity. Astronomers for centuries observed the movement of the planets. They never observed any movement of the earth. They recorded their observations, formulated hypotheses, and established laws about the positions and movements of the planets. Eventually, they formulated a theory that the planets were spheres that moved through space in epicyclic paths relative to the earth: the planets revolved about the sun, which revolved about the earth, whose position was fixed. Such a theory was adequate because it predicted the position of each planet at any given time. It was general because it imaginatively proposed that the planets were spheres in motion in space. (From observation, they could as well be two dimensional surfaces moving on a curved plane—an earlier theory.) Later, during the Renaissance, Copernicus proposed a theory claiming that the earth, too, was a sphere in motion, that the sun was fixed, and that the earth revolved in a circular orbit around it. His theory was adequate because it correctly predicted the positions of the planets. It was also general (imaginative): it not only accepted the imaginative proposals of the earlier theory, but it further claimed that the earth was a sphere in motion—a proposal not reinforced by observation. So both theories were adequate and general. Why was Copernican theory eventually accepted? Because it was *simpler*. Its simplicity lay in the fact that a system of concentric circles is more appealing to the human imagination—and easier to draw—than a system of epicycloids. Rigorously scientific arguments for the greater simplicity of Copernican theory take the form of long and complex mathematical equations showing that fewer and shorter formulas are needed to plot the paths of the planets if they revolve concentrically about a mid point than if they move in epicycles. But whether we appeal to our perceptual preference for concentric circles, or the mathematician's ease in plotting them, the Copernican view of the universe was simpler, and it was for this reason that it supplanted the earlier theory.

Linguistics has only recently used the methodology of empirical science to study human languages. Consequently, there are perhaps half a dozen fully developed competing theories of language in the world today, each of which aims to explain what linguists have observed about language. Our examination of the grammar of English will draw on the findings—observational and theoretical—of *two* such theories: American Structural Linguistics and Generative-Transformational Linguistics. I have two reasons for selecting them: (1) both have been applied to the detailed analysis of American English, and thus provide us with much factual information about it, and (2) both have significantly influenced materials and curricula in elementary and secondary schools in the United States. Since most readers of this book are preparing to teach English, a thorough knowledge of these two theories of language can make it possible to evaluate materials and curricula claiming to be linguistically based, and to use them effectively if indeed they are.

AMERICAN STRUCTURAL LINGUISTICS

The seeds of modern scientific linguistics in the United States were sown early in the twentieth century by two men: Edward Sapir and Leonard Bloomfield. Both were trained in studying the historical development of European languages. However, each man acquired another interest which, when combined with his training in the historical study of languages, provided the initial insights that were ultimately to foster the full blossoming of American Structural Linguistics. Sapir's other interest was anthropology; Bloomfield's was behaviorist psychology. Sapir's inclinations toward anthropology led him to an intense interest in American Indian languages. One of his earliest discoveries was that few traditional grammatical terms were relevant to the study of these exotic languages. Furthermore, he realized that many of these languages were rapidly becoming extinct. Thus faced with the need of developing a new descriptive method for analyzing these languages, he was motivated by a practical sense of urgency, rather than by theoretical considerations. Bloomfield was less practically motivated. He was interested in establishing linguistics as an empirical science, and he saw in behaviorist psychology an approach that could provide the means for doing so. For Bloomfield, language was a set of signals emitted in response to stimuli, and the scientific study of language was the study of the signals, since only these seemed to him to meet the empirical criterion of observability. Scientific linguistics, he held, should not concern itself directly with what there is to signal (with meaning), nor with how it is possible for humans to signal (with theories of mind).

Partly because of the concern for analyzing American Indian languages, and partly because of language-learning demands brought on by the Second World War, American Structural Linguistics became centrally concerned with practical linguistic description. Only peripherally did it extend and evaluate explicitly Bloomfield's theoretical proposals. But American structuralists followed Bloomfield, and interpreted very literally the dictum that an empirical science studies perceivable phenomena outside the mind. For descriptive purposes, a language was defined as a given collection of language signals, called a **corpus**. The linguist sat down with a speaker of a language and recorded his statements on a tape recorder or transcribed them in phonetic notation. He ignored any opinions the speaker had about the structure of the language. Later, in the absence of the speaker, the linguist would analyze his corpus. This analysis consisted of classifying and labeling various elements in the corpus at several levels. A linguistic corpus was considered to have a level of **phonological** structure, a level of **morphological** structure, and a level of **syntactic** structure. When all elements of the corpus were grouped and labeled at each level, the grammar of the language was complete.

We will examine the analytical methods of American structuralism in greater detail in chapters 2 and 3, but let me briefly illustrate them here. Imagine that an American structural linguist has interviewed a speaker of American English and recorded several hours of conversation. Assume, further, that the sentence in 1.1 is part of the recorded material. We write the sentence here according to the conventions of the English spelling system (its **orthography**). However, the linguist does not analyze the spelled sentence but a recording of the spoken sentence. Read the sentence aloud a few times and listen closely to how it sounds.

1.1 Tom needed two buses, but his wife's stupid brothers delivered a boat.

A careful phonetic transcription of 1.1 will record that the initial consonant sound of *Tom* (spelled *t*) is not exactly the same as the second consonant sound of *stupid* (also spelled *t*), and both of these are different from the final consonant sound of *boat* (likewise spelled *t*). All three sounds involve contact of the front part of the tongue with the ridge behind the upper teeth, but in *Tom* this contact is followed by an extra puff of air. There is no such puff of air following the contact of the tongue in *stupid*. And *boat* differs from the other two in that the tongue makes contact and remains in contact with the ridge behind the upper teeth even as the mouth closes to signal that the message has ended. Since the analyst wants to identify those elements of sound structure that play a role in the communication system of a language, he must carefully note distinctions like these. But, as he examines other portions of his corpus— making observations, formulating and testing hypotheses—he notices some general tendencies:

1.2a The final sound of *boat,* where the tongue remains in contact with the ridge behind the upper teeth, always occurs at the end of a statement when the speaker has finished what he had to say.
b The second sound of *stupid* always occurs between an "*s*-like" sound and a vowel.
c The initial sound of *Tom* occurs in contexts other than the previous two.

Using observations like those in 1.2, the analyst can establish a sound category in his grammar. Membership in the category derives both from the affirmative criterion that all the member sounds are pronounced by placing the front of the tongue in contact with the ridge behind the upper teeth, and the negative criterion that whatever differences there are between the sounds are insignificant and predictable. One practical consequence of establishing such a sound category is that an alphabet for English can use the same letter—as it does use the letter *t*—for all three sounds. The speaker of English knows as a matter of principle to pronounce the letter *t* one way at the end of a sentence, another way after *s* and before a vowel, and yet a third way in other sound contexts; thus there is no need to remind him of these differences by using three letters instead of one. Any such sound category, which groups similar sounds whose slight differences are predictable, is called a **phoneme.** When all the phonetic elements in a corpus are so grouped and an inventory of phonemes established, then the analysis is complete at the level of **phonology.**

Now, read 1.1 aloud again, this time paying careful attention to the pronunciation of *needed* and *delivered.* Remember that the American structural linguist ignores spelling and bases his analysis on pronunciation. Let us suppose that somewhere else in his corpus the verbs *need* and *deliver* occur, and that the analyst is able to determine that *need* and *needed* mean the same thing except that *needed* also communicates the notion of 'past time'. He likewise notices that the same relation holds between *deliver* and *delivered.* He first concludes that the idea of 'necessity' is communicated by *need* and the idea of 'bringing' by *deliver.* Next he concludes that the sounds appended to *need* and *deliver,* respectively, must embody the notion of 'past time'. But he notices that both a vowel and a consonant sound, *ed,* are added to *need* when it communicates the idea of 'past time', but only a consonant sound, *d,* is added to *deliver* when it communicates the idea of 'past time'. (This is not apparent from the spelling, but notice that the final letter *e* of *delivered* is silent.) The fact that the pronunciations *ed* and *d* both mean the same thing ('past time') is a reason to put them together into one meaning category. But this can be done effectively only if some principle can be found which predicts when each pronunciation is used. Careful analysis of a large corpus of English reveals (1) that 'past time' is signaled by *ed* when this meaning category is affixed to a verb ending in a *t* or *d* sound and (2) that only a consonant sound (usually *d,* but sometimes *t*) is appended when a verb ends in other sounds. Thus the structural linguist establishes a meaning category, called a **morpheme,** which groups together all sounds or combinations of sounds having the meaning 'past time'. When all meaningful elements in the corpus are grouped and an inventory of morphemes established, then the analysis is complete at the level of **morphology.**

Now, consider the partial sequence from 1.1, *Tom needed two buses.* This is a sentence. But the sequence in 1.3, containing the same meaningful elements, is not a sentence:

1.3   buses two Tomed need.

To describe the principles whereby 1.1 occurs in his corpus but 1.3 is excluded, the analyst takes note of facts like the following:

1.4a Certain meaningful elements, for example, *wife, brother, bus,* and *boat,* have *s* or *es* appended to them with the meaning 'more than one'; other elements, for example, *but, a, his, need,* and *deliver* do not.

b Many of these same elements, for example, *wife, brother*—and also *Tom*—can have *'s* appended to them with the meaning 'owns' or 'possesses'.

c Most of these same meaningful elements follow elements like *his, two,* and *a* in the corpus, but other elements, for example, *deliver* and *but* do not.

Observations like those in 1.4 lead the analyst to group *Tom, wife, brother,* and *boat* into a syntactic category based on the positions they occupy in the corpus relative to the positions of other meaningful elements. The category we are discussing is of course the class of nouns. The class of verbs is similarly defined—verbs occur in the corpus with the *ed* of 'past time' appended to them, and with the *ing* of the present participle, as in *delivering* and *needing;* elements like *wife, but, a* do not. American structural linguists call categories like nouns and verbs **form classes.** When all elements in a corpus are grouped into form classes, and when the principles of sentence structure are stated in terms of form-class sequences, the analysis is complete at the level of **syntax.**

The above brief demonstration of American structural analysis was presented just to give you a feeling for its method. The various concepts and technical terms will all be treated in greater detail later in this book. The discussion also serves as a guide to which portions of the book are based on American Structural Linguistics.

GENERATIVE-TRANSFORMATIONAL LINGUISTICS

In the early 1950s, when American Structural Linguistics was flourishing, Noam Chomsky was finishing graduate work. He refused to accept the structural axioms that a language was to be equated with a corpus in hand and that a grammar was a classification of the corpus. So he began to reformulate questions about language which had lain dormant for many years and which were thought to have been permanently put to rest by Bloomfield: questions about what it is that is coded into phonetic sequences (meaning), and about the nature of man's faculty to do such encoding (the nature of mind).

Chomsky's early work was a critical evaluation of American structuralist assumptions and methods. But he also extended the notion of empirical linguistic data and thus opened up new areas of inquiry which called for a much more imaginative theory of language than American structuralism was able to provide. In this section I present some of the arguments, mostly from the work of Chomsky, which led to the establishment of Generative-Transformational Linguistics.

Consider the American structuralist's notion of a language and his procedure for linguistic analysis. To the structuralist, a language *is* the corpus of data. When the corpus has been classified, the language is considered to be analyzed and its grammar written. But when this is done, even a child might say and understand things that are neither included in the corpus nor accountable for under any of the classifications derived from analysis of the corpus. This would be true even if—by some miracle—the structural analysis were based on a corpus containing every word of English that had ever been spoken or written.

It is not an exaggeration to say that virtually everything we say or hear is new, especially if we consider the total context of discourse. For example, the words in this paragraph have been used before. Likewise many of the phrases. However, most of the sentences have never been written or read before by anyone. And the paragraph as a whole most certainly has not. Yet I had little difficulty writing these sentences, and you are having little difficulty understanding them.

This fact, which we can call the innovative or creative aspect of language use, is of primary concern in Generative-Transformational Linguistics. A user of English could, if he lived long enough, formulate and understand a potentially infinite number of sentences. Furthermore, he is capable of formulating and understanding sentences of potentially infinite length, sentences such as these:

1.5a Mary gave the book to John, who gave it to Helen, who gave it to my friend, who gave it to the teacher, who gave it to Joe, who gave it to Albert, who gave it to his mother . . . .

b He is the man who wrote the book which won the prize which was donated by Mr. Smith, who was born in Calcutta, which is a large city which is located in India, where my father met Ghandi, who . . . .

No one ever will formulate an infinite number of sentences. Nor will anyone ever formulate a sentence of infinite length. But, because users of a language are potentially able to do so, the number of sentences and the length of sentences in a language is as infinite as anything in the physical world can be. Therefore, a language cannot be described fully by describing any finite number of sentences in it—by describing any corpus of data.

How then can we describe a language? We can do it by describing what the user possesses enabling him to produce and understand an infinite number of sentences, each one of potentially infinite length.

Because the human brain is finite in size and finite in capacity, generative-transformational linguists assume that the user of a language must possess a finite amount of knowledge with which he can produce an infinite number of sentences. Hence the term **generative.**

The language is defined as any and all outputs of this generative knowledge. The grammar of the language is a description of this knowledge (rather than of any corpus of utterances that are outputs of it). By describing this generative knowledge, the grammarian is describing all possible sentences.

This knowledge or generative capacity of the user of a language is referred to as **linguistic competence** and is distinguished from **linguistic performance.** The assumptions which underlie the distinction between competence and performance are these: the user of a language possesses a firm knowledge of the structure (generative system) of the language. However this knowledge is often interfered with by external variables like sneezes, lapses of memory, slips of the tongue, distractions, illnesses, tiredness. But when he lapses, the speaker always knows what he "meant" to say. Thus, what comes out of the speaker's mouth (his performance) is not to be taken as an exact representation of his real knowledge of the language (his competence).

The linguist's task has many analogues in the study of human behavior. Suppose, for instance, one knows nothing about the game of bridge and seeks to learn by observing others at play. The observer notes that, when the first player leads a card of a given suit, others generally play the same suit. As the hand progresses, the other players do not always do so. The observer will eventually infer the rule is that one must follow suit when one has cards of the lead suit in his hand. Knowledge of this principle is part of the "bridge competence" of the players. Now suppose a player, in the midst of an animated conversation or while refilling his glass, fails to follow suit when he is required to and can do so. The observer does not infer that the player no longer knows the rule, but simply that he failed to apply it. His performance did not accord with his competence. Thus we do not expect a bridge rule book to inform us that players who overindulge may fail to observe a certain rule or to list any of the endless other factors that can influence the performance of bridge players. We simply expect to be informed of the rules. So too a grammar should describe the "rules" the user knows and need not comment on instances of their misapplication.

However, certain difficulties accompany attempts to describe the linguistic competence of the user of English, or of any language. The linguist must (1) determine whose competence is to be analyzed and (2) devise means to bring this knowledge, called competence, under some kind of empirical scrutiny. Chomsky has asserted that linguistic theory is concerned primarily with an ideal speaker-listener. He means that the grammar the linguist writes (like the bridge rule-book) describes the principles according to which the user would behave if no extra-linguistic factors interfered with implementing these principles. Chomsky has not described the exact procedures linguists should follow to arrive at such a description of the competence of the ideal speaker-listener. In practice, generative-transformational linguists have assumed that persons who have little difficulty communicating with one another must possess essentially the same knowledge. The linguist may thus describe the competence of any user of English, including his own, and call his results a grammar of English. Having thus defined the object of his investigation, the linguist must still find means to study it. The competence of the user of English, since it is knowledge, is obviously not open to the kind of observation that is ordinarily considered integral to an empirical investigation: observation of perceivable phenomena, which exist outside the mind of the investigator and which are thus verifiable by other investigators. However, Chomsky has argued persuasively that generative-transformational theory is no less empirical than structural theory, even though it sets as its goal the description and explanation of mental processes underlying language rather than the description of the output of those processes. To do this, linguistics must broaden the notion of empirical linguistic data to include all of the following:

1.6a phonetic transcriptions
  b judgments about the sameness or difference of utterances
  c judgments about the acceptability of utterances
  d judgments about ambiguity that can be traced to structural origins
  e judgments about the sameness or differences of sentence types
  f judgments about the propriety of particular classifications or segmentations

In addition to the type of data considered empirical by the American structuralist (1.6a) a variety of judgments by the user of a language (1.6b to 1.6f) must be given empirical status. By thus studying the judgments of the user of a language in addition to the actual utterances he produces, the linguist is able to make inferences about linguistic competence. An example will demonstrate the empirical nature of data of the judgment type. Consider the sentences in 1.7.

1.7a The Czar asked the Kaiser to sign the treaty.
  b The Czar promised the Kaiser to sign the treaty.

The fact that any user of English will identify the one who signs the treaty as the Kaiser in 1.7a and the Czar in 1.7b is an objective phenomenon outside the mind of the investigator and constitutes a datum that may be used in writing a grammar describing the linguistic competence of the user of English.

An array of data of the type listed and exemplified in the previous paragraph has led generative-transformational linguists to make the following inferences about linguistic competence: (1) Sentences have an overt (**surface**) structure, which the user of a language knows and which is manifested in their sound or spelling. (The sentences in 1.7a and 1.7b would thus be said to be quite similar in their surface structures, differing only in the sound/spelling of their respective main verbs.) (2) Sentences also have a covert (**deep**) structure, likewise known to the user, but not necessarily manifested in their sound or spelling. (The sentences in 1.7a and 1.7b would thus be said to be significantly different in their deep structures, differing not only in the sound/spelling of their main verbs, but also in the functional relationships between their respective subjects and infinitive complements.)

A grammar constructed on the basis of the kinds of data listed in 1.6 is a model of linguistic competence—a set of theoretical terms and statements that both adequately accounts for all the available data and fulfills the criteria of generality and simplicity, by which scientific theories are evaluated. Such a model—the grammar of English—will perform the following tasks: (1) At the deeper levels of sentence structure, it will make it possible to explain the user's ability to interpret the meaning (semantic structure) of sentences in the language, including the user's intuitions about the meaning of individual lexical items and about constraints on their use in syntactic structures. It will explicitly assign an underlying structure in the form of a **constituent-structure tree diagram** to all sentences in the language. (2) At the surface level, the grammar will explain the ability of the user of a language to produce and to understand spoken and written sentences in their perceivable form. It will explicitly assign surface constituent-structure tree diagrams to all sentences. (3) The grammar will contain a system of syntactic processes (usually called **transformations**) which will explain the ability of the user of a language to relate deep and surface sentence structures. It will define the nature, number, and order of transformations which convert deeper-level structures into surface-level structures.

The above description of generative-transformational theory, like the earlier one of American structuralism, has been presented to provide a conceptual context for the details presented in later chapters, and to let you know which portions are based on Generative-Transformational

Linguistics. The technical terms mentioned in this section, and the previous section, will be illustrated and applied throughout the book. You are recommended to reread this chapter frequently as you proceed. Thus you will understand it better and also learn to interrelate the many details presented in later chapters. You are especially urged to review the section on scientific method since the presentation in later chapters makes constant reference to such concepts as adequacy, generality, and simplicity.

THE PLAN OF THIS BOOK

I have stated that this book aims to present a broad range of factual information about contemporary American English, using scientific linguistics, and that I draw on two theories of language for both facts and procedures. But these two theories differ drastically in how they define the object of scientific linguistic investigation and in how they go about studying it. The American structuralist studies a finite corpus of phonetic data for the purpose of classifying elements in it. The generative-transformationalist studies linguistic competence for the purpose of describing the user's capacity to generate an unlimited number of sentences. How can we derive a coherent presentation of the facts of English grammar from linguistic theories so much in conflict? We can do so because American Structural Linguistics not only predates Generative-Transformational Linguistics, as we have seen, but also precedes it on the logical hierarchy of empirical scientific method. As a theory of language, American structuralism does not rate high on the evaluative scale of generality: it never really goes beyond observations, hypotheses, and laws, being very much data-oriented. Generative-Transformational Linguistics, on the other hand, rates high in generality: it is a very imaginative model of unobserved mental structures underlying language, and even extends the notion of empirical data to include judgments. Because of this tendency of the two theories to emphasize opposite ends of the empirical hierarchy, it becomes both possible and pedagogically desirable to introduce the study of scientific linguistics by movement through structural to generative-transformational theory. In doing so, we are in a real sense retracing the steps of empirical scientific method as it has been applied to the study of language.

Thus, chapter 2 begins with a demonstration of the American structuralist method of identifying and classifying morphemes in a corpus. Many details of English morphology are then described within a structuralist framework—all the definitions and classifications of chapter 2 can be derived from observing the positions and relations of various types of morphemes in a corpus of English. Chapter 3 begins by attempting to treat English syntax from a structuralist point of view—by identifying and labeling form classes, and by describing sentence structure in terms of linear patterns of form classes. But as chapter 3 proceeds, new kinds of syntactic facts emerge, which cannot be handled by linear patterns. Alternate classificatory approaches are tried, but in the end, the theoretical evaluative criterion of simplicity demands abandonment of any kind of classificatory approach to syntax. I present arguments in chapter 4 to support this abandonment. These arguments reinforce the generative-transformational claim that a grammar of English cannot be based on the analysis of any corpus. Thus, we begin in chapter 4 to assemble the theoretical apparatus of generative-transformational theory. By the middle of chapter 5 the machinery is fully operative. The remainder of chapter 5 and all of chapters 6 and 7 develop a self-contained basic generative-transformational grammar of English. Chapter 8 takes the grammar as given, and shows how syntactic research expands and revises the basic grammar in order to account for an ever-expanding array of syntactic data. Chapter 9 outlines generative-transformational approaches to English semantics. Chapter 10 outlines both American structuralist and generative-transformational treatments of English phonology.

In addition to my conviction that a movement from American structural to generative-transformational theory follows the systematic ordering of empirical scientific method, I have two other reasons for basing my presentation on both of these theories rather than on generative-transformational theory alone. First, structural linguists have produced many detailed studies of English word structure. Generative-transformational linguists, while they have shown their theory capable of handling the facts of English word formation, have not produced extensive treatments of these facts. Any effective textbook must draw on the well-established and fully researched findings of a discipline. To the extent that a textbook like this plows new ground, it tends to become less comprehensible to its student users. Thus, if I hope to be accurate and detailed, I have no choice but to treat the facts of English word formation from a structural point of view. A second additional reason for starting with a structuralist treatment of English morphology is that it serves a useful purpose in preparing for later chapters, where a generative-transformational treatment of English syntax is developed in detail. From this perspective, the whole of chapter 2 can be viewed as an attempt to define inflectional suffixes so that later chapters can efficiently discuss their role in the syntax of the English auxiliary.

FOR FURTHER READING[1]

Toulmin (1960) treats empirical scientific method readably and informally; Bocheński (1965) treats it more formally but still clearly. Stageberg (1970) presents a detailed structuralist treatment of English with many exercises. The writings of Bloomfield (1933) and Sapir (1921 and 1950) represent the foundation works of American structuralism. Joos (1957) includes many technical articles on structuralist assumptions about language. For introductory generative-transformational treatments of English, consult Lester (1971) and Liles (1971). All of Chomsky's writings are foundation works of Generative-Transformational Linguistics; the first chapter of his book (1965) and portions of his article (1961) explicitly treat matters we have discussed in this introduction. Fodor and Katz (1966) include many technical articles on generative-transformational assumptions about language.

[1]Complete references are given in the bibliography at the end of the book.

Chapter 2

English Morphology

MORPHEMES

L et us begin by assuming that we are archeologists who wish to make inferences about the three primitive drawings and strings of geometric shapes contained in figure 2.1. Examine each one carefully; the three illustrations are not intended to form a sequential narrative.[1] Let us hypothesize that the geometric

Figure 2.1: Some primitive drawings accompanied by geometric symbols.

shapes are symbols which comment on the drawings and that we can provide rough meanings for the three sequences of symbols as follows:

2.1a △ ○ ▭ 'man bites dog'
  b ○ △ ▭ 'dog bites man'
  c △ ☆ ▭ 'man bites camel'

Linguists call the preliminary statements of meaning **glosses** and place them in single quotation marks. Each word is said to be a gloss for a

---

[1]This use of geometric shapes is an adaptation of a problem discussed by Cook (1967, pp. 21–22).

given geometric shape; the string of words can likewise be called a gloss for the string of shapes. The data in 2.1 constitute a **corpus,** or a **text.** Examine the corpus carefully. Which geometric symbol occurs only once in the corpus? Which gloss occurs only once? The star must therefore mean 'camel'. Which geometric symbol occurs in but two of the three strings? Which gloss occurs only in the two corresponding lines of glosses? The circle must therefore mean 'dog'. The triangle and rectangle occur in all three strings but the *position* of the triangle is different in 2.1b; the position of 'man' likewise changes. The triangle must therefore mean 'man' and, by elimination, the rectangle must mean 'bites'. We have thus assigned a gloss to each symbol.

But what in fact does mean 'dog' or 'man' in the communication system we have been examining? I have said that a circle means 'dog'. But in a technical mathematical sense there really are no circles in figure 2.1. Even the naked eye can detect that the "circles" are imperfectly drawn and that the two figures perceived to be circles are different in size and shape. Must we therefore retract our inference that a circle symbolizes 'dog'? Must we say that there are two, and maybe even more, symbols for 'dog': a small circle-like figure with an indentation on the upper right and a slightly larger circle-like figure with a protrusion on the upper right? What of different colored circles? Circles drawn with chalk? Circles traced in sand? Is each a different symbol for 'dog'? It seems not. A *circle* symbolizes 'dog'. This means that anything perceived to be a circle can be a symbol for 'dog' in the communication system we are considering. Thus the meaningful unit that symbolizes 'dog' is not any particular circle but the abstraction "circle." Let us move on to another array of data that will shed more light on the abstract nature of linguistic symbols.

Let us consider a corpus from a hypothetical human language. The data in 2.2 look more like the kind of data that linguists usually work with—only the specialist needs to decode archeological inscriptions, as we had to in the previous example. We can assume that the data and the glosses have been **elicited** from someone who knows the language and who also knows enough English to provide us with glosses. Linguists call such a person an **informant.** Examine carefully the corpus below.

2.2a	tekpasi	'birds sang'
b	datpasi	'children sang'
c	datsi	'a child sang'
d	lobasi	'robins sang'
e	losi	'a robin sang'
f	rofsi	'a boy sang'
g	disi	'a girl sang'

In 2.1 we were already provided with discrete symbols, each of which we initially presumed to correspond to one of the words in the gloss. In 2.2 we have an uninterrupted sequence of letters which we must somehow **segment**: we must discover which letters or combinations of letters correspond to which words or parts of words in the gloss. The procedure is nonetheless quite similar to that employed in the analysis of 2.1. The essence of the procedure is to note where changes in the gloss correspond to changes in the text, or inversely, where recurrent sameness in the gloss corresponds to sameness in the text. Examine the corpus again, this time drawing lines between groups of letters that seem to correspond to a word or part of a word in the gloss. Only 'sang', you probably noticed, occurs in every gloss, and only *si* occurs in every line of the text. We may initially look for a segment in the text which corresponds exactly to the indefinite article 'a', but we will find no recurrent corresponding segment in the text. However if we take 'a girl' as a meaningful unit which occurs only once in the glosses, we will notice that *di* likewise occurs only once and in the corresponding line in the text. Similarly, *rof* seems to correspond to 'a boy'. We are left with the following portions of the corpus unsolved:

2.3a	tekpa	'birds'
b	datpa	'children'
c	dat	'a child'
d	loba	'robins'
e	lo	'a robin'

Note that *dat* occurs in 2.3b and 2.3c, and *lo* in both 2.3d and 2.3e. But 2.3b and 2.3d contain an additional syllable. Is there a unit of meaning expressed in the glosses of 2.3b and 2.3d that might account for the additional syllable in the corresponding lines of the text? Yes. Both nouns are plural. We may tentatively conclude, then, that *pa* in 2.3b and *ba* in 2.3d mean something like 'more than one' and that *dat* is the singular 'child' and *lo* the singular 'robin'. We can now further infer that the *pa* in 2.3a likewise means 'plural', leaving *tek* to mean 'bird'. Let us now list the meaningful segments in the corpus along with the individual gloss of each:

2.4a	tek	'bird'
b	dat	'child'
c	lo	'robin'
d	rof	'boy'
e	di	'girl'
f	pa and ba	'plural'
g	si	'sang'

The most important fact to note from our analysis is that in 2.4f we have two segments for one meaning. Linguists have found this is not unusual in language. Indeed, even in the English glosses, we have a similar situation: the notion 'plural' is represented by the *s* in 'birds' and 'robins' but not so in 'children'. We can often find some system in the alternation of segments which have the same meaning. When the segments are pronounced quite similarly as in 2.4f, the alternation is usually conditioned by the pronunciation context. A hypothesis that emerges from the data of 2.2 is that the segment *pa* occurs after consonant sounds, and the segment *ba* after vowel sounds. Thus we may consider *pa* and *ba* to be systematically determined **variants** of one and the same unit of language, which—like the "circle"—is an abstraction. Just as the symbol for 'dog' in 2.1 was concluded to be anything perceived to be a circle, so in 2.2 the unit that means 'plural' is anything perceived to be . . . perceived to be what? Mathematics provided us with a ready-made perceptual abstraction for use in 2.1, but apparently no ready-made abstraction exists for our present purposes. Before discussing further how linguists treat such facts and resolve this need, let us examine yet another array of data, this time in English:

2.5a   boys, bags, tails, trains, hams
   b   tacks, bats, cuffs
   c   bushes, watches, judges
   d   oxen, brethren, children
   e   teeth, geese, feet
   f   data, criteria, alumni

Each English word in 2.5 contains two meaningful segments. Since the data are in English, I have not provided glosses. Such glosses could be in another language or they might even be pictures—of a boy, a train, and so forth. The gloss of the second segment in each word is of course 'plural'. The spelling of this segment is the same in 2.5a and 2.5b: an *s*. But in 2.5c to 2.5f each set of words manifests a different spelling of 'plural'. Furthermore, if we attend closely to the pronunciation of the words, we will note that although 2.5a and 2.5b both end in the letter *s,* the pronunciation of this letter is not the same in 2.5a as it is in 2.5b; in 2.5a the letter *s* represents a "z" sound, whereas in 2.5b it represents an "s" sound. Thus all of the following mean 'plural': (1) the "z" sound of 2.5a, (2) the "s" sound of 2.5b, (3) the *es* of 2.5c, (4) the *en* of 2.5d, (5) the vowels spelled *ee* as opposed to *oo* in 2.5e, and (6) the various vowel endings in 2.5f. This is why the linguist glossing an English text would write 'plural' in the gloss of every word in 2.5. And anyone knowing English will think 'more-than-one-of-whatever-it-is' when he hears any of the words in 2.5. Linguistics must take account of this recurrent sameness of gloss or meaning. It does so, in this case, by establishing an abstract unit of language that encompasses all the various sounds that mean 'plural'. Just as the notion "circle" encompasses an almost limitless variety of entities perceived to be circles, so a label like *es,* for instance, can be established to encompass any and all sounds or combinations of sounds that can be glossed 'plural' or that evoke the idea of plurality in the mind of someone knowing English. In this book, I label this particular abstraction *es.* I could alternatively have given it a number or simply called it 'plural'. Any such abstract label for a group of different sounds having the same gloss is what linguists call a **morpheme.**

WORDS

We have seen that a morpheme is an abstract meaning label attached to the smallest meaningful segments of sound in a language; usually one morpheme label will group together two or more segments with different pronunciations but with the same meaning. Our choice of the plural morpheme as an example from English should have made clear that a morpheme is not necessarily a **word.** Users of English feel that the plural morpheme is part of a word. And this is true. In fact, it is convenient to think of the domain of morphological analysis as the word: segmenting and labeling the morphemes that make up words, and subdividing morphemes into types according to the roles they play in forming words. When we treat the morphology of English, we study how words are put together. And this will be our concern throughout the remainder of this chapter.

If morphology treats the composition of words, then the discussion of morphemes contributes to defining what a word is. Thus this entire chapter constitutes such a definition. But even before beginning a detailed presentation of the facts, we should at least have a tentative definition in mind. Fortunately, the intuitions of native users of English are quite adequate; these are manifested in, and reinforced by, the conventions of English spelling: a word is a unit of language, which, when written or printed, is separated from other units by a space. But let us try to discover and make explicit some sources of these conventions. Two facts should be kept in mind: (1) that every word contains at least one morpheme, and (2) that many words contain two or more morphemes. Thus, once the morphemes of a language are identified and listed, a major task of morphology is to state how the morphemes group into words.

Consider the two-word sentence, *Birds sang.* Let us say that it contains three morphemes represented in the spelling by *bird, s,* and *sang.* If we asked a user of English to give us the meaning of *birds* (the question groups *bird* and the plural morpheme as one word), we would get a ready reply. If we asked for the meaning of *ssing* (this question attempts to group the plural morpheme and *sing* as one word), we would probably elicit a puzzled expression. Such reactions indicate that *bird* and *s* are somehow permanently associated for the user of English in a way that *s* and *sing* are not. This kind of association between or among morphemes constitutes an internal criterion for grouping two or more morphemes into one word: we do so if they tend to stay together.

There is another facet to this kind of coherence among morphemes. Consider the paired sentences in 2.6:

> **2.6a**   The *bird* sang.
> **aa**   The *birds* sang.
> **b**   I saw the *bird.*
> **bb**   I saw the *birds.*
> **c**   Joe gave food to the *bird.*
> **cc**   Joe gave food to the *birds.*
> **d**   Joe gave the *bird* food.
> **dd**   Joe gave the *birds* food.
> **e**   They photographed the tree and the *bird.*
> **ee**   They photographed the tree and the *birds.*

Each pair of sentences is the same except that in the double-lettered sentences the morpheme *bird* is accompanied by the plural morpheme. Observe that *birds* (with the plural morpheme) fits easily into the same positions as *bird.* But now consider the paired sentences in 2.7. Here we attempt to place *ssing* in a set of positions that *sing* can occupy in the sentences. (An asterisk placed in front of a linguistic form or linguistic sequence means that it is not likely to occur in English, or if it did occur, a listener or reader would have to work hard to make sense of it.)

> **2.7a**   The bird *sings.*
> **aa**   The bird *ssing.*
> **b**   The bird can *sing.*
> **bb**   *The bird can *ssing.*
> **c**   The bird will *sing.*
> **cc**   *The bird will *ssing.*
> **d**   The bird had been *singing.*
> **dd**   *The bird had been *ssinging.*
> **e**   We like the bird to *sing.*
> **ee**   *We like the bird to *ssing.*

Except for 2.7aa, the double-lettered sentences represent impossible orderings of morphemes in English; to obtain meaningful English sentences, it would be necessary for the *s* to appear elsewhere in the sentences, separated from *sing* and immediately following *bird.* The ability, shown in 2.6, of *bird* and *s* together to fill the same set of positions in English sentences as *bird* alone fills constitutes an external criterion for grouping the two morphemes together as one word, whereas the inability, shown in 2.7, of *s* and *sing* to fill the same set of positions as *sing* alone fills shows us why the two are not grouped together as one word.

Before going on to examine the various types of morphemes that can combine together into one word, I will use the two criteria we have just examined to formulate three definitions of a word. All three say essentially the same thing; they are expressed in progressively more technical terminology.

2.8a Words are the smallest meaningful units of language which tend to be internally indivisible and externally transportable from one position to another in sentences.

b Words are the smallest meaningful units of language which possess internal stability and positional mobility.

c Words are the smallest meaningful units of language having a fixed **composition** and a free **distribution**.

It is important to note that the internal criterion—stability among two or more morphemes—is irrelevant to the identification of several types of words in English because such words are always and only composed of just one morpheme. Morphemes like *a, the, some, this, that, two, three,* and *several* are words because they have considerable positional mobility and are not absolutely tied to the positions of some other morpheme (the way *s* is tied to morphemes like *bird*). But neither do they have other morphemes dependent on them. We know they are words because they have a relatively free distribution; the question of a fixed composition simply does not arise. Morphemes like *on, of, in, out,* and morphemes like *and, but, either, or,* are similarly said to be words on the basis of the external criterion alone.

ROOTS AND AFFIXES

The task of morphological analysis is not complete even when all the morphemes are properly grouped into words. The morphemes which compose a word may be of several types. An analyst must carefully observe a variety of facts differentiating such morphemes.

Consider the word *subtract,* which is composed of two morphemes, *sub* and *tract.* Even though their meanings are abstract, they are fairly consistent; *sub* meaning 'down' or 'under' and *tract* 'to pull' or 'to take'. Now, imagine a linguist analyzing an English corpus and looking for other occurrences of the morpheme *sub* and the morpheme *tract.* If he has access to a large corpus, he would find a very large number of words containing *sub.* Here is just a sampling:

> **2.9a** subdue, subject, submerse, submit, subscribe, subsidize, subsist, substitute, subsume, subvert
>
> **b** subjoin, sublease, sublet, submerge, subserve, subtend

However, even with access to the same large corpus, he would find relatively few words containing the morpheme *tract.* Here is a virtually complete list:

> **2.10** attract, contract, detract, distract, extract, protract, retract

The lists in 2.9 and 2.10 point out an important difference between *sub* and *tract.* If we view the word *subtract* as composed of two *positions* (one occupied by *sub,* the other by *tract*), we immediately notice that for each position there are only certain morphemes that can replace the one already there and still make up a genuine word. Very many morphemes can occupy the position of *tract* but only relatively few can occupy the position of *sub.* This is not an isolated phenomenon true only of the word *subtract.* Consider the word *express,* composed of the morpheme *ex* and the morpheme *press.* How many morphemes can you think of which can substitute for *press* after *ex?* Here is a partial list:

> **2.11a** exalt, excise, exclude, excuse, exempt, exhume, exonerate, expand, expect, expedite, expel, explain, explode, export, expunge, extol, extort, extract, extricate, exude
>
> **b** exclaim, exchange, expatriate, expose, extend

Now, how many morphemes can you think of that can substitute for *ex* before *press?* Here is a virtually complete list:

> **2.12** compress, depress, oppress, repress, suppress

Many other examples like these can be cited, examples which show that some morphemes occupy a position in words where there is a relatively unlimited potential for substituting other morphemes (linguists call such morphemes **roots**) and that other morphemes occupy a position where there is a relatively limited potential for substitution (these are called **affixes**). In our two examples, affixes came before the roots. Affixes may also follow roots. Consider the word *traction,* composed of the morpheme *tract* and the morpheme *ion.* It would be easy to show that many morphemes can replace *tract* in front of *ion* (for example, *tension, fusion, lesion, version, portion, plosion, fission*), and thus *tract* is a root, but that very few morphemes (perhaps only *able* and *or*) can replace *ion* after *tract,* and thus *ion* is an affix. Affixes preceding roots are called **prefixes,** and affixes following roots are called **suffixes.** But prefixes may also precede other prefixes, as in the word *decompression* where *de* is a prefix that precedes another prefix, *com,* and both precede the root *press.* And suffixes may also follow other suffixes as in the word *tractability,* where *ity* is a suffix that follows another suffix, *abil,* and both follow the root *tract.* Furthermore, a word may have both prefixes and suffixes (for example, *distractible, retraction, expressible, compression*). Linguists generally cite prefixes with a hyphen after them (for example, *sub-* and *ex-*) and suffixes with hyphens in front of them (for example, *-ion* and *-ible*).

Let us consider another phenomenon related to the classification of morpheme types. Hopefully, you will have asked yourself why the examples in 2.9 and 2.11 were divided into two groups under a and b. Reexamine these lists of examples, trying to determine a basis for the division. None of the roots in 2.9a or 2.11a can function as a word— none has a free distribution. The roots in 2.9b and 2.11b, on the other hand, can function as words. For these reasons, the roots in 2.9a and 2.11a are called **bound roots,** and those in 2.9b and 2.11b are called **free roots.** Here is a summary of the terms and definitions introduced in this section:

> **2.13a** *Roots:* morphemes which occupy a position in a word where the greatest potentiality for substitution exists
> (i) *Bound:* incapable of functioning as a word
> (ii) *Free:* capable of functioning as a word
>
> **b** *Affixes:* morphemes which occupy a position in a word where only a limited potentiality for substitution exists
> (i) *Prefixes:* affixes which precede roots and possibly other prefixes
> (ii) *Suffixes:* affixes which follow roots and possibly other suffixes

SOME ENGLISH PREFIXES

Examine the sampling of English prefixes in 2.14. Several others are treated in an exercise at the end of this chapter. I group the prefixes into six categories based on their meaning. These meaning categories are not exhaustive, but they do encompass a large number of English prefixes. Two examples of prefixes from each meaning type are given. As you examine the example words listed beside each prefix, notice that when a prefix is added to a root, the composite word is generally the same part of speech as the root without the prefix. Notice also that, while prefixes do not normally have as many pronunciation variants as did the -es morpheme we considered above, there is enough variation to reinforce our definition of a morpheme as an abstract meaning label which may group together a variety of pronunciations. In this regard, note especially the different pronunciations of *poly-* in *polyglot* and *polygamy* and the different pronunciations of *hyper-* in *hyperactive* and *hyperbole*.

2.14a	Number	bi-	bifocal, bilingual, biceps, bicycle
		poly-	polysyllabic, polyglot, polygamy
b	Time	post-	postwar, postelection, postclassical, postpone
		pre-	prewar, preschool, pre-19th century, premarital
c	Place	inter-	international, intercontinental, intertwine, interact, intermarry, interdependence, interplay
		sub-	subway, subsection, subconscious, sublet, subdivide, subcontract, subliminal
d	Degree	hyper-	hypercritical, hyperactive, hypersensitive, hyperbole
		ultra-	ultraviolet, ultramodern, ultraconservative, ultraliberal, ultramarine
e	Privation	un_1-	undo, untie, unzip, unpack, unleash, unhorse
		dis-	disconnect, disinfect, disown, dispose (of), disheartened, discolored, discontent, displeasure, dissatisfaction
f	Negation	non-	nonconformist, nonsmoker, nonpolitical, nondrip
		un_2-	unfair, unwise, unforgettable, unassuming, unexpected

DERIVATIONAL AND INFLECTIONAL SUFFIXES

Although I used prefixes as examples to distinguish between roots and affixes, I did note that affixes may also be suffixes and gave several examples. In fact, the majority of English affixes are suffixes. Let us now examine the behavior of some English suffixes.

Consider the verb root *treat* in the sentences of 2.15. It occurs in 2.15a without a suffix and in 2.15b and 2.15c with suffixes.

2.15a They treat their employees well.
  b That treatment helped cure the disease.
  c He treated his students fairly.

Note that the combination of the verb root *treat* and the suffix *-ment* in 2.15b results in a word that is a noun. (It is true that there is a noun root, *treat,* in English, as in the sentence *He bought me a treat,* but if we examine other words in English with the suffix *-ment,* such as *arrangement* and *amazement,* we find that *-ment* is clearly affixed to a verb root.) We may conclude that when the suffix *-ment* is affixed to a verb, the result is a noun. Now notice that when the verb root *treat* combines with the suffix *-ed* in 2.15c the result is still a verb. Thus *-ment* changes the part of speech of a root to which it is affixed, but *-ed* does not. Here is another example. The noun root *symbol* occurs without a suffix in 2.16a but with suffixes in 2.16b and 2.16c:

2.16a Purple is a symbol for royalty.
  b White flags symbolize surrender.
  c Both the circle and the triangle can be symbols.

Note that the combination of the noun root *symbol* with the suffix *-ize* in 2.16b results in a verb. Other examples of a noun root and *-ize* combining to form a verb are *hospitalize* and *vaporize.* We may conclude that when the suffix *-ize* is affixed to a noun, the result is a verb. But notice that when the noun root *symbol* combines with the suffix *-s* in 2.16c the resultant word is still a noun. Thus *-ize* changes the part of speech of a root to which it is affixed, but *-s* does not. Here is a list of the two roots and four suffixes we have just discussed with summary comments in parentheses:

2.17a treat (a verb root)
  b symbol (a noun root)
  c -ment (a suffix that changes verbs to nouns)
  d -ize (a suffix that changes nouns to verbs)
  e -ed (a verb suffix—that means 'past')
  f -s (a noun suffix—that means 'plural')

Suffixes like *-ment* and *-ize* which change the part of speech of words are called **derivational suffixes.** Suffixes like *-ed* and *-s* which do not change the part of speech of words are called **inflectional suffixes.** But let us look further into the behavior of these two types of affixes.

I noted earlier in this chapter that a root may have two or more suffixes attached to it. Here are two examples:

2.18a treatments
  b symbolized

Notice that in 2.18 each word is composed of a root, a derivational suffix, and an inflectional suffix. In 2.18a, -*ment* changes *treat* to a noun, and thus the -*s* that indicates plural in nouns can be added. In 2.18b, -*ize* changes *symbol* to a verb, and thus the -*ed* that indicates past in verbs can be added. Suppose we tried to reverse this order of affixation, reasoning as follows: if *treat* is a verb root, then -*ed* can be added giving *treated,* which is still a verb. Now if -*ment* changes verbs to nouns, why not add it to the verb *treated* giving the noun **treatedment?* But the combination of morphemes indicated by the spelling **treatedment* is in fact impossible in English. And so is the combination **symbolsize,* which might be formed by adding first an inflectional and then a derivational suffix to the root *symbol.* Such forms are not unreasonable, nor would they be without a certain usefulness. But they are evidently not used in English. And thus we have a second criterion for distinguishing between derivational and inflectional suffixes: inflectional suffixes can follow derivational suffixes in words, but derivational suffixes cannot follow inflectional suffixes. Notice that the inflectional suffixes -*ed* and -*s* occur only last in the words listed in 2.19.

> **2.19a** treatment
> **b** symbolize
> **c** treated
> **d** symbols
> **e** symbolization
> **f** symbolizable
> **g** treatments
> **h** symbolized
> **i** symbolizability
> **j** symbolizations

Before going on to discuss another criterion of distinction between derivational and inflectional suffixes, let me introduce two useful terms and illustrate them by reference to the words listed in 2.19. We have called *treat* and *symbol* roots. Thus we are able to say that *treatment* and *symbolize* are each composed of a root and a derivational suffix and that *treated* and *symbols* are each composed of a root and an inflectional suffix. But if we wish to discuss the linguistic form to which the last suffix is attached in 2.19e to 2.19j, we may face a terminological handicap. Consider *symbolizable* and *treatments.* We could say of course that -*able* is a suffix which derives an adjective from a root that is a verb (for example, *breakable*) and from a root-plus-another-affix that is a verb (for example, *symbolizable*). Or we could ignore the fact that -*able* is added just to a root in *breakable* and to a root-plus-another-affix in *symbolizable* and say that -*able* derives adjectives from *words* that are verbs whether the words are simple roots or roots plus one or more other suffixes. Nevertheless it seems useful to have terms that can refer either to roots or to combinations of roots and affixes, and that can indicate whether a derivational or inflectional suffix can be affixed to such a morpheme or combination of morphemes. Linguists often use the term **stem** to refer to any morpheme or combination of morphemes to which a given inflectional suffix can be affixed. Thus in the word *treated,* the root *treat* can also be called the stem of the *-ed* inflectional suffix. But in the word *symbolized,* the stem of the *-ed* inflectional suffix is *symbolize,* both a root and a derivational suffix. Similarly, the stem of the *-s* inflection in the word *symbolizations* is *symbolization,* a root plus two derivational suffixes. Similarly, linguists often use the term **base** to refer to any morpheme or combination of morphemes to which a given derivational suffix can be affixed. Thus while *treat* is a root in the word *treatment,* we call it a base relative to the derivational suffix *-ment.* In the word *symbolizable* the base of the derivational suffix *-able* is *symbolize,* a root and another derivational suffix. Similarly the base of the derivational suffix *-ity* in the word *symbolizability* is *symbolizable,* a root plus two derivational suffixes. Here are summary definitions of the terms stem and base:

 2.20a Stem: a root or a root plus other affixes to which a given inflectional suffix can be attached

   b Base: a root or a root plus other affixes to which a given derivational suffix can be attached

We now continue our examination of the distinctions between derivational and inflectional suffixes. We have seen that derivational suffixes change the part of speech of bases to which they are attached, but inflectional suffixes do not change the part of speech of stems to which they are attached. Secondly, derivational suffixes cannot follow inflectional suffixes, but inflectional suffixes must follow all derivational suffixes. Now consider the lists of words in 2.21, which demonstrate a third criterion of distinction.

 2.21a treatment, arrangement, amazement, judgment
  aa *killment, *buildment, *spendment
   b hospitalize, symbolize, vaporize
  bb *bookize, *chairize, *houseize

We noted earlier that the derivational suffix *-ment* changes verbs to nouns and that *-ize* changes nouns to verbs. The asterisked words in 2.21 demonstrate that *-ment* cannot change just any verb to a noun, nor can *-ize* change just any noun to a verb. In fact, if you try to add to the lists in 2.21a and 2.21b, you will find that both *-ment* and *-ize* operate on only very small groups of verbs and nouns respectively. Now compare the limitations on the operation of these two derivational suffixes with the ability of both inflectional suffixes we have so far examined to attach to virtually every stem of a part of speech: every noun has a plural, and *unique* every verb has a past. Thus, derivational suffixes may be affixed to only relatively few bases of a given part of speech. (This may be why English has several hundred derivational suffixes.) Inflectional suffixes may be affixed to all stems of a given part of speech. (This may be why, as we shall soon see, English has only eight inflectional suffixes.)

Here is a summary of the three differences between derivational and inflectional suffixes:

2.22 Derivational:
  a Usually change the part of speech of bases
  b Cannot follow inflectional suffixes
  c Usually affix to only small groups of bases of a given part of speech

Inflectional:
  a Never change the part of speech of stems
  b Must follow all derivational suffixes
  c Affix to virtually any stem of a given part of speech

SOME ENGLISH DERIVATIONAL SUFFIXES

Examine the eighteen derivational suffixes and example words in 2.23. They are in six groups of three, based on the change they effect in parts of speech. (Notations like N < V in 2.23c should be read "derives nouns from verbs.") Other derivational suffixes are treated in an exercise at the end of this chapter. As you examine the words in 2.23, notice two things: First, some derivational suffixes do not meet all three of our criteria of definition; for instance, the suffixes in 2.23a are affixed to noun bases and the resultant word remains a noun. Nonetheless the other two criteria classify these suffixes as derivational. Second, notice that derivational suffixes, like prefixes, do not ordinarily have many pronunciation variants, but they provide reinforcement for our definition of a morpheme as an abstract meaning label because they frequently produce pronunciation variants of morphemes in their bases. Notice how the morphemes *sane, vain,* and *chaste* change vowel pronunciation when *-ity* is affixed: *sanity, vanity, chastity.* And notice that the "k" sound at the end of *public, elastic,* and *fanatic* changes to an "s" sound when derivational suffixes are added: *publicity, elasticity, fanaticism.*

2.23a	N < N	-hood	neighborhood, sisterhood, bachelorhood, boyhood, brotherhood, childhood, maidenhood, knighthood
		-ship	lordship, township, fellowship, championship, friendship, membership, lectureship, kinship
		-ster	gangster, gamester, trickster, songster, punster, mobster, prankster, speedster
b	N < ADJ/N	-ism	idealism, impressionism, fanaticism, dualism, realism, imperialism, romanticism, patriotism
		-ity	sanity, vanity, rapidity, banality, elasticity, ability, actuality, agility, chastity, curiosity
		-ness	meanness, happiness, cleverness, usefulness, bitterness, brightness, darkness, goodness
c	N < V	-al	refusal, dismissal, upheaval, denial, survival, trial, approval, proposal
		-er	worker, writer, driver, employer, swimmer, preacher, traveler, teacher, baker
		-ment	arrangement, amazement, puzzlement, judgment, astonishment, treatment
d	V < ADJ/N	-en	ripen, widen, deafen, sadden, harden, lengthen, deepen, strengthen, neaten
		-ify	beautify, diversify, codify, amplify, simplify, glorify, nullify, Frenchify
		-ize	symbolize, hospitalize, publicize, popularize, modernize, idealize
e	ADJ < N/V	-ful	useful, delightful, pitiful, helpful, careful, awful, rightful, sinful, cheerful
		-ish	foolish, selfish, snobbish, modish, hellish, sheepish, Swedish, Jewish
		-able	acceptable, readable, drinkable, livable, commendable, comfortable, changeable
f	ADV < ADJ/N	-ly	happily, strangely, oddly, athletically, basically, semantically
		-wise	clockwise, lengthwise, weatherwise, educationwise
		-ward	earthward, homeward, eastward

ENGLISH INFLECTIONAL SUFFIXES

The eight inflectional suffixes of English are listed in 2.24. The word or phrase given first in parentheses serves both as a name and a rough designation of meaning. Next is the morpheme label, then words which end in the inflection. Each line represents a variant pronunciation of the suffix itself or a variant it requires in the pronunciation of certain stems. Examine the lists of examples, preferably by reading them aloud. Notice that 2.24a and 2.24b are noun inflections, 2.24c to 2.24f are verb inflections, and 2.24g and 2.24h are ordinarily adjective inflections. Notice also that many words given to exemplify the past tense inflection in 2.24d are spelled and pronounced the same as words listed with the past participle inflection in 2.24e. I shall comment below on this and other aspects of 2.24.

2.24a	(plural)	-es	boys, bags, tails, trains, hams
			tacks, bats, cuffs
			bushes, watches, judges
			wives, knives, thieves
			oxen, brethren, children
			teeth, geese, feet
			data, criteria, alumni
			sheep, fish, series
b	(possessive)	-poss	Jim's, Joe's, Mom's, Mr. Moore's
			Pat's, my wife's, Mike's
			the judge's, the witch's, the boss's
c	(present tense)	-prs	go/goes, buy/buys, sell/sells
			take/takes, bat/bats, buff/buffs
			push/pushes, watch/watches
			am/is/are, have/has, do/does
d	(past tense)	-pst	stayed, tried, behaved, barred
			walked, stopped, stuffed, watched
			sighted, banded, reminded
			chose, rose, spoke, stole, froze
			threw, knew, grew, slew
			took, stood, forsook
			bought, taught, fought
			cut, let, hit, bet
			went, did, had, made
e	(past participle)	-en	stayed, tried, behaved, barred
			walked, stopped, stuffed, watched
			sighted, banded, reminded
			bought, let, made
			taken, eaten, fallen, known

			broken, chosen, spoken, stolen
			written, given, driven, risen
			gone, done, been, seen
f	(present participle)	-ing	coming, going, buying, selling
g	(comparative)	-er	bigger, older, quicker
			better, worse
h	(superlative)	-est	biggest, oldest, quickest
			best, worst

The plural inflection, which we have labeled *-es,* is pronounced with "z," "s," "ez," and "en" sounds, or as a vowel change in a stem, or a change of vowel at the end of a stem—all of which I discussed earlier when illustrating the nature of morphemes; but the plural inflection can also have what is called a **zero** variant: the stems of *sheep, fish,* and *series* in 2.24a do not change pronunciation in any way when the *-es* inflection is added, as in *John bought three sheep.* Note also that the *-es* inflection can cause a pronunciation variant of a stem to appear: whereas the words *wife, knife,* and *thief* end in an "f" sound, the stems of their plurals end in a "v" sound.

Early in this chapter I defined a morpheme as an abstract meaning label, and I have reemphasized and illustrated this definition throughout the chapter. One reason I have done so is because it has important practical implications. Most of the remaining chapters of this book treat English syntax. As you will soon see, syntax is the study of the interaction of morphemes in sentences. Syntax ignores spelling and pronunciation variants. Thus it is important for you to learn to ignore variations such as the examples in 2.24 manifest, and to recall that the plural morpheme is always represented as *-es* no matter how it is pronounced and even if it is not pronounced at all.

The possessive inflection, labeled *-poss,* has three pronunciations: a "z" as in *Jim's,* an "s" as in *Pat's,* and an "ez" as in *the judge's.* But, again, we ignore such variations when discussing the behavior of this inflection and represent the morphemes in these three examples as *jim-poss, pat-poss,* and *the judge-poss.*

The present-tense inflection, labeled *-prs,* presents special problems. Many linguists speak of a "third person singular agreement inflection," which affixes to a verb in the present tense when the verb is preceded by *he, she, it,* or a noun that these pronouns can replace. This accounts for the "z," "s," and "ez" pronunciations at the end of some example words in the first three lines of 2.24c; it would also account for *is, does,* and *has* in the fourth line: all three "s-like" variants occur after third person singular nouns. But these "s-like" sounds add no more meaning to a verb stem than it communicates when preceded by *I, we, you, they,* or nouns these pronouns can replace. For this reason, we consider the "z," "s," or "ez" pronunciations to be variants of the *-prs* morpheme which alternate with a zero variant that occurs after *I, we,* and so forth. Thus the verb in both *We eat cheese* and *He eats cheese* is analyzed morphologically as *eat-prs.*

The past tense inflection, which we have labeled *-pst,* has a considerable number of pronunciation variants, many of which are exemplified in 2.24d. Notice two general tendencies: (1) a tendency to indicate 'past' by affixing a "d," "t," or "ed" pronunciation to the verb stem, as in *stayed, walked,* and *sighted* respectively, and (2) a tendency to indicate past by changing the pronunciation of a vowel in the verb stem, as in *chose, threw,* and *took.* Some variants, like *bought,* combine both tendencies. Some verbs, like *cut,* call for a zero variant. Other verbs seem to manifest the first tendency but also to call for a variant in the pronunciation of the stem: in *went, did, had,* and *made* a "d" or "t" pronunciation of the past tense inflection appears, but the pronunciation of the stem in each case varies somewhat from the ordinary nonpast pronunciations (*go, do, have, make*). The morphological representations of *went, did, had,* and *made* are *go-pst, do-pst, have-pst,* and *make-pst* respectively. The same kind of analysis is made of those verbs with past tense variants that change a vowel in the stem: *chose* is analyzed as *choose-pst, threw* as *throw-pst,* and *took* as *take-pst.*

The past participle inflection, which we have labeled *-en,* has a familiar variant pronounced "en" or "n" as in *taken, broken, written, gone.* Notice that *broken, written, gone,* and the words that accompany them in 2.24e change the pronunciation of a vowel in their stem when the *-en* inflection is affixed. However, even though the most frequently used verbs of English call for an "en" or "n" variant, most English verbs pronounce *-en* exactly like the past tense inflection. Notice that the first three lines of example words in 2.24e are the same as the first three lines in 2.24d. We may ask what determines whether a given occurrence of *stayed,* or *walked,* or *made* is to be analyzed as *stay-pst* or *stay-en, walk-pst* or *walk-en, make-pst* or *make-en.* In a later chapter, we shall examine detailed criteria for distinguishing these two inflections. Here, I wish only to demonstrate that the distinction is a real one and to discuss a simple procedure to determine which of the two inflections occurs in a given word. Notice that in *He sighted a UFO* the "ed" of *sighted* clearly means 'past', but in *UFOs are sighted every week* nothing about the sentence means 'past'. Similarly, the "ed" of *lived* in *He lived there last year* is clearly 'past', but the sentence *He has lived there for two years* implies that he is still living there, and is thus as much a comment on the present as on the past; we are not likely to say or hear a sentence like *He has lived there last year,* and the reason is of course that the "ed" of *lived* in this sentence is not a variant of the past tense inflection but of *-en.* Here is a procedure for deciding whether a given verb stem ending in "ed" has -pst or -en affixed. Find a verb like *take, break, write,* or *go* (whose pronunciation of -en is clearly distinct from -pst) and substitute it for the word in question. If, for instance, *go* were substituted for *live* in *He has lived there,* it would immediately be clear that *He has gone there* not *He has went there* is appropriate, and therefore that *lived* is to be analyzed as *live-en.*

The present participle inflection, which we have labeled -*ing,* presents few difficulties. Aside from the fact that the final "g" sound is sometimes dropped in conversation, it really has no pronunciation variants.

The comparative and superlative inflections, which we have labeled -*er* and -*est* respectively, have only a few pronunciation variants. When -*er* is affixed to the stem *good* it requires a variant of the stem, spelled "bett," to appear, and when -*est* is affixed, yet another variant, spelled "b," appears. But as with the other inflectional suffixes, we focus on the abstract and represent the morphemes of *better* and *best* as *good-er* and *good-est* respectively. *Worse* and *worst* would be analyzed similarly as *bad-er* and *bad-est.*

EXERCISES

1 All the words given below begin with a prefix. It is possible to sort them out and make a list, similar to the one in 2.14. (a) Make such a list and then (b) go to a college level dictionary and see how many other example words you can find for each prefix and add them to your list; then (c) identify the root of every example word on your list and determine whether it is bound or free.

decentralize	disloyal	irrelevant
decode	defrost	insane
semiconscious	amoral	asexual
discourteous	transmit	foreshadow
tricycle	disobey	supersonic
archduke	semiofficial	superstructure
archenemy	monoplane	asymmetrical
de-escalate	transplant	monotheism
transfer	protoplasm	foretell
semifinal	tripod	archtraitor
dislike	improper	prototype
illogical	monorail	forewarn

2 All the words given below end with a derivational suffix. It is possible to sort them out on the basis of the final suffix and make a list similar to the one in 2.23. Not all of the functional groups in 2.23 are represented; nor are there necessarily three suffixes in each group. (a) Make a list like 2.23, and then (b) confining your analysis to the last suffix only, try to find other words ending in the same suffix and add them to your list, then (c) identify the root of every example word on your list and determine whether it is bound or free.

alarmist	formalization	orchestrate
authorization	freighter	Parisian
Baptist	fruity	participant
capacitate	glorification	poisonous
cellist	glorious	Portuguese
certification	hyphenate	rainy
Chinese	icy	Republican
Christendom	Indonesian	riotous
civilization	informant	sandy
contestant	inhabitant	silken
creamy	Japanese	stardom
deodorant	journalese	starvation
earldom	juicy	steamer
earthen	kingdom	stylist
Elizabethan	leaden	thirsty
exploration	Londoner	traitorous
facilitate	meaty	typist
famous	modification	vaccinate
fixation	novelist	waxen
flowery	officialdom	wooden

3 Printed below is a passage by Henry David Thoreau with forty words italicized. Each italicized word ends in an inflectional suffix. Copy the words on a sheet of paper and beside each word write the morpheme label for the inflectional suffix it contains (*-es, -poss, -prs, -pst, -en, -ing, -er, -est*). The answers for the first five italicized words are printed below the passage.

At a certain season of our life we *are accustomed* to consider every spot as the possible site of a house. I *have* thus surveyed the country on every side within a dozen miles of where I live. In imagination I have *bought* all the *farms* in succession, for all were to be bought, and I *knew* their price. I walked over each *farmer's* premises, *tasted* his wild *apples,* discoursed on husbandry with him, *took* his farm at his price, at any price, *mortgaging* it to him in my mind; even put a *higher* price on it,—took every thing but a deed of it,—took his word for his deed, for I dearly *love* to talk,—cultivated it, and him too to some extent, I trust, and *withdrew* when I *had enjoyed* it long enough, *leaving* him to carry it on. This experience entitled me to be *regarded* as a sort of real-estate broker by my *friends.* Wherever I *sat,* there I might live, and the landscape *radiated* from me accordingly. What is a house but a sedes, a seat?— *better* if a country seat. I *discovered* many a site for a house not likely to be soon *improved,* which some might have *thought* too far from the village, but to my eyes the village was too far from it. Well, there I might live, I *said;* and there I *did* live, for an hour, a summer and a winter life; *saw* how I *could* let the *years* run off, buffet the winter through, and see the spring come in. The future *inhabitants* of this region, wherever they *may* place their houses, may be sure that they *have been antici-pated.* An afternoon *sufficed* to lay out the land into orchard, woodlot, and pasture, and to decide what fine *oaks* or *pines* should be left to stand before the door, and whence each blasted tree could be seen to the best advantage; and then I *let* it lie, fallow perchance, for a man *is* rich in proportion to the number of things which he can afford to let alone.

a. are   -prs
b. accustomed   -en
c. have   -prs
d. bought   -en
e. farms   -es

4 Indubitably the distinction we made in this chapter between derivational and inflectional suffixes is valid. However, some linguists disagree concerning the status of certain suffixes. For example, some linguists claim that *-ly,* which we listed in 2.23f as a derivational suffix, is in fact an inflectional suffix. Evaluate its status using the criteria listed in 2.22 and see if you can find out why there are doubts about it. What is your opinion—is *-ly* a derivational suffix or an inflectional suffix?

5 You may have noticed that every word treated in this chapter containing more than one morpheme had at least one root, but never more than one root—the other morphemes were affixes of various kinds. But English words can have more than one root. Here are some examples:

a. doghouse, facecloth, flowerbed
b. beekeeper, songwriter, stockholder
c. daybreak, headache, rainfall

We know that the elements between commas above are words not only because they manifest internal stability and positional mobility but also because they require a special kind of pronunciation pattern that has the effect of tying two roots close together. (Notice how especially loud the first syllable is in all the cited words.) Such words are quite common in English and are called **compounds.** There are many types of them. Notice how the words in (a) seem to be composed of two noun roots; those in (b) of a noun root, a verb root, and a derivational suffix; those in (c) of a noun root and a verb root. See if you can think of other compounds of each of the three types listed. Examine a passage of English prose and see how many compounds it contains. Look for yet other types besides the three types given here.

FOR FURTHER READING

Nida (1946) treats segmentation and the identification of morphemes and presents many problems for practice. Gleason (1961, pp. 51–127) surveys American structuralist morphology and discusses many details of English. Quirk et al. (1972, pp. 973–1008) treat English prefixes and derivational suffixes in some detail; they treat inflectional suffixes in considerable detail at various places throughout their work. Marchand (1969) presents the most comprehensive treatment of English prefixes and derivational suffixes. Joos (1957) includes highly technical articles about both general questions of morphology and specific details of English.

Chapter 3

English Constituent Structure

SYNTAX

We have seen that the linguist seeks to identify and list the morphemes of a language, to determine which are roots and which are affixes. He then classifies the roots as bound or free, the affixes as prefixes or suffixes, and the suffixes as derivational or inflectional. All these tasks belong to the process of compiling a dictionary. We may now ask: does a dictionary of English fully account for its structure and function? Think of your experience studying a foreign language or traveling abroad; does a knowledge of the vocabulary of a language or possession of a bilingual dictionary make it possible to use the language the way the natives do? It does not. We will now begin finding out why it does not.

Read aloud and compare the two sequences of English words in 3.1. Notice that both sequences contain the same words.

3.1a mornings the in beautiful most are mountains the
  b the mountains are most beautiful in the mornings

If you listened closely enough to your own reading, or if you now ask someone else to read the sequences aloud, you will notice that 3.1a reads like a list: the words are pronounced on a continuing monotone and perhaps with slight pauses between them. However, in reading 3.1b, the pitch of the voice rises and falls on the last word, and there are no pauses between the words. You might at this point want to say, "Of course! That's because 3.1b is a sentence and 3.1a is not." But let me risk belaboring the obvious, hoping to give some initial insight into just what a sentence is. When a user of English hears 3.1b, he does not just think of the dictionary meanings of *mountains* and *beautiful;* he also associates the beauty with the mountains. No such association is conveyed in 3.1a.

Furthermore, this association in 3.1b is limited to a specific period of time, mornings. In 3.1a, *mornings* bears no such relation to any other word or group of words in the sequence. The obvious observation is that the English language conveys meaning not only by using words, which are composed of meaningful morphemes, but by *ordering them in a meaningful way.*

We can isolate and observe these principles of order more clearly by examining the following sequence, composed partly of English morphemes and partly of italicized nonsense syllables.

> **3.2** it was *pab*ious and the *bepty crine*s *marn*ed and *surdle*d in the *dop*

The italicized syllables, because they are not English morphemes and would not be entered in an English dictionary, are by definition meaningless segments. But if we read this string as if it were an English sentence, thereby evoking the ordering principles of English, then these meaningless segments begin to take on meaning imposed on them by the context. A naive user of English, given this sequence to read, might in fact assume that the underlined segments are meaningful, but that he must look them up. But even before he goes to his dictionary, he already knows that *marn* and *surdle* are verbs. He knows this because they carry a verb suffix, the past tense inflection, and because their position in the string after the nouns and before the prepositional phrase is a position where verbs tend to occur in English. He knows that the words beginning *pab* and *bept* are probably adjectives because of their positions in the sequence relative to other words and because they carry adjectival derivational suffixes. He will infer that *dop* is a noun because of its position at the end of the sequence after *the;* but he will probably also infer that it specifies a place because it is in a prepositional phrase introduced by *in.*

The facts in the previous paragraph lead to this generalization: when English words are strung together according to certain ordering principles, meaning is conveyed by the ordering that is not contained in the glosses of the individual words in isolation. The linguist's description and explanation of these principles is termed **syntax.** This chapter and the next five chapters examine English syntax in some detail.

FORM CLASSES

Any attempt to describe English syntax must show why 3.1a and countless sequences of English words like it are not English sentences, and why 3.1b and countless other sequences are English sentences. We could suggest that a description of English syntax might resemble the description of English morphology. We saw in the last chapter that morphemes may combine together to form words. All such combinations can be fully described by *listing* them in a dictionary. Thus when a user of English encounters a sequence of sounds such as *dop* in 3.2, he evaluates it against a mental list of English morphemes and words, his internal dictionary, and rejects it as meaningless because it is not in this dictionary. Might it be possible similarly to make a list of all those sequences of English words that are sentences and in this way explain that 3.1a is rejected because it is not on the list?

No one has ever seriously proposed such an approach to syntax, and it is easy to see why. Read the sentence in 3.3 and ask yourself: (1) Is it an English sentence? (2) Is it likely to be on any such list of English sentences?

> **3.3** Even though my mother-in-law seems normal, she insists on mixing milk, eggs, and vodka with her blood-pressure medicine and drinking it out of a sterling-silver beer mug.

The answer to the first question is most assuredly *yes,* and to the second question *no.* Now it is true that new entries can be added to the dictionary of words, for example, *astronaut.* Might it not also be true that sentences like 3.3, when they occur and are found to be syntactically acceptable, can be added to the "dictionary" of sentences? There is a difference. Most users of a language, while they are capable of inventing new words (such as *dop* in 3.2) never do. Or if they do, in jest, the words will not be understood by most other users of the language. However, every user of English creates sentences like 3.3 as a normal function of his use of language. Whereas only several items in a given year are added to the list of morphemes and words in English, the list of English sentences probably doubles every day. You will notice that we are here reviewing an aspect of language use which was seen in the introduction to have important theoretical implications. There I claimed, and here I am simply illustrating again, that there is no effective limit on the number of sentences in English and therefore that any attempt to describe the syntactic versus nonsyntactic sequences of words by making a list cannot succeed.

How, then, can the task of syntactic description be approached? In light of the discussion of scientific method in chapter 1, it is clear that a description of the data is not a complete scientific description at all; it is a collection of observations. The process of scientific description begins when generalizations are made in the form of hypotheses. But hypotheses refer to categories (classes) rather than to specific instances. What this entails for the study of syntax is that words must be grouped into classes according to their roles in forming sentences. Once such groupings are achieved, the principles of sentence structure can be expressed by reference to these classes.

Consider the syntactic behavior of the words *teachers, students,* and *understood* in 3.4 and 3.5. Notice that the first two sequences in each case are sentences, but the other sequences are not. See if you can notice any patterns which would justify grouping these three words into two classes (two in one class, one in the other) on the basis of the positions they can occupy in sentences.

3.4a Teachers understood.
  b Students understood.
  c *Students teachers.
  d *Teachers students.
  e *Understood teachers.
  f *Understood students.
3.5a Students understood teachers.
  b Teachers understood students.
  c *Teachers students understood.
  d *Students teachers understood.
  e *Understood students teachers.
  f *Understood teachers students.

The material in 3.4 illustrates that certain combinations of two of the words we are considering qualify as English sentences, but others do not; the material in 3.5 illustrates that certain combinations of three of the words qualify, but others do not. Notice that in the two-word sentences (3.4a and 3.4b) either *teachers* or *students* can occupy the first position. However, as 3.4c to 3.4f indicate, neither *teachers* nor *students* can occupy the second position in the two-word sentences. These observations indicate that *teachers* and *students* probably belong to the same syntactic class, but that *understood* probably belongs to another syntactic class. This hypothesis is reinforced by the data in 3.5: in these three-word sentences, *teachers* or *students* may occupy either the first or the last position, but *understood* must occupy the middle position. We thus have reason to place *students* and *teachers* in one syntactic class, call it class I, and *understood* in another syntactic class, call it class II, and tentatively to define the classes as follows:

3.6a A word is a member of class I if it can precede a word of class II in a two-word sentence or if it can precede or follow a word of class II in a three-word sentence.
  b A word is a member of class II if it can follow a word of class I in a two-word sentence or occur between two words of class I in a three-word sentence.

You probably noticed that what we are calling class I words are of course **nouns,** and class II words are **verbs.** But it is most important to keep in mind that the definitions of these classes are here based on their *positions* in sentences, and not on any real or supposed aspect of their meaning. We do not, for instance, define a noun as "the name of a person, place, or thing"; we define it according to its positions relative to the positions of other classes in sentences. And we do not define a verb as "an action or state of being"; we define it, too, according to its positions in sentences. And having thus defined *teachers* and *students* as nouns, we can test whether another word is a noun by substituting the word for *teachers* or *students* in those positions which these words can occupy in sentences. When "nouns" and "verbs" are thus defined strictly according to their positions in sentences, linguists call them **form classes.** Linguists prefer this term to the more familiar term, **parts of speech,** because they wish to exclude semantic connotations—such as that a noun names a person, place, or thing—from the notion of the form class. Let us examine a few of the principal form classes of English and try to provide fairly explicit definitions based on their positions in sentences.

We begin by further refining, first the definition of a noun, and then that of a verb. Fully adequate definitions of form classes by position require considerable observation plus subtle and detailed formulation. Consider, for example, the sequences in 3.7, which should be sentences according to the definitions in 3.6, but which in fact are not.

3.7a *Teacher understood.
b *Student understood teacher.

If we maintain the definition of a noun in 3.6a, we must claim that *teacher* and *student* are not members of the same form class as *teachers* and *students.* But our treatment of English morphology indicates that *student* is the same form class as *students* and *teacher* the same as *teachers.* We know this because the plural suffix of *teachers* and *students* is an inflectional suffix, and inflectional suffixes by definition do not change the form class of their stems. Thus we must revise the provisional definition of a noun in 3.6a so that it can encompass *teacher* and *student,* even though *teacher* and *student* cannot occupy the positions described in 3.6a. You may already have noticed that the definition in 3.6a applies to plural nouns, and this is why the sequences in 3.7 are not sentences. Now, examine the sequences in 3.8, which are sentences.

3.8a The teacher understood.
b The student understood the teacher.

If we introduce the word *the* in front of a singular noun, then it can combine with a verb to form a sentence as in 3.8a, or it can precede and follow a verb as in 3.8b. Let us reformulate the definition of a noun to include these new facts:

> **3.9** A word is a noun if, with the plural inflection affixed, it can precede a verb in a two-word sentence or precede and follow a verb in a three-word sentence, or, without the plural inflection but preceded by the word *the,* it can combine with a following verb to form a sentence, or, still accompanied by *the,* both precede and follow a verb to form a sentence.

The definition in 3.9 might possibly be refined, clarified, and shortened, but even so it will retain a certain degree of complexity. For this reason, let us follow the practice of linguists, and define form classes not by describing their positions but by presenting *examples* of their positions. Thus instead of 3.9, we say that a word is a noun if it can fit in any of the positions represented by a line in 3.10.

> **3.10a** _____ understood.
> **b** _____ understood _____.
> **c** The _____ understood.
> **d** The _____ understood the _____.

The defining sequences in 3.10 are sometimes called **diagnostic patterns,** or **test frames.** A given word will not necessarily fit in all the diagnostic positions, but if it fits in any one, then it is a noun. We have already seen that singular nouns cannot fit in 3.10a and 3.10b. Notice, however, that plural nouns can fit in all the positions—at least *teachers* and *students* can. Let us try some other words. What about *but, on, come, since, happy?* Test them and see for yourself. None of them is a noun, because none of them can occupy any of the diagnostic positions. What about *blood?* Notice that it seems inappropriate to place it in any of the initial diagnostic positions—for reasons having more to do with meaning than syntax. But it can fit in the second position of 3.10b and 3.10d, and so it is a noun.

Because we had to start somewhere, we defined nouns by reference to diagnostic patterns which use specific words. But having done so, we are now able to define verbs by means of patterns that refer to nouns as a class rather than to any specific noun. We will use the symbol N to stand for the class of nouns, and define a verb as any word which can occupy any one of the diagnostic positions in 3.11.

> **3.11a** N _____.
> **b** N _____ N.
> **c** The N _____.
> **d** The N _____ the N.

We have seen that *understood* occupies all the positions. But many verbs are limited in their ability to fill the various diagnostic patterns in 3.11. For example, *came* and *went* can occupy 3.11a and 3.11c, as in *John came, The boy went*. But they cannot occupy 3.11b and 3.11d (**John came Bill, *The boy went the ball*). And verbs like *prefer* and *discuss* can occupy 3.11b and 3.11d (*John preferred eggs, The boy discussed the problem*) but not 3.11a and 3.11c (**John preferred, *The boy discussed*). Now consider the sentences in 3.12, which provide evidence that the diagnostic patterns in 3.11 are not complete enough to define all verbs—at least all the inflected forms of verbs:

3.12a Harold was breaking the agreement.
   b William had broken the agreement.
   c The agreement was broken by Edward.

The presence of *-ing* and *-en* seems to indicate that *breaking* and *broken* are verbs. But neither *breaking* nor *broken* can fill any of the positions of 3.11. We might solve the problem in one of two ways: (1) we could expand the set of diagnostic patterns to include the following:

3.13a N was _____ N.
   b The N was _____ the N.
   c N had _____ N.
   d The N had _____ the N.
   e N was _____ by N.
   f The N was _____ by the N.

or (2) we could simply claim that if *any* of the inflected or uninflected variants of a stem can fit any of the diagnostic positions, then the stem is a member of the class being defined. In any case I wish here only to indicate some of the complexities involved in defining form classes by position. I will later expand our approach to syntax to include treatment of all the matters hinted at so far and many other matters as well. For this reason I do not intend our definitions of form classes here to be complete but only to illustrate the technique, both so that we can evaluate the technique and so that we can make use of the form classes here defined to examine additional aspects of English syntax.

But before we do, let us look at a few other form classes. In defining nouns and verbs, we used the word *the* in the diagnostic frames. And now that we have defined nouns and verbs, we have at least begun an implicit definition of the form class to which *the* belongs. Let us assume that the diagnostic frames in 3.14 comprise at least part of the definition of this new class:

3.14a _____ N V.
   b _____ N V _____ N.

What words can fit in the positions defined by 3.14? The italicized words in 3.15 and 3.16 all seem to qualify.

 3.15a *The* teacher understood.
  aa *The* teacher understood *the* student.
  b *This* teacher understood.
  bb *This* teacher understood *this* student.
  c *A* teacher understood.
  cc *A* teacher understood *a* student.
  d *Some* teachers understood.
  dd *Some* teachers understood *some* students.
 3.16a *Old* teachers understood.
  aa *Old* teachers understood *old* students.
  b *New* teachers understood.
  bb *New* teachers understood *new* students.
  c *Happy* teachers understood.
  cc *Happy* teachers understood *happy* students.
  d *Young* teachers understood.
  dd *Young* teachers understood *young* students.

If the diagnostic frames in 3.14 exclusively define just one form class, then all the italicized words in 3.15 and 3.16 belong to the same form class. But now examine the sequences in 3.17:

 3.17a The young student understood.
  b *Young the student understood.
  c *The the student understood.
  d *Young young student understood.

If the words *the* and *young* were indeed members of the same form class, we might expect all the sequences in 3.17, not just the first, to qualify as sentences. But since only the first qualifies, we may want to claim that the two words are members of different form classes and that the two classes precede a noun in a fixed order (3.17a) but not in reverse order (3.17b). Nor (seemingly) can two occurrences of either class precede a noun (3.17c and 3.17d). Having hypothesized that the italicized words in 3.15 are of a different form class than those in 3.16, we can soon find many more differentiating positions. We find for instance that two occurrences of the latter class *can* precede a noun:

 3.18 *Happy old* teachers understood.

We also find that the latter class of words can occupy a position in a sentence quite unlike the positions so far noted:

 3.19a The student is *young*.
  b Teachers are *old*.

In light of these several observations, let us establish two form classes, **determiners** and **adjectives,** and define them in the following ways. First we define adjectives as words that can occupy one of the positions in 3.20:

3.20a The _____ N V.
  b The _____ N V the _____ N.
  c The _____ _____ N V.
  d N is/are _____ .

The diagnostic frames in 3.20 succeed in distinguishing adjectives from determiners in that adjectives but not determiners may occupy the positions defined. Notice that nouns can occupy the position defined in 3.20d (as in *Teachers are helpers*). We could refine the diagnostic pattern in 3.20d to exclude nouns, but I wish here only to distinguish adjectives from determiners. In fact, I would like to be able to list diagnostic patterns for determiners that would exclude adjectives and thereby define determiners more positively. This is not easy to do without bringing in other form classes I wish to ignore for the present. Moreover it is not easy because several adjectives can precede a noun, and determiners must precede any adjectives. Thus any position in front of one or several adjectives can usually be filled either by a determiner or another adjective. So let us mix negative and positive criteria and define a determiner as any word which cannot fill any of the diagnostic positions in 3.20, but which can fill one of the diagnostic positions in 3.21:

3.21a _____ ADJ N V.
  b _____ ADJ N V _____ ADJ N.

All the italicized words in 3.15 meet both the negative and positive criteria of the definition of determiners.

So far we have defined four form classes: nouns, verbs, adjectives, and determiners. These four classes account for all the words in all the numbered sentences in this section except the words *is* and *are* in 3.19a and 3.19b. Let us now consider these words briefly. Examine the sentences in 3.22 and compare them with their counterparts in 3.23:

3.22a The student is happy.
  b Teachers are old.
  c The teacher was new.
  d Students were young.
3.23a The student is a chemist.
  b Teachers are helpers.
  c The teacher was the leader.
  d Students were guides.

A verb like *understand* can be substituted for *is, are, was,* and *were* in

3.23. (All these words, along with *am, being,* and *been,* are inflected forms of the morpheme *be.*) The fact that a verb and *be* can occupy the same position would give us reason to claim that *be* is a verb. But *understand,* and most other verbs, cannot substitute for *be* in 3.22. Thus we also have a reason to claim that *be* is not a verb. Another reason can be seen by comparing any sentence in 3.23 with a similar sentence formed by substituting a verb for *be:*

> **3.24a** Teachers *are* helpers.
> **b** Teachers *understand* helpers.

Even though *are* and *understand* seem to occupy the same position in 3.24, anyone who speaks English will feel that the sentences are structurally different. There is something about *are* that causes the user of English to think that *teachers* and *helpers* refer to one and the same group of people. But *understand* requires *teachers* and *helpers* to be conceived of as different groups. Thus the diagnostic frame N _____ N when applied to *be* should be differentiated in some way from when it is applied to verbs. For *be,* some notation would indicate that both nouns had identity of reference. In any case, there is ample reason to claim that *be* and all of its inflected forms *(am, is, are, was, were, being, been)* are not members of the form class of verbs. Traditionally, *be* has been called the **copulative verb,** or the **copula.** We shall not make up a new form class name for it; rather, we shall treat it as a class in itself, simply writing *be* in diagnostic patterns and sentence analyses whenever we wish to refer to it or any one of its inflected forms.

It has not been my goal in this section to define all the form classes of English, nor to define any class exhaustively. The whole of my treatment of English syntax will be an ongoing presentation and refinement of such definitions. I have, however, defined five classes in sufficient detail to discuss how form classes can be used in the larger task of describing the principles of English syntax. Here are the five classes with the abbreviations I shall use throughout the book to refer to them:

> **3.25a** Nouns: N
> **b** Verbs: V
> **c** Adjectives: ADJ
> **d** Determiners: DET
> **e** Copula: be

LINEAR SENTENCE PATTERNS

In the previous section, we defined five form classes on the basis of their relative positions in English sentences. Having done so, we can make general statements about sentence structure, using these classes.

Consider the sets of sentences in 3.26 to 3.29 and notice how the linear form-class pattern associated with each set explains why the sequences of words in each set are sentences:

3.26a N + V
Women work.
Children play.
Teachers understand.

b DET + N + V
A woman works.
Some children play.
This teacher understands.

3.27a N + V + N
Women build cars.
Children play games.
Teachers understand students.

b DET + N + V + N
The women build cars.
Some children play games.
That teacher understands students.

c N + V + DET + N
Women build the cars.
Children play some games.
Teachers understand those students.

d DET + N + V + DET + N
A woman builds the cars.
Some children play some games.
This teacher understands those students.

3.28a N + be + ADJ
Women are diligent.
Children are happy.
Teachers are informative.

b DET + N + be + ADJ
The women were diligent.
Some children are happy.
Those teachers are informative.

3.29a N + be + N
Women are workers.
Children are people.
Teachers are adults.

b DET + N + be + N
A woman was leader.
Some children are poets.
These teachers are women.

c N + be + DET + N
Women were the leaders.
Children are the future.
Teachers are the coaches.
d DET + N + be + DET + N
A woman was the leader.
Some children are the musicians.
These teachers are the coaches.

The sentence-pattern formulae and examples in 3.26 to 3.29 identify several basic types of English sentences. Those in 3.26 and 3.27 indicate that some English sentences contain a verb; those in 3.28 and 3.29 that some sentences instead contain the copula, *be.* If a sentence has a verb, the verb may end the sentence, as in 3.26a, or the verb may be followed by a noun, as in 3.27a. If the sentence has *be,* it cannot end in *be.* (There is no such pattern listed.) However, *be* (unlike a verb) can be followed either by an adjective, as in 3.28a, or a noun, as in 3.29a. The subpatterns (b, c, and d) under each of the headings of 3.26 to 3.29 account for the fact that wherever a noun appears in any of the patterns a determiner may accompany it.

Notice how the use of form-class patterns to describe the syntactic sequences of English is more economical than an attempt to list all the sentences of English. The patterns in 3.26 to 3.29 each describe three sentences. With little effort, you can add hundreds of other example sentences to each set of three. And so a scientific step in the direction of descriptive simplicity is made possible by recourse to patterns of form classes. Here are some additional linear sentence patterns for English, each one presented with one example sentence. They are divided into the same four pattern types as 3.26 to 3.29. The lettered subtypes correspond to the subtypes according to determiner placement of the patterns in 3.26 to 3.29. Notice that the patterns in 3.30 to 3.33 are developed by placing adjectives in front of the nouns in the patterns presented in 3.26 to 3.29.

3.30a ADJ + N + V
Young women work.
b DET + ADJ + N + V
Some happy children play.
3.31a ADJ + N + V + N
Old teachers understand students.
aa N + V + ADJ + N
Teachers understand new students.
aaa ADJ + N + V + ADJ + N
Old teachers understand new students.

b   DET + ADJ + N + V + N
The young women build cars.

bb   DET + N + V + ADJ + N
The women build new cars.

bbb   DET + ADJ + N + V + ADJ + N
The young women build new cars.

c   ADJ + N + V + DET + N
Happy children play some games.

cc   N + V + DET + ADJ + N
Children play some new games.

ccc   ADJ + N + V + DET + ADJ + N
Happy children play some new games.

d   DET + ADJ + N + V + DET + N
This old teacher understands those students.

dd   DET + N + V + DET + ADJ + N
This teacher understands those young students.

ddd   DET + ADJ + N + V + DET + ADJ + N
This old teacher understands those young students.

3.32a   ADJ + N + be + ADJ
Happy women are diligent.

b   DET + ADJ + N + be + ADJ
Some young children are happy.

3.33a   ADJ + N + be + N
Young children are people.

aa   N + be + ADJ + N
Children are happy people.

aaa   ADJ + N + be + ADJ + N
Young children are happy people.

b   DET + ADJ + N + be + N
These new teachers are women.

bb   DET + N + be + ADJ + N
These teachers are happy women.

bbb   DET + ADJ + N + be + ADJ + N
These new teachers are happy women.

c   ADJ + N + be + DET + N
Young women were the leaders.

cc   N + be + DET + ADJ + N
Women were the new leaders.

ccc   ADJ + N + be + DET + ADJ + N
Young women were the new leaders.

d   DET + ADJ + N + be + DET + N
Some young children are the musicians.

dd   DET + N + be + DET + ADJ + N
Some children are the new musicians.

ddd   DET + ADJ + N + be + DET + ADJ + N
Some young children are the new musicians.

I have, in 3.30 to 3.33, listed 28 linear sentence patterns, which, when added to the twelve presented in 3.26 to 3.29, give us forty such patterns for English. We noted above that nouns may have two and even three or more adjectives in front of them. If we were to develop the list of patterns further by placing two adjectives in front of every noun, the total list of patterns would exceed 100; if we were to place three adjectives in front of the nouns, the total number of patterns would exceed 200. Now recall that we have made use of only five form classes of English in the discussion of linear sentence patterns. English has many more form classes: auxiliary verbs, prepositions, conjunctions, and adverbs are among the more common. When these are taken into consideration, we soon realize that an inventory of linear sentence patterns for English must run into the tens of thousands, probably hundreds of thousands. In fact, if we expect sentence patterns to explain sentences like those in 3.34, which reprints 1.5, then it appears that there is no limit on the number of sentence patterns in English, since there is no effective way to limit the length of an English sentence.

> **3.34a** Mary gave the book to John, who gave it to Helen, who gave it to my friend, who gave it to the teacher, who gave it to Joe, who gave it to Albert, who gave it to his mother . . . .
>
> **b** He is the man who wrote the book which won the prize which was donated by Mr. Smith, who was born in Calcutta, which is a large city which is located in India, where my father met Ghandi, who . . . .

And so sentence patterns, while they make it possible to simplify syntactic descriptions, do not seem to make it possible to simplify enough. I shall return to the question of how we can make even simpler statements about English sentence structure after we consider an even more serious deficiency of linear sentence patterns.

CONSTITUENT STRUCTURE

Consider the sentence in 3.35. Notice first that it illustrates yet another possibility for greatly increasing the inventory of English sentence patterns: the fact that two nouns can occur together in an English sentence. Notice also that the sentence is basically a variation of the $N + V$ pattern (for example, *Teachers understand*). But neither of these facts is what makes this sentence especially interesting. See if you can notice something else about it.

> **3.35** $ADJ + N + N + V$
> Spanish book publishers arrived.

Read the sentence aloud, saying the word *Spanish* louder than the word *book*. Now read it again, this time saying the word *book* louder than the word *Spanish*. Did you notice that the sentence has a different *meaning* for each reading? Here are the two readings with paraphrases which clarify the differences. (Italics indicate loudness.)

3.36a *Spanish* book publishers arrived.
(Publishers of Spanish books arrived.)
b Spanish *book* publishers arrived.
(Spanish publishers of books arrived.)

In 3.36a, the books treat Spanish; the publishers might be of any nationality. In 3.36b, the books might treat any subject; the publishers are of Spanish nationality.

We saw earlier that syntax describes those principles which order words meaningfully into sentences. So it is clearly the task of a syntactic description of English to explain how a sequence of the same four words (*Spanish book publishers arrived*) manifesting only one linear pattern of form classes (ADJ + N + N + V) can have two different meanings. We can only suppose that there must be more to the principles of syntax than a linear sequencing of form classes, and therefore that it is not enough to describe the syntax of 3.36a and 3.36b by saying that they both manifest the pattern ADJ + N + N + V. The difference between 3.36a and 3.36b seems to derive from differences in *grouping* of the form classes within the linear sequence. The paraphrases in 3.36 capture this grouping. Another way to indicate the difference in grouping is to use brackets as in 3.37. The brackets in 3.37a indicate that *Spanish* is more closely related to *book* than to *publisher* (that is, it "modifies" *book*, but not *publisher*); the brackets in 3.37b indicate that *book* and *publisher* are more closely related to each other than either is to *Spanish* (thus *Spanish* "modifies" the both of them as a unit).

3.37a [ADJ + N] + N + V
Spanish book publishers arrived.
b ADJ+[N + N] + V
Spanish *book* publishers arrived.

The ambiguity of the phrase *Spanish book publishers* is a vivid example of an aspect of sentence structure that holds for all sentences: sentences are not simply linear patterns of discrete form classes each of which is an element unto itself and each of which bears equal structural relationships to any and all other form classes in the sequence. Rather, sentences are sequences of *grouped* form classes. A description of the principles of English syntax must not only define the linear order of form classes but also the grouping of the classes. Here, for instance, are complete groupings for 3.36a and 3.36b. Examine them carefully. Try to interpret the meaning of the notation and try to determine why it is the way it is.

3.38a $[[ADJ + N] + N] + [V]$
 Spanish book publishers arrived.
  b $[ADJ + [N + N]] + [V]$
 Spanish *book* publishers arrived.

First notice that *both* sentences are basically divided into two groups: *Spanish book publishers* and *arrived*. This grouping derives from syntactic ordering principles of English: *arrived* (the second "group") is an action performed by whatever entity is identified in the first group. (A sentence like *publishers arrived* would have the same basic division into two groups and for the same reason.) The *differences* between the two readings of the sentences in 3.36 occur completely within the first of the two basic groups into which both sentences are divided in 3.38. Now consider the notational device in 3.39. It represents another way of making the very same claims as 3.38 about the structural grouping of the words and form classes in the two sentences we have been considering.

3.39a

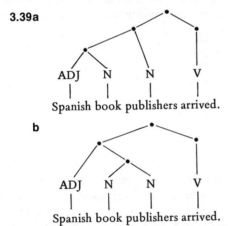

Spanish book publishers arrived.

  b

Spanish book publishers arrived.

The diagrams in 3.38 are called **bracketings**. The diagrams in 3.39 are called **inverted-tree diagrams**. Both notational systems equally represent the fact that the sequences of morphemes are grouped. However the tree diagram makes it clearer that the structure of the groupings is **hierarchical**. This means that the groups are not strung out side by side. Rather some groups are included in other groups. Thus in 3.39a *Spanish* and *book* are very closely related and constitute one group, but the two together bear a closer relation to *publishers* than either or both bear to *arrived*. And of course, *arrived* is predicated of the entire phrase *Spanish book publishers*.

Let us consider the implications of hierarchical structure further. In chapter 2 we examined and defined various morpheme types on the basis of their positions within words. In this chapter we have examined and defined several form classes on the basis of their positions within sentences. Morphemes that could substitute for one another in the same position within words were classed together and called roots, prefixes, suffixes, and so forth. Words that could substitute for one another in the same position within sentences were classed together and given a form-class label. But we have now discovered that the very notion of "position in a sentence" is defined hierarchically, not linearly. We must thus establish syntactic classes and provide category labels for *groups*. We must be able to label any word or group of words by virtue of its ability to occupy a given position in a hierarchical structure. In terms of tree diagrams such as those in 3.39, this means that any word or group of words that can appear in a tree where one of the dots appears must share a categorical label for being able to do so, and the tree diagram must contain the label instead of a dot. For example, we already know that *publishers* is a noun, but it can in a real sense be more than a noun. It shares with the entire phrase *Spanish book publishers* the ability to combine with *arrived* to form a complete sentence:

3.40

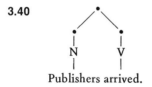

Publishers arrived.

And so, in relation to *arrived, publishers* and *Spanish book publishers* are the same: they both can occupy the position in a hierarchical structure tree in front of the position where a verb can appear, and together with a verb can form a sentence. For these reasons, we must establish a syntactic category which defines such a position in a tree diagram: we will call the members of this category **noun phrases** and use the abbreviation NP to represent them in tree diagrams. Use of this new category label calls for revisions in the diagrams of 3.39 and 3.40, as shown in 3.41.

3.41a

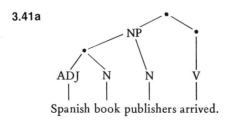

Spanish book publishers arrived.

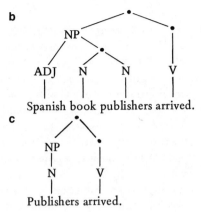

b

ADJ   N   N   V

Spanish book publishers arrived.

c

NP

N   V

Publishers arrived.

Now, notice that in all the diagrams in 3.41 there is a dot in the tree above the form-class label V, and on the same level as the label NP. We may now argue that just as *publishers* and *Spanish book publishers* are called NPs because they both can combine with *arrived* to form a sentence, so too a verb like *understood* and a verb and noun phrase like *understood students* should be given a label which reflects that they both can combine with a noun phrase to form a sentence. Because they can, let us call them **verb phrases,** and assume that the label VP should appear in the diagrams of 3.41 in place of the dot to the right of the label NP. Fully adequate arguments supporting the existence of categories like NP and VP would require much more space, and more complex reasoning, than I can give them here. I have said enough, however, to show that labels at higher levels in tree diagrams are necessary, and to give some idea of the basis for establishing the labels NP and VP.

I now introduce some technical terms to provide a vocabulary for talking about tree diagrams when the need arises. The discussion will refer to the diagram in 3.42.

3.42[1]

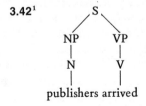

S

NP   VP

N   V

publishers arrived

Linguists use the term **constituent structure** to refer to the fact that sentences have a hierarchical structure of groups within groups such as we have been considering. All elements in the tree diagram of a sentence,

[1]From this point on we shall not observe the sentence conventions of initial capitalization or terminal punctuation in tree diagrams.

(1) the higher level category labels, (2) the form-class labels, and even (3) the words or morphemes at the bottom of the diagram, are called the **constituents** of the sentence. Thus, the sentence in 3.42 is said to have seven constituents: S, NP, VP, N, V, *publishers,* and *arrived.* (S is a category label that designates the entire sequence as a sentence.) NP and VP are said to be the **immediate constituents** of S because they are directly attached by upward lines to S with no intervening category labels. N, V, *publishers,* and *arrived* are also constituents of S but, because other category labels intervene, they are not immediate constituents. N is an immediate constituent of NP; it is in no way a constituent of VP because no upward lines attach it to VP. *Publishers* is a constituent of NP but not an immediate constituent. V is an immediate constituent of VP but in no way a constituent of NP. *Arrived* is a constituent of VP but not its immediate constituent. *Publishers* is an immediate constituent of N, and *arrived* an immediate constituent of V.

Constituent structure may also be represented by a system of *labeled* bracketings. Such notational diagrams are difficult to interpret, but every bit as adequate and explicit as tree diagrams. Here, for example, is the labeled bracketing that corresponds exactly to the tree in 3.42:

3.43 $[_S [_{NP} [_N \text{publishers}]_N]_{NP} [_{VP} [_V \text{arrived}]_V]_{VP}]_S$

A subscript category label inside a left bracket and outside a right bracket indicates that every element between the pair of brackets is a constituent of the labeled type. Thus the brackets $[_S \ldots]_S$ in 3.43 indicate that the entire sequence is a sentence. The brackets $[_{NP} \ldots]_{NP}$ and $[_{VP} \ldots]_{VP}$ indicate that the immediate constituents of the sentence are a noun phrase and a verb phrase and that all constituents within each pair of brackets constitute a noun phrase and a verb phrase respectively. The brackets $[_N \ldots]_N$ indicate both that the noun phrase in this sentence contains a noun (the N brackets are inside the NP brackets) and that *publishers* is a noun (it is inside the N brackets). Similarly, the brackets $[_V \ldots]_V$ indicate both that the verb phrase contains a verb (the V brackets are inside the VP brackets) and that *arrived* is a verb (it is inside the V brackets). Linguists use labeled brackets instead of tree diagrams to represent constituent structure when they need to conserve space on the printed page. We will need labeled bracketings later to express certain aspects of constituent structure in transformations.

EXERCISES

1 In this chapter I called *be* a copula but chose not to label it COP. Rather, I decided to make *be* its own category label. This implies that *be* is the only member of that form class which, though not a verb, can begin a verb phrase and, unlike a verb, can be followed by either an adjective or a noun phrase with the same reference as the initial noun phrase. Actually, my decision to treat *be* as the sole member of the copula class aims to simplify the presentation later in this book rather than fully to account for the copula in English, which may indeed have other members. Consider the italicized words in (1):

(1)a Joe *seems* happy.
   b They *look* sick.

Seem and *look* share with *be* the ability to precede an adjective and to relate it as an attribute to the initial noun phrase. There is thus reason to call them copulas. But now consider the sequences in (2):

(2)a *Joe seems a student.
   b *They look friends.

Unlike *be* (*Joe is a student, They are friends*), *seem* and *look* apparently do not allow a noun phrase to follow. Are they therefore not copulas after all? See if you can think of other words like *seem* and *look* which allow predicate adjectives to follow them. And try to discover other characteristics which can help you decide whether they should indeed be classed with *be* or perhaps be given a form-class label all their own.

2 The noun phrases listed below manifest the same kind of ambiguity as the phrase *Spanish book publishers.* To clarify for yourself the two possible interpretations of each phrase, read each one aloud twice, first emphasizing the first word, then the second. You can then gain valuable experience interpreting tree diagrams and labeled bracketings if you use both notations to represent each one of the two possible interpretations of each phrase on the list. The answer for the first phrase is given below the list.

a. American history teacher
b. black board eraser
c. civil engineering student
d. excess profits tax
e. foreign language teacher
f. freshman English teacher
g. local newspaper editor

Here are the two interpretations of (a) represented in tree diagrams:

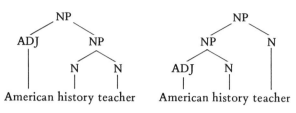

Here are the two interpretations of (a) represented in labeled bracketings:

[$_{NP}$ [$_{ADJ}$ American]$_{ADJ}$ [$_{NP}$ [$_N$ history]$_N$ [$_N$ teacher]$_N$]$_{NP}$]$_{NP}$

[$_{NP}$ [$_{NP}$ [$_{ADJ}$ American]$_{ADJ}$ [$_N$ history]$_N$]$_{NP}$ [$_N$ teacher]$_N$]$_{NP}$

3 The following sentence is an especially dramatic example of the role of constituent structure in organizing the message a sentence conveys: *The president fired the counselor with zeal.* Read the sentence a few times and see if you can determine why it is especially interesting. The sentence has at least three quite different readings each of which depends in some measure on the hierarchical grouping we choose to assign (that is, in all three cases the meanings of the words and the linear form-class patterns tend to remain constant). In the first reading, the phrase *with zeal* tells *how* the president performed the action of firing. *(How did he do it? With zeal.)* In the second reading, the phrase *with zeal* tells *which* counselor was fired. *(Who did he fire? The counselor with zeal.)* In the third reading, the president put zeal *into* (imbued) the counselor. *(What did he do to the counselor? He fired him with zeal.)* These three interpretations represent three different *groupings* of the words into higher-level constituents. Using either tree diagrams, or brackets, try to represent these different groupings.

FOR FURTHER READING

Of all the references, Fries (1952) presents the most comprehensive treatment of English form classes and linear sentence patterns. Hockett (1958) discusses English constituent structure at length. You will find readable treatments of many issues covered in this chapter in either Francis (1958) or Gleason (1961).

Chapter 4

English Phrase-Structure Rules

THE NATURE AND OPERATION OF PS RULES

At the beginning of the last chapter we wondered if we could provide a means for evaluating whether a given sentence is syntactically acceptable by listing all the sentences of English. We did not even give the proposal serious consideration; rather, we set out to generalize about sentence structure and developed the notion of form classes for this purpose. We hoped to describe English syntax by listing a set of linear form-class patterns for all the possible syntactic sequences in English. We found that, while such a set of patterns was indeed simpler than a list of all the sentences in English, thousands of patterns would nonetheless be necessary. We hoped for even greater simplicity. But before setting out to achieve greater simplicity, we paused to consider an aspect of sentence structure that makes linear sentence patterns inadequate: they in no way account for hierarchical constituent structure. So here is where we stand in our quest for both an adequate and economical means of describing the principles of English syntax: instead of an inventory of linear sentence patterns, we can develop an inventory of tree diagrams, one for every possible constituent structure in English. For instance, in 4.1 to 4.4 there are provisional tree diagrams for the first example sentence under each pattern in 3.26 to 3.29. Until we devise a means, later in the chapter, for representing tense inflections, the ordinary spelling of inflected forms of both verbs and *be* will appear in trees and in provisional rules.

4.1a

women work

b

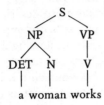

a woman works

4.2a

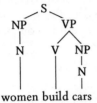

women build cars

b

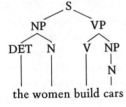

the women build cars

c

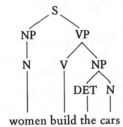

women build the cars

d

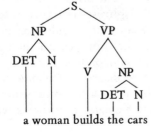

a woman builds the cars

4.3a

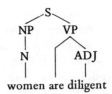

women are diligent

b

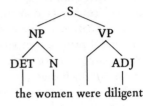

the women were diligent

4.4a

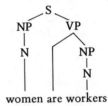

women are workers

b

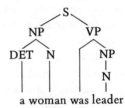

a woman was leader

c

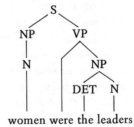

women were the leaders

d

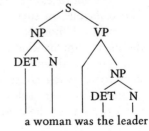

a woman was the leader

Just as twelve sentence patterns were necessary in 3.26 to 3.29 to account for these twelve sentences, so in 4.1 to 4.4 twelve tree diagrams are necessary. And just as we easily increased the inventory of patterns from twelve to fifty by putting in adjectives, and then showed how the total could just as easily increase into the thousands, so we could do the same with the inventory of tree diagrams. Thus, while tree diagrams can indeed represent constituent structure, they are no more descriptively economical than linear sentence patterns. Let us explicitly apply the empirical principle of simplicity on a very small scale, evaluating not the entire inventory of thousands of English tree diagrams but just the small subset of such diagrams contained in 4.1 to 4.4. Ask yourself if it is possible to represent all of the information about the twelve sentences diagrammed in 4.1 to 4.4 by recourse to simpler descriptive principles. Notice the large amount of repetition contained in the tree diagrams: every diagram, for instance, holds this much structure in common:

4.5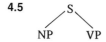

Would it not be simpler to say once, as a matter of principle, that all the sentences are composed of a NP and a VP? Notice too that of a total of twenty noun phrases in the twelve tree diagrams ten are composed of a noun and ten of a determiner and a noun. Would it not be simpler to say once instead of ten times that a noun phrase may be composed of a noun alone and once instead of ten times that a noun phrase may be composed of a determiner and a noun? Notice that six verb phrases begin with a verb and six with a variant of *be*. Would it not be simpler to state each option once instead of six times? The answer to these questions, and others we could raise about unnecessary repetition in the inventory of tree diagrams, is of course yes. It would be simpler to make such general statements about constituent structure once, and in doing so have the statements account for any and all sentences to which they apply. We could make these general statements in words, for example, *A sentence is composed of a NP and a VP.* But linguists have developed a formal notational system to make just such general statements about constituent structure more explicitly, comprehensively, and briefly than in words. The principles in such a system are called **phrase-structure rules** (or **PS rules**). Although the nature and operation of PS rules can involve the most complex kind of mathematical speculation, you can understand them and use them quite adequately if you think of them as a set of directives for drawing constituent-structure tree diagrams. Examine the set of phrase-structure rules in 4.6. The arrow in each rule means that what is on the left of the arrow can have as immediate constituents what is on the right of the arrow, or, in terms of tree diagrams, what is on the left of the arrow can have lines drawn from it directly to what is on the right of the arrow. As you examine the PS rules, notice how they provide for every label, every line, and every word of the twelve sentences in 4.1 to 4.4.

4.6a   S → NP + VP
   b   VP → V
        VP → V + NP
        VP → are + ADJ
        VP → was + ADJ
        VP → were + ADJ
        VP → are + NP
        VP → was + NP
        VP → were + NP
   c   NP → N
        NP → DET + N
   d   V → build
        V → builds
        V → work
        V → works
   e   ADJ → diligent
   f   DET → a
        DET → the
   g   N → woman
        N → women
        N → leader
        N → leaders
        N → workers
        N → cars

The PS rule in 4.6a expresses once and for all what the inventory in 4.1 to 4.4 repeats in all twelve diagrams: that the immediate constituents of all twelve sentences are NP and VP. The first line in 4.6b expresses once what is repeated in the trees in 4.1a and 4.1b: that a VP may have a V as its sole immediate constituent. The second line in 4.6b expresses once what is repeated four times in 4.2a to 4.2d: that a VP may have a V and NP as its immediate constituents. Similar descriptive economy is achieved by each of the PS rules in 4.6.

Here is an example of how the PS rules in 4.6 provide a description of a sentence. We take as our example 4.1a *(Women work)*. First, 4.6a provides for this much of the constituent structure:

4.7

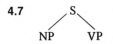

Next, 4.6b provides for the branch from VP to V:

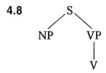

4.8

Then 4.6c provides for the branch to N:

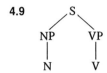

4.9

The third PS rule in 4.6d then provides for the branch to *work:*

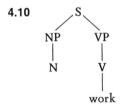

4.10

Finally, the second PS rule in 4.6g provides for the branch to *women:*

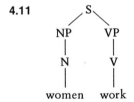

4.11

And so the grammar is able to provide a syntactic description of the sentence *Women work,* without having to make up a description especially for it before the need arises to use the sentence. You may find it useful to take a pencil and paper in hand and demonstrate to yourself, as we have done for 4.1a, how the PS rules in 4.6 do indeed define all twelve tree diagrams in 4.1 to 4.4. It is worth emphasizing that sentence descriptions provided by PS rules are not taken from any kind of ready-made inventory. Rather, the rules *create* a description when the need arises. For this reason such grammars are termed **generative:** because they generate constituent structures rather than store them.

Phrase-structure rules will play a central role in our description of English syntax. By generating constituent-structure trees, they adequately describe the hierarchical groupings in sentence structures. And they do this with maximum simplicity because they make it possible to generalize about sentence structure, but at the same time to apply the generalizations to the description of individual sentences. PS rules are also a much more viable basis for a *psychological* theory of syntax: they make it reasonable to impute to the user of English knowledge akin to the linguist's description of English grammar; it is more reasonable to suppose that humans, who have finite memories and quite varied intellectual abilities, produce sentences by applying general principles, rather than through having memorized thousands upon thousands of constituent structures.

Now let us look again at the PS rules in 4.6 and see how we can express them with greater simplicity, thus achieving even more descriptive economy. The discussion will focus on the rules in 4.6b, reprinted here in 4.12:

> **4.12a** VP → V
> **b** VP → V + NP
> **c** VP → are + ADJ
> **d** VP → was + ADJ
> **e** VP → were + ADJ
> **f** VP → are + NP
> **g** VP → was + NP
> **h** VP → were + NP

4.12a and 4.12b express two possibilities for verb-phrase structure: a VP may contain a V alone or a V followed by an NP. Since both rules call for an initial verb, it would be simpler to say so once instead of twice. We can do this in formal notation by using *parentheses:*

> **4.13** VP → V + (NP)

The notation in 4.13 means that when the rule operates, a line must be drawn in the tree from VP to V but there is an optional choice whether to draw a second line to NP. Thus both 4.12a and 4.12b are expressed by 4.13. Now consider 4.12c to 4.12e. All three are alike except that each offers an alternate choice of a variant of *be: are, was,* or *were.* One rule which offered this same choice of alternates would be simpler than three which unnecessarily repeat the notation VP → and the notation + ADJ. We can combine the three rules into one in formal notation by using *braces:*

> **4.14a**
> $$VP \rightarrow \begin{Bmatrix} are \\ was \\ were \end{Bmatrix} + ADJ$$
> **b** VP → {are, was, were} + ADJ

The notations in 4.14a and 4.14b are identical in meaning: when elements are listed vertically between braces *or* horizontally separated by commas, and when a rule containing them operates, then one of the elements must be drawn into the tree, but only one. Now notice that the last three rules in 4.12 can be treated similarly, but also notice that they express the same alternate choice among *are, was,* and *were.* Thus, whenever there is a choice among *are, was,* and *were* in the initial position in a VP, there is a choice between ADJ and NP in the second position. And so we can summarize all of the last six lines of rules in 4.12 as follows:

4.15
$$VP \rightarrow \begin{Bmatrix} are \\ was \\ were \end{Bmatrix} + \begin{Bmatrix} ADJ \\ NP \end{Bmatrix}$$

And by using an outer set of braces, we can summarize *all* the rules of 4.12 as follows:

4.16
$$VP \rightarrow \begin{Bmatrix} V + (NP) \\ \begin{Bmatrix} are \\ was \\ were \end{Bmatrix} + \begin{Bmatrix} ADJ \\ NP \end{Bmatrix} \end{Bmatrix}$$

Carefully compare 4.16 with 4.12 recalling that they are absolutely equivalent. But notice that 4.16 has no repetition whatever, and thus, from the point of view of scientific description, it is the simplest possible account of the verb phrases in the twelve constituent-structure trees in 4.1 to 4.4.

Using parentheses to express optional choice and braces to express required choice of one of a set of alternates, we can now summarize all of the PS rules in 4.6 as follows:

4.17a $S \rightarrow NP + VP$

b $VP \rightarrow \begin{Bmatrix} V + (NP) \\ \{are, was, were\} + \begin{Bmatrix} ADJ \\ NP \end{Bmatrix} \end{Bmatrix}$

c $NP \rightarrow (DET) + N$

d $V \rightarrow \{build, builds, work, works\}$

e $ADJ \rightarrow diligent$

f $DET \rightarrow \{a, the\}$

g $N \rightarrow \{woman, women, leader, leaders, workers, cars\}$

THE ENGLISH AUXILIARY

Let us now take a closer look at some details of English sentence structure. We begin with the hypothesis that the phrase-structure rules in 4.17 can generate not only the twelve sentences they were made up to describe but also the whole range of English sentences as well. We will test this hypothesis against sets of English sentences. In each test, we will find that the rules are inadequate, and we will revise and expand them as needed. But we shall soon see that they do not need very much expansion to become adequate to generate an exceptionally large number of English constituent structures.

Examine the sentences in 4.18 to 4.21, asking yourself whether the PS rules in 4.17 can generate constituent structure diagrams for each of them.

4.18a William writes plays.
  b William wrote plays.
4.19a William will write plays.
  b William would write plays.
4.20a William has written plays.
  b William had written plays.
  c William will have written plays.
  d William would have written plays.
4.21a William is writing plays.
  b William was writing plays.
  c William will be writing plays.
  d William would be writing plays.
  e William has been writing plays.
  f William had been writing plays.
  g William will have been writing plays.
  h William would have been writing plays.

In 4.22 it is demonstrated that the PS rules in 4.17 can indeed generate trees for the sentences in 4.18.

4.22a

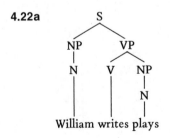

William writes plays

b

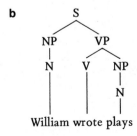

William wrote plays

The sentences in 4.19 to 4.21, however, pose problems. Let us begin with the pair of sentences in 4.19. The words *will* and *would* either represent another occurrence of the form class of verbs, in which case the PS rules must be changed to generate two verbs in a verb phrase, or these two words represent a form class other than verbs, thus requiring a new category label in addition to a change in the PS rules. If they are the same form class as verbs, they should be able to substitute for a verb, or interchange positions with a verb. But they can do neither *(*William woulds plays, *William write will plays)*. We conclude that they are members of a form class other than verbs. For the moment, let us call them **auxiliaries**. The words *has* and *had* in 4.20a and 4.20b pose a similar problem. They do seem to be able to substitute for a verb *(William has plays)*, but not with *has* having the same meaning as in *William has written plays*. And they cannot interchange positions with a verb *(*William written has plays)*. So we will call them auxiliaries too. But now consider 4.20c and 4.20d where the sequences *will have* and *would have* occur. Since the order cannot be inverted *(*William have will written plays)*, we conclude that *will* and *would* on the one hand and *have, has,* and *had* on the other hand cannot all be members of the same form class. If we wish to call them all auxiliaries, then we must find a way of distinguishing at least two subclasses of auxiliaries. But now consider the sentences in 4.21. If you examine all eight sentences, and argue as I have done in this paragraph, you will conclude (1) that *is* and *was* are also auxiliaries, but (2) auxiliaries of yet a *third* subclass.

How can we revise the PS rules in 4.17 so that they can generate these three types of auxiliary verbs each in its proper position. See what you think of 4.23, where 4.23a is a revision of the first PS rule in 4.17, and 4.23b is an entirely new PS rule.

4.23a $S \rightarrow NP + (AUX) + VP$

b $AUX \rightarrow \left\{ \begin{array}{l} \left[\begin{array}{l} \left\{ \begin{array}{l} \text{will} \\ \text{would} \end{array} \right\} + \text{(have)} + \text{(been)} \end{array} \right] \\ \left\{ \begin{array}{l} \text{has} \\ \text{had} \end{array} \right\} + \text{(been)} \\ \left\{ \begin{array}{l} \text{is} \\ \text{was} \end{array} \right\} \end{array} \right\}$

Assuming, of course, that the nouns *William* and *plays* and the various inflected forms of the verb *write* are added to the right of the arrow in the PS rules which introduce nouns and verbs, then the revised PS rules can generate trees like the one in 4.24, which is the constituent structure of 4.21e.

4.24

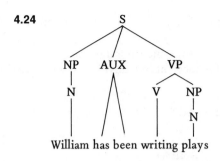

William has been writing plays

Now, the rules in 4.23, which generate trees like·the one in 4.24, are a step in the right direction, but they are far from fully satisfactory for several reasons. (1) They do not explain why certain sequences of auxiliaries precede only specified inflected forms of a verb. (Notice that *written* appears only immediately after *have, has,* or *had,* and *writing* appears only immediately after *been, is,* or *was.*) (2) The PS rules in 4.23 also fail to account for tense in any unified way. (Notice that the first auxiliary stem, if there is an auxiliary, manifests *-prs* or *-pst,* whichever is called for, and in the absence of an auxiliary, the verb manifests the tense suffix.) The PS rules do not even indicate explicitly the presence of tense morphemes, not to mention treating them in such a way that unnecessary repetition is avoided in the rules. (3) The PS rules in 4.23 fail to show that the variant forms of *have* share a sameness of function and so do the variant forms of *be:* this sameness would call for one and only one appearance of *have* and, likewise, only one appearance of *be* in PS rules in order to achieve a great amount of descriptive simplicity.

But there are yet other facts about English auxiliaries which the PS rules in 4.23 fail to take account of. There is the fact that *will (will-prs)* and *would (will-pst)* are but two of a larger class of words which can occupy the initial auxiliary position. *Can, could, may, might, shall, must,* and *should* are others. The PS rules should account for these words too.

In view of the observations in the previous two paragraphs, we must conclude that adequate PS rules for the English auxiliary must show (1) that tense is a separate category which always affixes to the first auxiliary stem, if there is one, and to the verb stem otherwise, (2) that there is a separate subclass of auxiliaries including words like *can, may, will,* and *shall,* this class occurring before other auxiliaries, (3) that *have* itself constitutes an auxiliary subclass which is positioned after words like *can, may, will,* and *shall* and which is functionally tied to the *-en* inflectional suffix, and (4) that *be* itself constitutes an auxiliary subclass which is positioned after other auxiliaries and which is functionally tied to the *-ing* inflectional suffix.

Here is a set of PS rules which incorporates the rules in 4.17, but which also accounts for the facts about auxiliaries we have just examined:

4.25a S → NP + AUX + VP

b VP → $\begin{Bmatrix} V + (NP) \\ be + \begin{Bmatrix} ADJ \\ NP \end{Bmatrix} \end{Bmatrix}$

c NP → (DET) + N

d AUX → TNS + (M) + (PERF) + (PROG)

e TNS → $\begin{Bmatrix} \text{-prs} \\ \text{-pst} \end{Bmatrix}$

f M → {can, may, will, shall, should, must, . . .}

g PERF → have-en

h PROG → be-ing

i V → {build, work, write, . . .}

j ADJ → {diligent, . . .}

k DET → {a, the, . . .}

l N → {woman, leader, car, William, play, . . .}

Notice that the category label AUX in 4.25a is not in parentheses. This indicates that every English sentence has an auxiliary. We must claim this because every English sentence has a tense suffix, and since TNS is introduced as a category of AUX, then every sentence must contain AUX. Rule 4.25d claims that, in addition to TNS, the higher level AUX category may have up to three other immediate constituents. The first constituent is labeled M, for **modal**, a label for words like *can, may, will,* and *shall*. The second constituent is labeled PERF, for **perfect**. The third constituent is labeled PROG, for **progressive**. PS rule 4.25e indicates that either *-prs* or *-pst* may be immediate constituents of TNS. PS rule 4.25f indicates that *can, may, will, shall, should,* or *must* may be immediate constituents of M. The ellipsis dots indicate that there are other modals in English. PS rule 4.25g indicates that *have* and the inflectional suffix *-en* are always immediate constituents of PERF. The functional tie between these two morphemes is thus accounted for. PS rule 4.25h indicates that *be* and the inflectional suffix *-ing* are always the immediate constituents of PROG. The functional tie between these two morphemes is thus accounted for.

In 4.26, I show the constituent-structure tree that the newly revised set of PS rules generates for sentence 4.21e, which we chose earlier in 4.24, to exemplify the output of the provisional PS rules in 4.23.

4.26

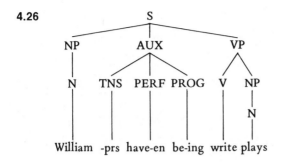

The PS rules in 4.25 present a kind of dilemma. In order to simplify the account of inflectional suffixes (to show that tense attaches to the first AUX stem or V, to show that *-en* is functionally tied to *have,* and to show that *-ing* is similarly tied to *be*) the rules place these suffixes in positions that they do not in fact occupy in English sentences. You will see later that a truly adequate account of English syntax will often require us to analyze constituent structure in such a seemingly contradictory manner. Until then, you must simply learn to live with an apparent contradiction: our grammar consistently positions the inflectional suffixes *-pst, -prs, -en,* and *-ing* in front of the stems they in fact *follow* in sentences.

In 4.27 (on the following page), I represent the constituent structure of all of the sentences in 4.18 to 4.21. If no morpheme appears in a given sentence under a given category label in AUX, then the label is not part of the tree for that particular sentence.

The rules applying to the auxiliary will be more meaningful and useful if we pause now to examine each of the categories of AUX in greater detail. Many of the comments will deal with the meanings of the AUX categories, and thus go beyond syntax, which is the proper subject matter of this chapter. But knowledge of the meanings of the AUX categories will make it easier for you to understand the rules which explain the syntax of the auxiliary.

I stated above that tense occurs in every English sentence. This means that either *-prs* or *-pst* is affixed to some stem in every sentence. The rules further claim that there are two and only two tense affixes in English. Some grammars also apply the term tense to perfect and progressive, and thus you may have heard expressions like "present perfect tense." We reserve the term as a label for occurrences of either *-prs* or *-pst.* The term *present* is actually a bit of a paradox because verbs with the *-prs* suffix usually do not refer to current situations at all, but to habitual, or repeated events. In *John sells shoes,* John may very well be sleeping

4.27

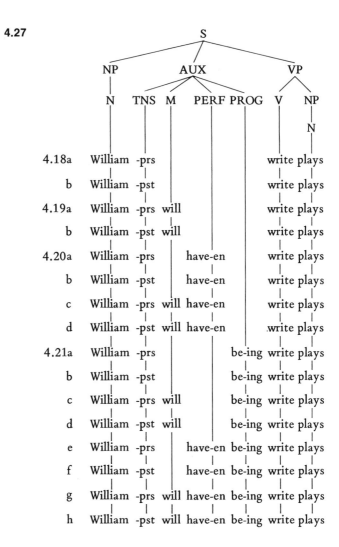

when the sentence is spoken. The sentence *Students go to ball games on Saturdays* might be spoken on a Tuesday. Verbs with *-prs* can even refer to *future* events, as in *The team returns tonight.* The *-pst* suffix, which does in fact refer most often to events prior to the present, can however manifest a meaning that has nothing to do with time: a verb with *-pst* can refer to *hypothetical* situations, as in *If the president walked in, I would faint.* Both *walked* and *would* contain *-pst,* but neither verb refers to actions or events prior to the time the sentence is spoken. If anything, the events are *future* (though they may never occur at all). In view of these comments on the tense inflections, it is important to emphasize that the occurrence of *-prs* or *-pst* in a sentence is not primarily a matter of meaning, it is determined by the form of the verb. Remember that one of the two suffixes must occur in every sentence. When you analyze sentences, if the relevant inflected stem has no change or if it has an "*s*-like" termination, then affix *-prs;* if it has a change in vowel, or if it has a "*d*-like" termination, then affix *-pst.*

The PS rules in 4.25 define modals syntactically as members of a substitution class in AUX following TNS and preceding PERF. There is also an interesting morphological characteristic which sets modals off from other auxiliaries, and from verbs: when they occur with a third person singular subject, such as *he, she,* or *it,* the "*s*-like" variant of *-prs* which occurs with other AUX or verb stems does not appear (**Helen cans speak French, *He shoulds turn himself in).* The semantics of modal verbs is so complex that I can only hint at the issues here. Most modal verbs can have more than one meaning. Sometimes the meanings are strikingly different, sometimes subtly so. In 4.28 I list some meanings of *can, may, will, shall, should,* and *must.* Examine the meanings and the example sentences.

4.28a	can	Ability	Mike can play tennis.
		Permission	Yes, Joey. You can go to the movies.
		Potentiality	A redwood can grow to several hundred feet.
b	may	Potentiality	It may rain.
		Permission	Yes, Joey. You may go to the movies.
c	will	Certainty	The sun will rise tomorrow.
		Command	All sophomores will report for registration at 10 A.M.
d	shall	Promise	I shall be there.
		Legal command	Legislative power shall be vested in the Congress.
e	should	Weak obligation	You should study for the test.
		Possibility	If he should come, tell him.
f	must	Strong obligation	You must pay your taxes.
		Deduction	The rug is wet. It must have rained.

Notice that modals as a class communicate information about the speaker's attitude toward the happenings of a sentence: whether he thinks the statement is certain, possible, probable, required, true, and so forth. Notice also that I have listed the same meaning with two modals in some instances. But it is easy to see that in such cases the meanings are not exactly identical. For instance, *can* and *may* both express permission, but *can* does so in less formal social contexts, and *may* in more formal contexts. And the kind of potentiality expressed by *can* and *may* is not the same; the former seems to derive from inner potencies of some noun; the latter from a kind of cosmically conditioned potency. You may wish to consult the works cited at the end of this chapter for detailed discussion of the meanings of modals.

I did not discuss *could, might,* and *would* in the previous paragraph. This is because I consider them to be the past of *can, may,* and *will* respectively. The sentences in 4.29 illustrate this.

> **4.29a** I can come.
> **aa** Yesterday, I said I could come.
> **b** I may come.
> **bb** Yesterday, I said I might come.
> **c** I will come.
> **cc** Yesterday, I said I would come.

Thus, whenever you encounter *could, might,* or *would* in sentences later in this book, learn to think of them as *can-pst, may-pst, will-pst.* There are certain oversimplifications in such a procedure; for example, *might* seems capable of replacing *may* in 4.29b with no real change in meaning and thus could perhaps be analyzed as *might-prs.* But I wish to overlook some of the semantic subtleties of modals in order to direct your attention to questions of syntax. You may wonder why I do not treat *should* as the past of *shall.* We would certainly achieve a satisfying symmetry if we could do so. But it seems that we cannot. Compare the pair of sentences in 4.30 with the pairs in 4.29. While the second sentence in 4.30 is an acceptable English sentence, *should* can in no way be taken to mean *shall-pst:*

> **4.30a** I shall come.
> **b** Yesterday, I said I should come.

In 4.30a the speaker is promising to come. In 4.30b, the speaker is expressing the fact that he had an obligation to come, not that he promised to come. For this reason you should learn to think of *should* as *should-prs.*

I noted earlier that the presence of the category PERF in AUX is signaled by the stem *have* and the suffix *-en* attached to the following stem. I defended grouping these two disconnected morphemes as constituents of the same category because they were functionally tied. In syntactic terms, this meant that one morpheme does not occur in an English sentence without the other. In semantic terms, this means that when these two morphemes are present in AUX, a sentence conveys certain information which it would not otherwise convey and that this information cannot be communicated by either morpheme alone. Ordinarily, the presence of *have-en* means that the event the sentence describes has *duration*. Compare the sentences in 4.31.

4.31a John lives in Florida.
  b John has lived in Florida for ten years.

In 4.31a, John may have moved to Florida yesterday; we have no way of knowing. In 4.31b, John began living in Florida at some time in the past, has continued living there, and still lives there. All this is communicated by the presence of *have-en*. But now read 4.31b again without the words *for ten years.* The sentence can still have the meaning we just discussed, but it can also have another meaning, a second meaning of *have-en*. It can refer to an *indefinite time in the past* when John lived in Florida, without implying that he still lives there. *Have-en* can have yet a third meaning, one which is actually quite common. Consider the two short dialogs in 4.32:

4.32a Do you speak French?
    I studied it.
    Well, do you still speak it?
  b Do you speak French?
    I have studied it.
    Good, you can translate this sentence.

4.32b indicates that *have-en* can *relate some past event or situation to a current event or situation as a cause or explanation.* Here are some other examples: (1) We walk into a cold room, look at the open window, and say *Someone has left the window open,* thus explaining the cause of the coldness. (2) Speaking of President Nixon, we say *He has given some significant speeches.* We are commenting on his present performance as president. About Dwight Eisenhower we would say rather *He gave some significant speeches.* In fact, speakers of English rarely use the perfect in reference to any deceased person, because to do so implies that the person is living. Now, notice how, in the various contexts of 4.33, the same sentence can have all three meanings which I have attributed to *have-en:*

4.33a Duration:
    I have lived in Florida for ten years, and I plan to stay here for the rest of my life.
  b Indefinite time in the past:
    I was born in Pennsylvania, but *I have lived in Florida,* California, and Texas.
  c Relating past to present as cause or explanation:
    You need advice on where to stay in Orlando?
    Don't worry, *I have lived in Florida.*

All of these facts of course strongly reinforce the decision to analyze *have* and *-en* as constituents of the same category, PERF. None of the meanings which I have discussed can be attributed to either of these morphemes alone.

I noted earlier that the presence of the category PROG in AUX is signaled by the stem *be* and the suffix *-ing* attached to the following stem. I defended grouping these two disconnected morphemes as constituents of the same category because they were, like *have* and *-en*, functionally tied. In syntactic terms, this meant that one morpheme does not occur in an English sentence without the other. In semantic terms, this means that when these two morphemes are present in AUX, a sentence conveys certain information it would not otherwise convey, and that this information cannot be communicated by either morpheme alone. Ordinarily the presence of *be-ing* means that the event the sentence describes is *in progress.* Compare the two sentences in 4.34.

> **4.34a** We study linguistics.
> **b** We are studying linguistics.

The AUX of 4.34a contains only *-prs* and thus, as you have seen, is a comment on something that is done habitually, but which very likely is not happening when such a sentence is spoken. The presence of *be-ing* in 4.34b ties the study of linguistics to the time when the sentence is spoken. Actually 4.34b is ambiguous because *be-ing* can communicate another meaning besides progressive. In a sentence like *We are studying linguistics tonight,* the action of studying is not in progress; rather it is *anticipated.* But as with *have-en,* whichever meaning is communicated, it is communicated by the presence of both *be* and *-ing,* thus reinforcing the decision to analyze the two morphemes as constituents of the one category, PROG.

ENGLISH PREPOSITIONAL PHRASES

Let us begin this section, as we did the last, by examining an array of sentences and evaluating them in the light of our current set of phrase-structure rules, those in 4.25. Ask yourself whether the PS rules in 4.25 can generate constituent-structure trees to account for all the words in the sentences in 4.35.

> **4.35a** The girls are studying French *with enthusiasm.*
> **b** Kate had been kind *at Harvard.*
> **c** Richard teaches Russian *in the evening.*
> **d** The Norwegians have invaded Burma *for some reason.*

Careful examination of these sentences reveals that the PS rules in 4.25 provide constituent-structure trees for all but the italicized portions of the sentences. These italicized portions manifest two difficulties: (1) they end in a noun phrase, but the PS rules do not allow for a second noun phrase following a verb as in 4.35a, 4.35c, and 4.35d, nor for a noun phrase after an adjective as in 4.35b, and (2) each italicized portion begins with a word which does not qualify as a member of any form class so far discussed. Furthermore, these words, *with, at, in,* and *for,* seem to relate the noun phrases following them to the rest of the sentence. These words are of course **prepositions,** and the italicized portions in 4.35 are **prepositional phrases.** I shall use the label P for the former category, and the label PP for the latter. Proof of the existence of a form class of prepositions can easily be adduced by trying to substitute other words in the positions which *with, at, in,* and *for* occupy in the sentences of 4.35. Proof that the entire italicized sequence in each sentence should be grouped into a single PP category derives from the already mentioned fact that the preposition seems to relate the NP following it to the rest of the sentence, as well as from certain other facts which I will now discuss. Examine the sentences in 4.36. Ask whether the PS rules can generate them, and also compare them with the sentences in 4.35.

4.36a   The girls are studying French *how?*
  aa   The girls are studying French *enthusiastically.*
  b   Kate had been kind *where?*
  bb   Kate had been kind *there.*
  c   Richard teaches Russian *when?*
  cc   Richard teaches Russian *then.*
  d   The Norwegians have invaded Burma *why?*
  dd   The Norwegians have invaded Burma *deliberately.*

The single-lettered sentences in 4.36 represent unusually ordered but nonetheless quite acceptable questions in English. The double-lettered sentences represent possible answers to these questions. Both the question words and the words which substitute for them in the answers occupy positions where form classes so far discussed cannot appear. We thus have reason to establish yet another form class for English. The class is of course the class of **adverbs,** which I shall label ADV. Now notice that the prepositional phrases in 4.35 are also appropriate answers to the question word adverbs in the corresponding sentences of 4.36. This not only reinforces the claim that PPs are indeed unitary categories in constituent structure, it also raises the problem of how to represent the fact that a PP can substitute for an adverb.

To clarify the problem raised in the previous paragraph, let us focus on just these three sentences:

4.37a The girls are studying French *how?*
   b The girls are studying French *enthusiastically.*
   c The girls are studying French *with enthusiasm.*

The italicized word or words in these sentences provide evidence that (1) there is a position toward the end of an English sentence which requires a category label, but (2) the position may be occupied either by a single word or by a prepositional phrase. Thus we need a label for the position as such, and also labels for the two types of constituents the position may have: single words or prepositional phrases. Here is a proposal, which I shall modify almost immediately, for how the PS rules could account for these facts:

4.38a $S \rightarrow NP + AUX + VP + (Adverbial)$
   b $Adverbial \rightarrow \begin{Bmatrix} PP \\ ADV \end{Bmatrix}$
   c $ADV \rightarrow \{how, enthusiastically, \ldots\}$

Incorporation of rules like this into the full set of PS rules would provide trees like those in 4.39, where I diagram fully only the relevant portions of the sentences in 4.37.

4.39

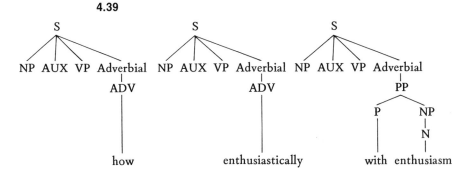

I add the suffix *-ial* to *adverb* simply to designate a more general category than adverbs. I could also use an expression like adverb phrase. The proposal in 4.38 would suffice were it not for sentences like this:

4.40 The girls were studying French enthusiastically at the pool yesterday for some reason.

The sentence in 4.40 has four adverbials: one answers the question *how?* *(enthusiastically)*, one answers the question *where?* *(at the pool)*, one answers the question *when?* *(yesterday)* and one answers the question *why?* *(for some reason).* Thus there are (at least) *four* positions at the end of a sentence where either a single word adverb or a PP may appear. And on the basis of the four question-word adverbs, *how, where, when,* and *why,* we can distinguish four *subtypes* of adverbials: (1) **adverbials of manner,** which I will label ADVM, (2) **adverbials of place,** which I will label ADVP, (3) **adverbials of time,** which I will label ADVT, and (4) **adverbials of reason,** which I will label ADVR. I define an ADVM as any word or phrase which can substitute for the question-word adverb *how.* I define an ADVP as any word or phrase which can substitute for the question-word adverb *where.* I define an ADVT as any word or phrase which can substitute for the question-word adverb *when,* and I define an ADVR as any word or phrase which can substitute for the question-word adverb *why.* Here then are revisions in our PS rules which will be incorporated the next time the entire set appears:

4.41a $S \rightarrow NP + AUX + VP + (ADVM) + (ADVP) + (ADVT) + (ADVR) \ldots$

b $\begin{Bmatrix} ADVM \\ ADVP \\ ADVT \\ ADVR \end{Bmatrix} \rightarrow \begin{Bmatrix} PP \\ ADV \end{Bmatrix}$

c $PP \rightarrow P + NP$

d $P \rightarrow \{with, at, in, for, \ldots\}$

e $ADV \rightarrow \begin{Bmatrix} \text{enthusiastically, there, then, deliberately, } \ldots \\ \text{how, where, when, why, } \ldots \end{Bmatrix}$

Notice the ellipsis dots at the end of 4.41a. These indicate that there are other types of adverbials in English, but I shall not treat them at this time. The rules in 4.41, in conjunction with rules I have discussed previously, will generate the tree in 4.42 for the sentence in 4.40.

4.42

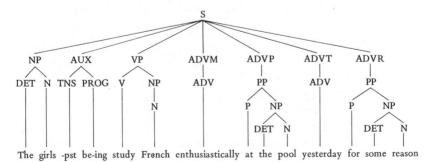

The girls -pst be-ing study French enthusiastically at the pool yesterday for some reason

Thus far in this section, I have introduced the notion of prepositional phrases, given reasons to support the need in English for such a category in constituent structure, and provided rules for generating PPs in appropriate places in trees. The PPs so far discussed have all been adverbials of various kinds. But not all PPs are adverbials.

Consider the sentences in 4.43, and ask whether the italicized prepositional phrases can substitute for any of the question-word adverbs defining the four types of adverbials included in our revised rules.

4.43a The speaker will be talking *about taxes.*
   b The secretary conferred *with experts.*
   c A defendant depends *on a lawyer.*
   d Carnegie had given a contribution *to the railroads.*

Questions ending in *how, where, when,* or *why* instead of the PPs in 4.43 would not elicit any of these PPs in reply, which means that none of the question-word adverbials can properly substitute for them. In fact, the question sequences that seem to correspond to the sentences in 4.43 are these:

4.44a The speaker will be talking *about what?*
   b The secretary conferred *with who(m)?*
   c A defendant depends *on who(m)?*
   d Carnegie had given a contribution *to what?*

Since none of the prepositional phrases in 4.43 can substitute for the question words which define adverbials, we must conclude that these PPs are not adverbials and thus provide rules to account for them. The sentences in 4.45 will help us to do this.

4.45a The speaker will be talking *about taxes* with sincerity.
   b The secretary conferred *with experts* before the conference.
   c A defendant depends *on a lawyer* during a trial.
   d Carnegie had given a contribution *to the railroads* for some reason.

The sentences in 4.45 show that the PPs we are considering *precede* adverbials. Of course we may interchange the order of the prepositional phrases in each sentence. But I claim that the order given in 4.45 is the more natural order, and wish to develop PS rules that will generate this preferred word order. (We will see in later chapters how a grammar accounts for alternate ordering of essentially the same meaningful elements.) To see how, exactly, the PS rules should position nonadverbial prepositional phrases, consider the following situation, in relation to 4.45c: Suppose we meet a friend and commence a conversation. The friend says, without explanation, *A defendant depends*. Such a sentence would confuse us, and we would probably say something like *A defendant depends on what?* Such a response is evidence that a prepositional phrase beginning with *on* has an intimate tie to the verb *depend*. In fact, the preposition *on* almost seems to be part of the verb. Another kind of evidence for this close functional tie of PPs like *on a lawyer* to the verb *depend* is presented in 4.46:

> **4.46a** During a trial, a defendant depends on a lawyer.
> **b** *On a lawyer, a defendant depends during a trial.

An adverbial prepositional phrase like *during a trial* can naturally be moved to the front of a sentence. A prepositional phrase like *on a lawyer* ordinarily cannot. 4.46b is not an absolutely impossible sequence, but to achieve sufficient naturalness, the word *lawyer* must be pronounced especially loudly, thus indicating that a very unusual reordering of constituents is manifested in such a sequence. In any event the following points are clear: (1) certain prepositional phrases are not adverbials; (2) these should precede adverbials in constituent structure; (3) the PS rules should show that these PPs have a close tie to verbs, thus explaining that the meaning of some verbs seems to expect certain PPs to follow them and also explaining that these PPs are loath to move to the front of a sentence (that is, they seem to be "locked into" a tree more tightly than adverbial PPs). Before I present revisions of the PS rules to account for these facts, let us consider one further aspect of nonadverbial PPs. For this purpose examine the sentence in 4.47:

> **4.47** The secretary conferred *with experts about policy* before the conference.

Both of the italicized prepositional phrases are nonadverbial prepositional phrases because neither can appropriately substitute for a question word adverbial, and both are "expected" by the verb. (If someone says *The secretary conferred,* listeners are very likely to ask *With whom?* or *About what?*) Thus our revised PS rules must make room for at least two such PPs in close relation to a verb. Here is a proposed revision of the VP rule, which makes room for up to two PPs inside the VP and thus accounts for the close tie of certain PPs to a verb:

$$\textbf{4.48} \quad VP \rightarrow \left\{ \begin{array}{l} V + (NP) + (PP) + (PP) \\ be + \left\{ \begin{array}{l} ADJ \\ NP \end{array} \right\} \end{array} \right\}$$

With this revision, the PS rules will generate the tree in 4.49 for the sentence in 4.47.

4.49

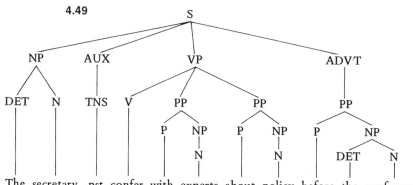

The secretary -pst confer with experts about policy before the conference

I shall use the expression **verb phrase prepositional phrases** to refer to PPs in the VP and the expression **adverbial prepositional phrases** to refer to PPs in adverbials. I have not exhausted the possibilities for verb phrase prepositional phrases. Consider the sentences in 4.50:

> **4.50a** You will be fond *of Helen* after the honeymoon.
>   **b** The voters had been happy *with Herbert* before the depression.

Neither of the italicized PPs can substitute for the question words defining our four types of adverbials, but the VPs in the sentences of 4.50 do not contain a V, and thus our new rule for placing PPs after a verb is of no use. The VPs in 4.50 each contain *be* + ADJ. Notice that in 4.50a *of Helen* seems to manifest the same kind of tie to the adjective *fond* which *on a lawyer* had to *depends* in 4.45c. (If someone said *You will be fond*, we are likely to respond *Of what?*) And the phrase *of Helen* is similarly prevented from easy movement to the front of the sentence. To capture both of the facts, let us create a category, the **adjective phrase**, which we will label ADJP, for the purpose of showing the close tie between adjectives and PPs like those in 4.50. And so, we make yet another revision in the VP rule to allow it to introduce adjective phrases, and we add a new rule to show that, as immediate constituents, the ADJP may have either an adjective alone or an adjective followed by a PP:

4.51a $VP \rightarrow \begin{Bmatrix} V + (NP) + (PP) + (PP) \\ be + \begin{Bmatrix} ADJP \\ NP \end{Bmatrix} \end{Bmatrix}$

   b $ADJP \rightarrow ADJ + (PP)$

With these revisions, the PS rules will generate the tree in 4.52 for the sentence in 4.50a.

4.52

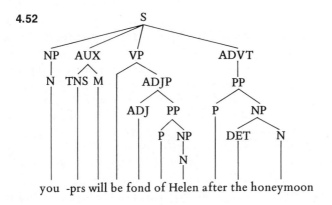

you -prs will be fond of Helen after the honeymoon

Sometimes the distinction which I have drawn between adverbial prepositional phrases and verb phrase prepositional phrases is difficult to apply in individual cases. Consider the sentences in 4.53:

4.53a Napoleon sent a message *to the troops.*
   b Oscar has been looking *at television.*
   c Teachers were sad *about the holiday.*

I have used the question-word adverbs, *how, where, when,* and *why,* as the very basis of our definitions of four types of adverbials. Thus, I have claimed, a PP is an adverb of a given type if it can substitute for one of these question words. One can argue that *to the troops* in 4.53a can substitute for *where* and is thus an adverbial of place. The same can be said of *at television* in 4.53b. Similarly, one can argue that *about the holiday* can substitute for *why* and is thus an adverbial of reason. But, on the other hand, I have argued that PPs that seem to fulfill a specific semantic expectation of a verb or adjective and that are awkward if placed at the front of a sentence belong inside the verb phrase. The PPs in 4.53 seem to fulfill these VP criteria as well, in spite of possibly fulfilling the adverbial criterion. I do not intend to resolve the issue. I do hope, however, that this section has shown that there is indeed a distinction between PPs closely tied to a VP and PPs which seem to relate to the sentence as a whole (adverbials). When analyzing sentences like those in 4.53, we must consider all the evidence and make a decision accordingly. Some linguists claim that it is unlikely for two adverbials of a given type to appear in one sentence. If this is so, then we can test the constituency of PPs like the ones in 4.53 by trying to add another adverbial of the suspect type to the sentence. If we can do so naturally and if the evidence for VP constituency is strong, then we should probably claim that the PS rules will put the PP inside the VP. The sentence in 4.53b provides a good example of this technique. It is very natural to say *Oscar has been looking at television in the living room.* The PP *in the living room* is very obviously an ADVP. This, coupled with the fact that *at television* seems to fulfill a semantic expectation of *look,* indicates that we should treat *at television* as a verb phrase prepositional phrase.

It may be some comfort to know that the question of prepositional-phrase constituency is one of the most lively issues in linguistic research, and many problems have just begun to be resolved. I shall have more to say about some of these issues in chapter 9.

I now present, in 4.54, the whole set of PS rules developed in this chapter to account for English constituent structure. Notice that I identify each rule with a lower case roman numeral. This follows the custom of linguists, and also makes it easier to refer to the rules later in the book.

4.54 i $S \rightarrow NP + AUX + VP + (ADVM) + (ADVP) + (ADVT) + (ADVR) \ldots$

ii $VP \rightarrow \begin{cases} V + (NP) + (PP) + (PP) \\ be + (\begin{cases} ADJP \\ NP \end{cases}) \end{cases}$

iii $\begin{cases} ADVM \\ ADVP \\ ADVT \\ ADVR \end{cases} \rightarrow \begin{cases} PP \\ ADV \end{cases}$

iv $ADJP \rightarrow ADJ + (PP)$

v $PP \rightarrow P + NP$

vi $NP \rightarrow (DET) + N$

vii $AUX \rightarrow TNS + (M) + (PERF) + (PROG)$

viii $TNS \rightarrow \begin{cases} \text{-prs} \\ \text{-pst} \end{cases}$

ix $M \rightarrow \{can, may, will, shall, should, must, \ldots\}$

x $PERF \rightarrow have\text{-}en$

xi $PROG \rightarrow be\text{-}ing$

xii $V \rightarrow \{build, work, write, \ldots\}$

xiii $ADV \rightarrow \begin{cases} \text{enthusiastically, there, then,} \\ \text{deliberately,} \ldots \\ \text{how, where, when, why,} \ldots \end{cases}$

xiv	ADJ → {diligent, fond, happy, . . .}
xv	P → {with, at, in, for, . . .}
xvi	DET → {a, the, this, that, . . .}
xvii	N → {woman, leader, car, William, play, . . .}

Two aspects of these rules require additional comment. Notice that in rule ii, the braces enclosing ADJP and NP are themselves enclosed by parentheses. This is to account for sentences like the following:

4.55a Joe was in Chicago.
   b The test is in the morning.

The VPs in 4.55 have no constituents other than the morpheme *be*. Thus the rules must allow for selection of neither alternate after *be* in rule ii. But notice that when *be* is the only constituent of the VP, an adverbial must follow it. Some linguists account for this by listing certain adverbials as VP constituents following *be* in addition to listing them as immediate constituents of S. The only reason I do not do so is to make our PS rules easier to learn. Thus, even though our PS rules are fairly comprehensive, they will occasionally ignore certain details. A later chapter will show how one of the tasks of syntactic research is to revise and refine the PS rules.

The second point I wish to make about the PS rules in 4.54 is that rule ix and rules xii through xvii all end in ellipsis dots. The dots allude to the entire English dictionary. The PS rules assume that an analysis and classification of all the words in English into form classes has been accomplished and that these rules are selecting from complete lists of words of each form class to generate English constituent structures.

EXERCISES

Draw the constituent structure tree diagrams which our PS rules generate for the following sentences.

1. Edgar may have solved the problem.
2. John may be a teacher after graduation.
3. Someone stole a book from that woman.
4. Those turtles might have been kidnapping a frog yesterday.
5. Albert has been a diplomat in Asia.
6. Mary has been reciting poetry to children in the morning.
7. The club should be paying dues to the treasurer today.
8. Alfred had been conscientious then.

9. An alarm may be sounding at the university.
10. He was a revolutionary for profit.
11. I have been having headaches during class.
12. Some Eskimos may be planning a revolution.
13. Herb had been playing the trumpet for enjoyment.
14. Some officials could be lying to the people.
15. Paul had been a skeptic before the vision.
16. Those people are striving for peace.
17. Rod has been earning money through poetry.
18. The witness was being stubborn about the information.
19. Some voters are working for the party energetically.
20. The players might have been fumbling the ball for fun.
21. The president may have been in California before the election.
22. Harold had been fighting the Danes successfully in the north.
23. The judge was being cooperative at the hearing.
24. Canada should be negotiating with Europe about tariffs.
25. Harriet slept quietly by the window yesterday.
26. Richard will be writing to Congress about the deficit.
27. Those men might have been arguing with some politicians yesterday.
28. The negotiators were trying for a compromise cautiously.
29. The governor must have been playing monopoly for relaxation.
30. The dean had been an anthropologist in Cuba before the revolution.

FOR FURTHER READING

Lyons (1969) treats technical aspects of PS rules. Liles (1971) and Lester (1971) present complete sets of PS rules for English. Different versions of PS rules for English can be found in Chomsky (1957 and 1965). Joos (1964) presents a most comprehensive treatment of the categories of the English auxiliary. Ehrman (1966) discusses readably and completely the meanings of the modals. Lakoff and Ross (1966) discuss additional criteria for determining the verb phrase constituency of prepositional phrases.

Chapter 5

Transformational Syntax of English Simple Sentences: I

INADEQUACY OF PHRASE-STRUCTURE RULES

Early in chapter 3, we speculated whether we could describe the syntactic sequences of English merely by making a list of English sentences. We found that such a list would be endless. We then tried to treat syntax as a list of linear patterns of form classes and found that the list of patterns, if not endless, would be unmanageably long. But our principal objection to linear sentence patterns was their failure to even acknowledge, much less explain, the hierarchical constituent structure of sentences. We solved the latter problem in chapter 4 by opting for tree diagrams rather than linear patterns, but the problem of numbers still remained: even the number of tree structures in English would be very, very large. And then another objection to an inventory of tree structures arose: any such inventory would repeat unnecessarily, in diagram after diagram, many generalizations about English sentence structure and thus would violate the canon of simplicity by which grammars, as theories of language structure, must abide. We solved this simplicity problem with phrase-structure rules, wherein each statement about sentence structure is given once, and then applied by convention to the generation of any and all sentences that manifest the structure. PS rules seemed also, and finally, to solve the problem of numbers—they seemed able to account for endless numbers of sentences without the need for endless lists of sentences or of patterns or of trees.

But now examine each sentence in 5.1, especially the double-lettered sentences, and ask yourself: (1) Is this an English sentence? (2) Will our PS rules, as they now stand, provide a diagram for it?

> **5.1a** Richard sent a message to Henry.
> **aa** Richard sent Henry a message.
> **b** The troops came home quietly.
> **bb** Quietly, the troops came home.
> **c** Rip is sleeping.
> **cc** Is Rip sleeping?

The answer to the first question is yes for every sentence in 5.1; the answer to the second question is yes for the single-lettered sentences, but no for the double-lettered sentences: 5.1aa contains two NPs in a VP, and our rules allow for only one; 5.1bb has an adverb in front of the initial sentence NP, and our rules allow adverbs only to follow the VP; 5.1cc contains a form of *be* (with a *-prs* inflection) in front of the initial sentence NP, and our rules allow such morphemes to occur only in the AUX, which must follow the initial sentence NP. Thus our PS rules, as they stand, are inadequate because they are not able to generate these three perfectly acceptable English sentences. Does this mean that we will be forced to discard PS rules as we did inventories of linear patterns and inventories of trees? Since PS rules have shown themselves to be useful and flexible, we need to examine this problem closely before we decide their fate. Let us see if we can revise our rules to make them capable of generating the double-lettered sentences in 5.1.

The PS rules could be made to generate 5.1aa by adding another NP to PS rule ii; here is how it would look (the additional NP is italicized and parts of the rule are left out):

$$\textbf{5.2} \quad VP \rightarrow \left\{ \begin{array}{l} V + (NP) + (NP) + (PP) + (PP) \\ \ldots \end{array} \right\}$$

The rules could be made to generate 5.1bb by adding an optional ADVM in front of the NP in rule i:

$$\textbf{5.3} \quad S \rightarrow (ADVM) + NP + AUX + VP \ldots$$

And the PS rules could generate 5.1cc by revising rule i to allow *is* (TNS + *be*) to precede the initial NP:

$$\textbf{5.4} \quad S \rightarrow (ADVM) + (TNS + be) + NP + AUX + VP \ldots$$

But we are on the wrong track when we attempt to account for the double-lettered sentences in 5.1 by revising the PS rules, and for two reasons. The first has to do with the old problem of numbers, the second with adequacy to a new kind of linguistic data. First, an examination of any page of any book will turn up very few sentences that our rules, as now formulated, can generate. Most sentences are quite complex, having dependent clauses, subordinating conjunctions, and adverbs in many different places. Many sentences are questions, negations, commands. If we attempted to revise our rules to account for all of these phenomena, we would soon need a list of rules that would fill a sheet of paper the size of a football field. But, and this is important, such a list of rules would not necessarily be infinitely complicated. Thus, while the problem of size can make a purely PS grammar cumbersome, it does not in itself disqualify such a grammar as a possibly complete description of English syntax. A second objection disqualifies PS rules as fully adequate to the task of syntactic description.

Consider again the solution proposed in 5.4 to the problem posed by 5.1cc *(Is Rip sleeping?)*. Imagine that 5.4 has indeed replaced PS rule i; now let us proceed to apply the revised rules to generate 5.1cc. In 5.5 I show the only tree that the revised rules can generate for this sentence.

5.5

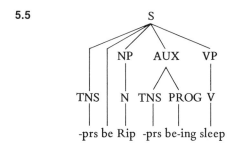

First, notice that since PS rule vii requires TNS in every AUX, there is a second *-prs* in the tree. Second, notice that the only way the grammar can generate the *-ing* of *sleeping* is by including the category PROG in the AUX. But this gives us another *be* in the tree. Thus even our revised rules are incapable of generating 5.1cc; rather, they have generated the nonsensical sequence *is Rip is sleeping*. So it was not enough simply to add TNS + *be* in front of the NP in PS rule i. Now, it would probably be possible, with much labor and at the expense of creating great complexity, to revise the PS rules in such a way that the choice of TNS + *be* by rule i would exclude the choice of these morphemes by rule vii, and we could account for *-ing* in the question by some other revision of rule vii. But all such revisions, even if possible, are undesirable for other reasons. If such revisions were allowed, the grammar would fail to account for the fact that *be* in 5.1cc is the very same *be* as in 5.1c: even though, in the question, *be* is separated by *two* stems from *-ing,* it still joins -*ing* in signaling the presence of the category PROG. And users of English are fully aware of this fact. They perceive an essential sameness of structure between a question like *Is Rip sleeping?* and the statement that answers it: *Rip is sleeping.* If a grammar is to be fully *adequate,* it must explain such relations among sentences in addition to explaining why morphemes occur in a certain order.

DEEP STRUCTURE AND SURFACE STRUCTURE

Until now, we have considered it the task of a syntactic description to explain why certain sequences of English morphemes are sentences (why they manifest a recognizable English constituent structure) and why other sequences are not. We have just looked at another kind of fact which a fully adequate description of English syntax must explain. All three pairs of sentences in 5.1 exemplify this new kind of fact. Users of English perceive an essential sameness of constituent structure between the two sentences in each pair. We have already examined this aspect of the last pair: *be* marks the category PROG, even though its position is different in 5.1c and 5.1cc. Similarly, *Henry* is the recipient of the *message* in both 5.1a and 5.1aa, even though the relative positions of these two noun phrases differ. And in 5.1b and 5.1bb, *quietly* tells *how* the troops came home, whether it is first or last in the sentence. Now, we must still find a way to account for the *difference* in word order between the sentences of each pair. But we must do this and, if possible, also explain the *sameness* that holds between the two sentences of each pair. The grammar can perform both tasks if it can generate two constituent structures for each sentence, one which would be the *same* for both sentences in a pair, and one which would *differ* for each of the sentences in a pair. As it turns out, our PS rules are formulated in such a way that they already can generate a constituent-structure tree that, except for the positioning of auxiliary affixes, adequately accounts for the word order of the first sentence in each of the three pairs we are considering. We can solve both problems of description of the second sentence (how it is *like* the first and how it *differs* from the first) if we attribute to it the same constituent structure that the PS rules generate for the first sentence and then find a way to have our grammar generate yet another tree for it—one which will show how all the morphemes finally come to occupy the positions they occupy in the sentence as written or spoken.

Thus the PS rules would generate the structure in 5.6 as part of the description of both 5.1a *(Richard sent a message to Henry)* and 5.1aa *(Richard sent Henry a message)*.

5.6

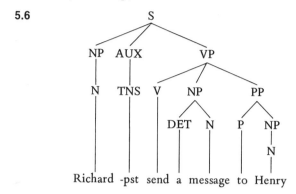

Richard -pst send a message to Henry

In providing this tree as part of the description of both sentences, the grammar makes it possible to explain the fact that Henry *receives* the message in both sentences—we can perform, on this tree, the task of interpreting meaningful relations by claiming that NPs in PPs introduced by *to* are *recipients*. But having made such an interpretation possible, the grammar must now show that 5.1aa, while originally structured as 5.6, somehow changes its structure into a tree that we may diagram as in 5.7.

5.7

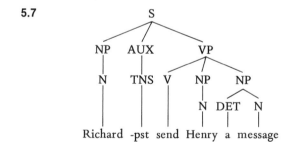

Richard -pst send Henry a message

To show how 5.6 changes to 5.7, we need a new kind of structural principle in our grammar. We already have principles that *build* trees, line by line, category by category: PS rules; we need a different kind of principle, one that can take a fully developed constituent-structure tree and *change* it: *add* something to it, *delete* something from it, or *move* something from one place to another in it. We call principles of this new type **transformations.** Constituent-structure trees which are the direct product of PS rules and on which no changes have been worked by transformations we call **deep structures,** and trees that result when all changes worked by transformations have been carried out we call **surface structures.**

THE NATURE AND OPERATION OF TRANSFORMATIONS: INDIRECT OBJECTS

Reexamine the tree in 5.6 and carefully compare it with the tree in 5.7. How do the two trees differ? Can you compose a sentence that might serve as a directive to a typist or a draftsman who has 5.6 in hand and must change it to 5.7? Try to formulate the directive in such a way that it could be applied generally; that is, try to refer to general categories in the tree rather than individual morphemes. Here is such a directive:

> **5.8**   Given any deep-structure tree which has a VP composed of a V, NP, and PP, and where the PP is introduced by the preposition *to,*
> then one may delete *to* and move the NP that accompanied *to* in the PP to a position between the V and the other NP.

The statement in 5.8 is a transformation. But it is presented informally, in words. We noted in the last chapter that phrase-structure rules could be stated informally, but that the notation we ultimately adopted—with category symbols, arrows, parentheses, and braces—made it possible to be explicit, comprehensive, and brief. The same is true of transformations. Some are so complex that several paragraphs would be necessary to state them informally. For this reason, linguists have developed a formal symbolic notation for the expression of transformations. Read 5.8 again and notice that there are two parts to it, a "given" part and a "then" part: it first defines certain characteristics of a deep-structure tree, and then specifies certain changes to be made in the tree. Notice also that the second part of the statement uses the word *may.* Other transformations use the word *must* as we shall see. Here is how the "given" portion of the transformation can be represented in formal symbolic notation:

5.9   SD: $X \, [_{VP} \, V \, NP \, [_{PP} \, [_P \, to] \, _P \, NP]_{PP} \, Y]_{VP} \, Z$

The abbreviation SD stands for the phrase **structural description;** thus the entire statement in 5.9 means: "Here is the kind of tree to which this rule is relevant." The brackets make it possible, as we saw in chapter 3, to represent hierarchical constituent structure with a linear notation. Another way of representing exactly the same information as 5.9 is given in 5.10 (5.9 is preferred simply to save space).

5.10   SD**:**

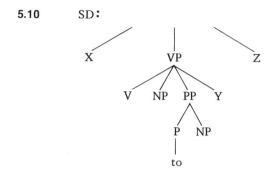

How does the symbolic notation in 5.9 (and 5.10) relate to the statement in 5.8? The letters X, Y, and Z in 5.9 are needed to capture the notion expressed by the words "any deep-structure tree" in 5.8. These letters are called **variables** and stand for *any* and *all* (or *no*) constituents which the PS rules might allow in the various positions the variables occupy. As 5.8 makes clear, the transformation can effect a change in the VP when, and only when, the VP is structured a certain way. The bracketed notation of 5.9 represents a VP with a V, NP, and PP introduced by *to,* exactly the same specifications as 5.8. The variable X indicates that the change may be carried out no matter what precedes the VP, the variable Z indicates that the change may be carried out no matter what follows the VP, and the variable Y indicates that the presence in the VP of other elements after the PP introduced by *to* is irrelevant to the operation of the transformation. We could use ellipsis dots (. . .) instead of X, Y, and Z variables to represent such notions, but linguists normally use variables. Thus the formal symbolic notation of 5.9 is identical in meaning to the "given" clause of 5.8. Now we must extend the formal notation of 5.9 so that it can express the "then" clause of 5.8. In 5.11 I show the complete formal symbolic representation of this transformation.

5.11   INDIRECT OBJECT MOVEMENT (OPT)
SD: X " [$_{VP}$ V " NP [$_{PP}$ " [$_P$ to] $_P$ " NP] $_{PP}$ " Y] $_{VP}$ " Z
SC: 1   2   3   4   5   6   7 $\Rightarrow$
      1   2 5 3   0   6   7
COND: Sometimes must apply; sometimes cannot

The abbreviation SC stands for the phrase **structural change**. Here is how the "then" clause of 5.8 is represented in 5.11: index numbers are assigned to the various elements in the SD; we do this by inserting double quotation marks in the structural description between the indexed elements. (Often dashes are used, but I wish to avoid confusion with the hyphen that marks a suffix.) Thus the number 1 in 5.11 stands for the variable X; the number 2 stands for V; the number 3 stands for the NP between the V and PP; the number 4 stands for *to,* and so on. The double-lined arrow at the end of the first line of index numbers means "make the following change(s)." The numbers in the second line represent the status of the various indexed elements after the changes are made. By putting 0 in the place of 4 (which indexes *to*), the transformation expresses the fact that *to* is deleted; by moving 5 (which indexes the NP accompanying *to* in the PP) between 2 and 3, the transformation expresses the fact that this NP, which originates in the PP, is placed immediately after the V and before the NP that it followed in the deep structure.

Certain other aspects of 5.11 require comment. Transformations are customarily given names by linguists, and these names are usually printed in capital letters. I have named the transformation under discussion INDIRECT OBJECT MOVEMENT. We noted earlier that this transformation may be applied but does not have to be. For this reason, we say that it is **optional** and indicate as much in the formal notation by placing (OPT) after the name. This means that a deep structure to which this rule applies can result in a syntactically correct English sentence whether this rule operates on it or not. (We will see shortly that some transformations are **obligatory**—OBL—which means that if they apply to a tree, they must operate on it in order to have a syntactically correct English sentence.) Finally, many transformations have **conditions,** indicated by COND in 5.11. These can be quite complex, and in the case of the INDIRECT OBJECT MOVEMENT transformation, they are. You need to be aware of the existence of conditions, and I will note them as I discuss each transformation, but the scope of this book does not ordinarily allow full discussion. The conditions on INDIRECT OBJECT MOVEMENT, hinted at in 5.11, derive from facts like the following. Normally, it is possible in English to have pairs of sentences like those in 5.12, where the first pair repeats 5.1a and 5.1aa:

5.12a   Richard sent a message to Henry.
  aa   Richard sent Henry a message.
   b   Joe gave a present to Eloise.
  bb   Joe gave Eloise a present.
   c   Some students mailed a letter to the senator.
  cc   Some students mailed the senator a letter.

Each pair of sentences in 5.12 comes from the same deep structure, the double-lettered sentences by optional application of the INDIRECT OBJECT MOVEMENT transformation. But sometimes there is no option; sometimes the rule is obligatory. The single-lettered sentences in 5.13, where this transformation has not been applied, are unacceptable.

Notice that the deep-structure NP which immediately follows the V in 5.13a and 5.13b is a noun clause.

5.13a *I told that I was innocent to the judge.
aa I told the judge that I was innocent.
b *He wrote that he was studying to his father.
bb He wrote his father that he was studying.
c *They asked a question to the child.
cc They asked the child a question.

Thus, even though INDIRECT OBJECT MOVEMENT is ordinarily optional, under certain conditions it is required. Now consider the sentence pairs in 5.14. These, too, illustrate exceptions to the optionality of INDIRECT OBJECT MOVEMENT, but in these cases the transformation is *blocked,* not required as in 5.13.

5.14a I am writing it to John.
aa *I am writing John it.
b John explained the situation to Bill.
bb *John explained Bill the situation.
c I said some words to the judge.
cc *I said the judge some words.

After you spend some time working with the concepts I am only now introducing, you may wish to return to the sentences in 5.13 and 5.14 to see if you can define precisely the conditions that determine when the normally optional INDIRECT OBJECT MOVEMENT transformation is obligatory and when it is blocked.

THE APPLICATION OF TRANSFORMATIONS: AUXILIARY INFLECTIONS

I have developed a view of syntax where two quite different kinds of structural principles participate in the generation of sentences: (1) PS rules generate deep-structure trees, and (2) transformations generate surface-structure trees from deep-structure trees.

Now let us look again at 5.1a and 5.1aa. I have shown how the application of INDIRECT OBJECT MOVEMENT in the generation of 5.1aa accounts for the difference between it and 5.1a. But I have not yet shown how the surface structure of either of these two sentences is finally generated. Here is why: A surface constituent structure must position the morphemes of a sentence exactly as they occur in speech or writing. Let me demonstrate by focusing on 5.1aa *(Richard sent Henry a message).*

Here is what our grammar presently has to say about this sentence. First, the PS rules generate this deep structure for it:

5.15

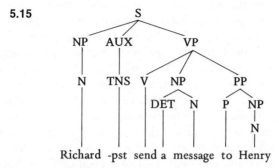

Richard -pst send a message to Henry

Second, the INDIRECT OBJECT MOVEMENT transformation changes the deep structure of 5.15 into the structure in 5.16:

5.16

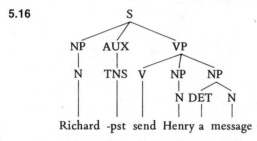

Richard -pst send Henry a message

But 5.16 is still not an adequate surface structure for 5.1aa because the inflectional suffix *-pst* precedes the stem that it must follow in a spoken or written sentence; that is, the surface structure must instead look something like the following:

5.17

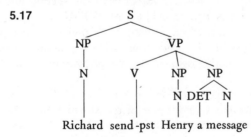

Richard send -pst Henry a message

In 5.17, the *-pst* inflection appears as a suffix of the stem *send.* How can the grammar be made to specify explicitly this change of position? You saw in the last chapter why it was necessary to analyze the various categories of the auxiliary as was done, with inflectional suffixes preceding their surface stems. You saw, for instance, that *have* and *-en* work together to indicate the presence of the category PERF, and you saw that tense inflections had to be listed first by the auxiliary rule in order to explain that the first stem of the auxiliary carries this inflection if there is a stem in the auxiliary and that the first stem in the VP carries it if there are no stems in the auxiliary. Now, having added transformations, as descriptive devices, to our grammar, I can show how the various inflectional suffixes of the English auxiliary are correctly positioned. If 5.17, and sentences like it, were the only sentences needing explanation, we could simply formulate a transformation that moved tense inflections from a position in front of a verb stem to a position following the stem. But we need a transformation that will move any auxiliary inflection from in front of any potential stem to a position following such a stem. Here is a formal symbolic statement of such a rule:

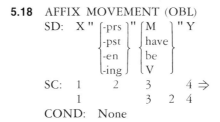

5.18   AFFIX MOVEMENT (OBL)
SD: X " [-prs] " [M   ] " Y
              [-pst]   [have]
              [-en]   [be]
              [-ing]   [V   ]
SC: 1   2   3   4 ⇒
      1   3   2   4
COND: None

This transformation is fairly uncomplicated. It reads as follows: given any one of the four inflectional suffixes that are indexed as element number 2 and that occur immediately in front of any one of the stem types indexed as number 3 (M, *have, be,* or V), then move the inflection to a position following the stem. (This change is shown by moving the number 2 to the other side of the number 3 in the second line of the SC.) The transformation is named **AFFIX MOVEMENT** and it is obligatory. This transformation when applied to 5.16 changes it into 5.17 and thus makes it possible for the grammar to generate a surface-structure tree which correctly positions the morphemes of 5.1aa (*Richard sent Henry a message*).

Our grammar now consists of an ordered set of PS rules, which generate deep-structure trees, and a pair of transformations, which help change deep-structure trees into surface-structure trees. Transformations are said to "apply" or "not apply" to a tree according to whether the tree "meets" the structural description (SD) of the rule. The list of transformations is considered to be ordered; thus, when more than one transformation applies in the generation of a given sentence, each one must apply in the order in which it is listed, and each successive transformation on the list operates on the tree that has resulted from the application of those preceding it on the list. Let us now discuss all of these matters further. What does it mean to say that a transformation "applies" to a tree structure? It means that the SD of a transformation is matched to a given tree. If there are category symbols in a tree to which each index number of its SD can be assigned, then the transformation applies to the tree. Here, in 5.19, is an *analysis* (application of the index numbers) of the deep structure of *Richard sent Henry a message* showing how the IN-DIRECT OBJECT MOVEMENT transformation applies. The rule is reprinted in 5.20 for convenience of reference and comparison. Recall that the variable X refers to everything preceding the V in a tree, which in 5.19 is *Richard -pst;* the variable Y refers to whatever in the VP may happen to follow the PP introduced by *to;* the variable Z refers to whatever may happen to follow the VP in a tree. Both Y and Z are said to be **null** (nonexistent) as this transformation applies to the structure in 5.19. (We indicate this by using ellipsis dots.)

5.19

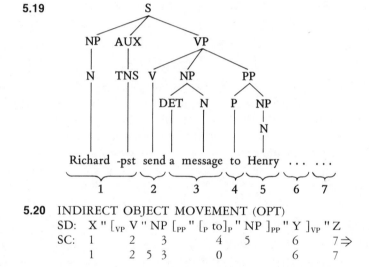

5.20 INDIRECT OBJECT MOVEMENT (OPT)
SD: X " [$_{VP}$ V " NP [$_{PP}$ " [$_P$ to]$_P$ " NP]$_{PP}$ " Y]$_{VP}$ " Z
SC: 1   2   3   4   5   6   7 $\Rightarrow$
     1   2   5 3   0   6   7

Now notice, if we take the indexed items of 5.19 and make the changes as indicated by the SC of 5.20, here is the quite correct sequence of morphemes which results:

5.21 Richard -pst send Henry a message

         1   2   5   3

I have said that transformations take a tree and change it into another tree. It is not enough for a transformation to account for the linear order of morphemes as the INDIRECT OBJECT MOVEMENT transformation has just done by correctly producing the sequence in 5.21. The INDIRECT OBJECT MOVEMENT transformation should also be able to define precisely the configuration of the constituent-structure tree associated with 5.21. But notice, the number 4 in the SC refers to [p to] p in the SD; thus, *to* and the label P categorizing it in the tree are deleted by the rule. But the category label PP is not deleted by the rule. Nor would we want it to be, for if it were, then everything in the PP would automatically be deleted as well, and we do not wish to delete the NP *Henry,* but to move it. Thus, the tree that results when this transformation is applied still contains an unnecessary branch and PP category label, as shown in 5.22.

5.22

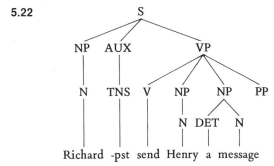

Current research in transformational grammar is much concerned with problems like the above. One solution to the problem in 5.22 is a proposed convention of "tree pruning" in the application of transformational rules. Such a convention calls for the automatic deletion of any categories left with nothing in them as the result of the operation of some transformation. If we adopt such a convention, then the extra PP branch in 5.22 is automatically deleted and the output tree of the INDIRECT OBJECT MOVEMENT transformation is the tree in 5.23. And it is this tree that now stands ready to be analyzed by the SD of the next transformation on the list, AFFIX MOVEMENT. The tree in 5.23 is here presented as analyzed and index-numbered by AFFIX MOVEMENT. AFFIX MOVEMENT is reprinted in 5.24 for convenience of reference and comparison.

5.23

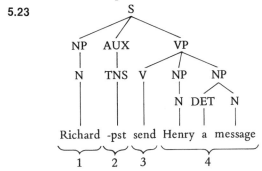

5.24 AFFIX MOVEMENT (OBL)

SD: X " $\begin{bmatrix} \text{-prs} \\ \text{-pst} \\ \text{-en} \\ \text{-ing} \end{bmatrix}$ " $\begin{bmatrix} \text{M} \\ \text{have} \\ \text{be} \\ \text{V} \end{bmatrix}$ " Y

SC: 1   2   3   4 $\Rightarrow$
     1   3   2   4

COND: None

If we take the indexed items in 5.23 and make the changes called for by 5.24, the following quite correct linear sequence of morphemes results:

5.25 Richard send-pst Henry a message

         1   3   2   4

But, again, the transformation does not contain enough explicit information about the exact shape of the resultant tree. The transformation moves *-pst,* but it leaves the category labels AUX and TNS with nothing to categorize. We can invoke the tree-pruning convention to have both of these labels deleted. Nonetheless, there remains yet another problem: nothing in the transformation indicates how the repositioned *-pst* is branched into the tree resulting from the transformation. There are at least two reasonable possibilities, as indicated by the dotted lines in 5.26. (Nothing in the AFFIX MOVEMENT transformation would prohibit branches even from NP or N.)

5.26

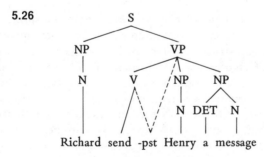

Richard send -pst Henry a message

Now, it seems likely that *-pst* is a constituent of V and not a constituent of VP, since, as we saw in chapter 2, there are good reasons for treating suffixes as *parts* of words, dependent on their stems for positional mobility. But the point to note is that AFFIX MOVEMENT as formally stated in our grammar does not make this explicit. This problem, and many other problems like it, are resolvable by expansion and refinement of the notational conventions for formal symbolic statement of transformations, and professional linguists are hard at work on just such expansions and refinements. But since the principal aim in this book is to use transformations as vehicles for examining a broad range of facts of English, I will adopt an analytical-display technique that enables us to bypass such problems. As a result, *and even though transformations operate on trees, taking trees as input and providing trees as output,* I shall not ordinarily present the entire trees that result from the application of transformations; I shall simply keep a linear record of the effect of a transformation on the ordering of the morphemes in trees. Here in 5.27, for instance, is how the analytical-display format represents how the grammar generates 5.1aa, which we have examined at such length.

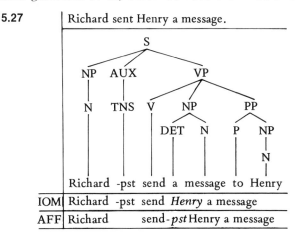

5.27 | Richard sent Henry a message.

IOM	Richard	-pst	send	*Henry*	a message
AFF	Richard		send-*pst*	Henry a message

On the line at the top of the display in 5.27, I write the surface structure of the sentence in normal orthography. In the space immediately below, I draw the deep structure, which is the tree generated by the PS rules and not yet affected by any transformations. Then, in a column on the lower left, I list the transformations that need to apply to the deep structure in order to produce a sequence of morphemes corresponding to the sentence written at the top. (Notice that the names of transformations are abbreviated, simply to save space.) Beside the name of each transformation, and on the same horizontal line with it, there is a linear record of the change the transformation has wrought on the sequence of morphemes. Those morphemes directly affected by the rule are italicized. Thus *Henry* is italicized in the first such line of 5.27 because the INDIRECT OBJECT MOVEMENT transformation (IOM) has moved it. In the next line of the analytical display, *-pst* is italicized because the AFFIX MOVEMENT transformation (AFF) has moved it. Notice that the last line of 5.27 lists all the morphemes of the surface structure in their proper surface order.

Before we proceed to the discussion of additional transformations, consider the analytical display in 5.28.

5.28 | The committee has given Marshall a raise.

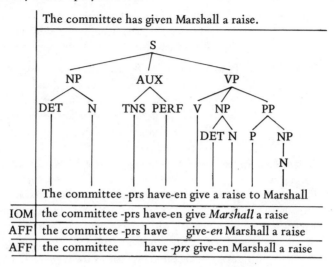

IOM	the committee -prs have-en give *Marshall* a raise
AFF	the committee -prs have give-*en* Marshall a raise
AFF	the committee have -*prs* give-en Marshall a raise

Notice that the deep structure in 5.28 contains two inflectional suffixes, and thus the AFFIX MOVEMENT transformation must apply *twice* to generate the correct surface sequence. (The rule is not formulated so that it can move more than one affix at a time.) Next, notice that I chose first to move -*en* (the rightmost affix) and then moved -*prs*. Either order would have provided the correct result. Using a right to left order will probably make it easier for you to keep track of what you are doing when you begin to practice analyzing sentences later in this chapter.

PASSIVES

Throughout the remainder of this chapter and the next two chapters, I will present, at the beginning of each section, a series of sentences for examination and evaluation in light of both the PS rules and transformations studied up to that time. Ordinarily, the entire set of sentences will provide evidence of the application of some new transformation. Some of the sentences will also show the effects of previously discussed transformations so that you can review them and observe how transformations interact. Learn to ask the following general questions about a sentence: (1) Can the PS rules and the transformations so far discussed generate it? (2) If not, what additions need to be made to the grammar in order to account for it? A useful tactic in seeking answers is to try to diagram the sentence as if the PS rules alone operated to generate it. Let us try this tactic on the sentences in 5.29.

5.29a The bomb was thrown by an arsonist.
   b The forgery could have been detected by an expert.
   c The lobbyist was given a refund by the government.

Notice the words *was thrown* in 5.29a. The first word is past, so under TNS in the deep-structure diagram, we would draw a line to *-pst*. This leaves the surface morpheme sequence *be throw-en* to be accounted for, which would require *be-en* to precede *throw* in deep structure (so that AFFIX MOVEMENT could reposition the *-en* in surface structure). But the PS rules do not provide for the sequence *be-en* in deep structures; only the *have-en* of PERF and the *be-ing* of PROG can be generated, not *be-en*. How then can we account for *be-en* in the surface sequences of 5.29? Let us explain any new surface structural characteristics of sentences as the work of transformations operating on deep structures. But before we can speculate on the nature of the transformation needed to account for *be* and *-en* in the sentences of 5.29, we must have some idea about the configuration of the deep-structure tree such a transformation will operate on.

Recall that we added transformations to our grammar not only (1) to account for the positioning of morphemes in surface structures, but also (2) to account for sameness of meaningful relations existing among surface sentences with different positionings of morphemes. Thus, we decided earlier to attribute the same deep structure to *Richard sent a message to Henry* and *Richard sent Henry a message*. So it is not enough to note that the sentences in 5.29 contain two morphemes, *be* and *-en,* which the PS rules cannot generate. We must ask ourselves whether each sentence as a whole is significantly the same in its meaningful relations as some other sentence which the PS rules can generate. This kind of question is the everyday concern of the professional linguist. As newcomers to linguistics, you may not easily find a ready answer. But, hopefully, you may already have thought (the heading of this section is certainly a clue!) that the sentences in 5.29 are passive sentences and that every sentence is related to a sentence that the PS rules *can* generate: its so-called active counterpart. Here are the active counterparts of the sentences in 5.29:

5.30a An arsonist threw the bomb.
   b An expert could have detected the forgery.
   c The government gave the lobbyist a refund.

Compare the sentences in 5.30 with their counterparts in 5.29. Users of English readily accept the claim that the counterpart sentences are closely related in meaning despite the differences in the surface morphemes. For example, in both sentences, we know that *an arsonist* performed the action of throwing, even though this NP is in a PP at the end of 5.29a and is the initial NP of 5.30a. And we know that the bomb moved through the air in both sentences, even though it is the initial NP of 5.29a and follows the verb in 5.30a. Because of this essential sameness of meaningful relations and because our PS rules readily generate deep structures for the sentences in 5.30, let us claim that the deep structures thus generated underlie both the active sentences and their passive counterparts. In 5.31, for example, the deep structure of both 5.29a and 5.30a is depicted.

5.31

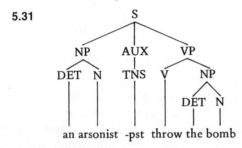

By assigning both sentences the deep structure in 5.31, we explain their sameness of meaningful relations. But now we need a transformation that can take 5.31 and convert it into the surface sequence of morphemes in 5.29a. Here are 5.29a and 5.30a listed together, so you can compare them closely. How do they differ?

5.29a The bomb was thrown by an arsonist.
5.30a An arsonist threw the bomb.

Besides the previously noted differences in the position of NPs, 5.29a contains three morphemes which are not present in 5.30a: *be, -en,* and *by.* When we first studied the English auxiliary in chapter 4, we were struck with the fact that a stem and an inflection *on the following stem* in a surface structure can work together to mark the presence of a meaningful category in an English sentence. We noted this in the case of *have* and *-en* marking PERF, and *be* and *-ing* marking PROG. The same phenomenon appears in passive sentences like 5.29a: the surface indicator of passive is the presence of the morpheme *be* and the inflection *-en* on the following stem. For this reason, the grammar should, at some point in the generation of passive sentences, show that *be* and *-en* work together to indicate that the sentence is passive. It can do this by having the two morphemes appear together in the auxiliary labeled PASS, just as *have* and *-en* appear labeled PERF and *be* and *-ing* appear labeled PROG. But, whereas the latter two auxiliary categories are introduced into the AUX by the PS rules, the PASS category needs to be introduced by a transformation. Thus, I propose the tree in 5.32 as the output of the PASSIVE transformation.

5.32

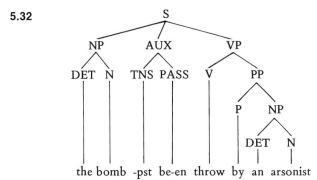

the bomb -pst be-en throw by an arsonist

It is the task, then, of the PASSIVE transformation to change the deep-structure tree in 5.31 into the tree depicted in 5.32. You might want to try your hand at either an informal or formal statement of such a transformation before you examine the formulation given in 5.33, which not only generates 5.32 but the full range of passive sentences in English.

5.33 PASSIVE (OPT)
SD: $X''NP'' [_{AUX}Y'']_{AUX}$ $[_{VP}V''NP''Z'']_{VP}$ W
SC: 1 2 3 4 5 6 7 $\Rightarrow$
     1 5 3$[_{PASS}$be-en$]_{PASS}$ 4 6 $[_{PP}[_{P}$by$]_{P}2]_{PP}$ 7
COND: Sometimes blocked

This is one of the more complex rules treated in this book—complex because it makes many changes at one time. Let us examine the output line of the SC comparing it from left to right with the input line:

5.34a The NP (5) which was in the VP is now the initial NP of the sentence.
b A new category, PASS containing the morphemes *be-en,* is placed in the AUX to the right of whatever (Y) is already there.
c A PP containing the P *by* is created to the right of whatever (Z) ends the VP, and
d the NP (2) that was the initial NP of the input tree is placed within this newly created PP. (The variable W stands for any adverbials that may appear in the sequence.)

The SD of the PASSIVE transformation implies that it can operate on any deep structure where the verb is followed by a noun phrase. But it cannot always do so. Notice that the double-lettered attempts to generate passive counterparts for the single-lettered sentences in 5.35 are unlikely English sentences:

5.35a   The war cost two hundred billion dollars.
  aa *Two hundred billion dollars was cost by the war.
  b Drab colors become you.
  bb *You are become by drab colors.
  c The bureaucracy lacks compassion.
  cc *Compassion is lacked by the bureaucracy.
  d The dictionary weighs ten pounds.
  dd *Ten pounds is weighed by the dictionary.

The condition stated in 5.35 hints at these limitations. I shall not discuss them further, except to call your attention to the fact that the subjects of all the single-lettered sentences of 5.35 are in no sense "agents." That is, they do not do anything. Thus it seems that the PASSIVE transformation expects the deep-structure subject to be some kind of an agent.

In 5.36 the deep structure of 5.31 *(The bomb was thrown by an arsonist)* is analyzed and indexed by the PASSIVE transformation.

5.36

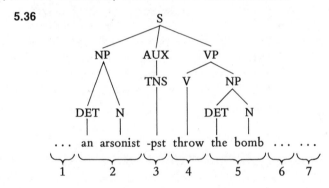

Examine 5.37 for the sequence of morphemes that results from the application of the PASSIVE transformation; it is indexed according to the output line of the SC.

5.37 ... the bomb -pst be-en throw ... by an arsonist ...
      1   5   3 $[_{\text{PASS}}$be-en$]_{\text{PASS}}$ 4 $6[_{\text{PP}} [_{\text{P}}$by $]_{\text{P}}$ 2 $]_{\text{PP}}$ 7

The complete tree which corresponds to this linear sequence of morphemes is that in 5.32. Now examine 5.38 for the complete analytical display showing how the grammar generates 5.29a. Notice that two AFFIX MOVEMENT transformations must apply to complete the generation of the surface sequence.

5.38 | The bomb was thrown by an arsonist.

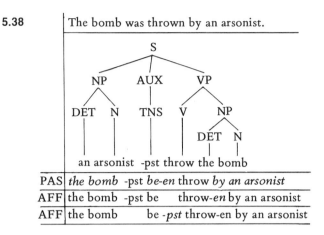

PAS	*the bomb* -pst *be-en* throw *by an arsonist*
AFF	the bomb -pst be throw-*en* by an arsonist
AFF	the bomb be -*pst* throw-en by an arsonist

Notice that when recording the effect of the PASSIVE transformation in an analytical display, we italicize the two NPs which changed position (in 5.38 these are *an arsonist* and *the bomb*) and also italicize the three morphemes which the PASSIVE transformation adds to the sequence (*be-en* and *by*). See if you can draw analytical displays for 5.29c *(The lobbyist was given a refund by the government)* and 5.29b *(The forgery could have been detected by an expert)*. In addition to PASSIVE, you will need three AFFIX MOVEMENT transformations to generate 5.29b. And to generate 5.29c, you will first need to apply INDIRECT OBJECT MOVEMENT, then PASSIVE, and finally, two AFFIX MOVEMENT transformations.

THE ORDERING OF TRANSFORMATIONS

Elsewhere in this chapter, I have stated that the list of transformations is ordered. This means that if two or more transformations apply in generating a given English sentence, they must apply in the order in which they are listed in the grammar. The first to apply takes the deep-structure tree as input and makes the called for changes in it. As its input, each subsequent transformation takes the output tree of that transformation which applied immediately beforehand and then proceeds to make the called for changes in it. As we continue to develop a basic transformational grammar for English through to the end of chapter 7, I will, as far as possible, introduce and discuss transformations in the order in which they must apply. I cannot always do so, however, because I want you to be able to practice using transformations for sentence analysis as soon as I introduce them. Thus I have already introduced and discussed AFFIX MOVEMENT, even though it must follow all but one of the sixteen transformations in the basic grammar. I have introduced it because it applies to almost every sentence, and without it, we could not complete the analysis of practice sentences. The order in which transformations must apply in the generation of English sentences is shown in the Appendix, where all the PS rules and transformations of the basic grammar are listed.

Let us look briefly at some evidence which shows why transformations are ordered. Specifically, we ask why INDIRECT OBJECT MOVEMENT must be listed, and therefore applied, before PASSIVE. Examine the sentences in 5.39. See if you can determine the shape of their deep structures, and the transformations applied in generating their surface structures.

> **5.39a** The government mailed a check to Frank.
> **b** The government mailed Frank a check.
> **c** A check was mailed to Frank by the government.
> **d** Frank was mailed a check by the government.

All four sentences in 5.39 have the same deep structure, but different transformations apply to generate their respective surface structures. In 5.40 (on the following page) you will find a combined analytical display which shows the common deep structure once, and then shows how different combinations of the three transformations so far discussed account for the four different sentences in 5.39. The letters in 5.40 indicate which surface sequences of morphemes correspond to which sentences in 5.39.

Carefully examine the generation of 5.39d in the four lines terminating in 5.40d. Because the INDIRECT OBJECT MOVEMENT transformation first moves *Frank* to the position immediately following the verb in the verb phrase, the PASSIVE transformation is then able to transport it to the front of the sentence, producing the perfectly acceptable sequence of morphemes manifested in 5.39d. If the transformations were ordered differently, with PASSIVE preceding INDIRECT OBJECT MOVEMENT, the grammar could not possibly generate the surface structure of 5.39d because PASSIVE cannot lift *Frank* out of a PP; it can only move the NP immediately after the verb to the front of the sentence.

Let us consider two counter arguments to our claim that INDIRECT OBJECT MOVEMENT and PASSIVE must be listed and applied in the order given. The first is a general argument against the necessity to order transformations at all. If transformations are allowed to apply in any order, the argument goes, problems like the one described at the end

5.40

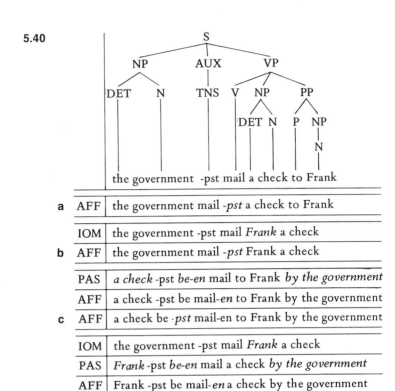

a	AFF	the government mail *-pst* a check to Frank
	IOM	the government -pst mail *Frank* a check
b	AFF	the government mail *-pst* Frank a check
	PAS	*a check* -pst *be-en* mail to Frank *by the government*
	AFF	a check -pst be mail-*en* to Frank by the government
c	AFF	a check be *-pst* mail-en to Frank by the government
	IOM	the government -pst mail *Frank* a check
	PAS	*Frank* -pst *be-en* mail a check *by the government*
	AFF	Frank -pst be mail-*en* a check by the government
d	AFF	Frank be *-pst* mail-en a check by the government

of the preceding paragraph would not arise: PASSIVE could indeed be listed before INDIRECT OBJECT MOVEMENT but allowed to apply either before it or after it as needed. A very complex argument based on many empirical details of English syntax can be raised against unordered transformations, but I have not discussed enough of these details to use them effectively now. I can however raise a simple logical argument based on the principle of *simplicity* in evaluating scientific theories. Ask yourself which of these two claims is simpler: (1) INDIRECT OBJECT MOVEMENT and PASSIVE are English transformations which account for all relevant sentences if applied just in the order listed; (2) INDIRECT OBJECT MOVEMENT and PASSIVE are English transformations which account for all relevant sentences if they can be applied *either* in the order listed *or* in the reverse order. Assume that the transformations named in (1) are formulated exactly the same as the two named in (2). Thus (1) and (2) are competing theoretical explanations of passives and indirect objects in English, each making use of the same two transformations. Let us call the two transformations A and B in order to compare (1) and (2) more clearly. The explanation in (1), which claims *A then B,* is simpler than (2), which claims *Either A then B or B then A.* The very length of (2) is indication of its greater complexity. Thus a set of ordered transformations is inherently more desirable on scientific grounds than an unordered set. But even if we accept the desirability of ordered rather than unordered transformations, why is the order INDIRECT OBJECT MOVEMENT then PASSIVE to be desired in the present instance? We have already seen that if the order is reversed, the grammar cannot generate 5.39d because PASSIVE can move only a noun phrase immediately following the verb to the front of the sentence. But why not formulate the PASSIVE transformation in such a way that it can move not only a noun phrase immediately after a verb but also a noun phrase in certain prepositional phrases to the front of the sentence, thus enabling PASSIVE to be ordered before INDIRECT OBJECT MOVEMENT? Such an alternate formulation of the PASSIVE transformation is possible, but it would be much more complex than the present formulation and thus undesirable—again because it violates the evaluative criterion of *simplicity:* not only would the SD of such a transformation have to indicate the two alternate types of structures to which it could apply, but the SC for the second alternate would have the added task of deleting a preposition when a word like *Frank* in 5.39d were moved out of a deep-structure PP to the front of the sentence. Thus, for reasons of simplicity, we should accept both the general claim that transformations are ordered and the specific claim that INDIRECT OBJECT MOVEMENT is ordered before PASSIVE. It is well beyond the scope of this book to discuss, for every transformation introduced, why it is ordered before or after every other. I will, however, treat questions of ordering from time to time. You may assume that reasons of the type just adduced support the ordering I present for the sixteen transformations in the basic grammar. Works cited at the end of this chapter discuss the ordering of transformations, sometimes at considerable length.

EXERCISES

Provide analytical displays for the eight sentences listed below.

1. The legislature may have owed the taxpayers a rebate.
2. The judge was handed the verdict by the bailiff.
3. The courts can grant Elizabeth a divorce.

4. A bottle was thrown at the umpire by a fan after the game.
5. The ambassador could be offering the terrorists a compromise secretly.
6. Drugs are sold to some adolescents by bankers.
7. Walter had been offered an ambassadorship by the president before the election.
8. Those women may have been shown the film by an activist.

FOR FURTHER READING

Chomsky's two books (1957 and 1965) are basic references on all the matters of this chapter. Grinder and Elgin (1973, chapter 6) treat the form and application of transformations. Burt (1971) discusses the ordering of transformations in considerable detail. Ross (1967) treats technical problems of transformational formalism exhaustively. Fillmore's monograph on indirect objects (1965) is comprehensive, but quite within the grasp of someone who has read this chapter. Quirk et al. (1972) treat many aspects of English passive sentences in various places throughout their work.

Chapter 6

Transformational Syntax of English Simple Sentences II

SENTENCE NEGATION

Examine the sentences in 6.1 in light of our phrase-structure rules for generating deep structures and in light of those transformations already treated.

6.1a The boys must not bring beer.
  b Nicholas has not been listening to the chancellor.
  c The rich are not paying taxes.
  d The informer was not honored by the enemy.

All of the sentences in 6.1 are of course negative sentences. The specific characteristic of each sentence our grammar cannot account for is the presence of the word *not*. This word is not a member of any form class so far discussed. Traditional grammars sometimes call it an adverb, but if we apply the substitutional criteria which we have used to define the class of adverbs, we find that *not* fails to qualify: it cannot answer any of the question words which adverbs answer, nor can it occupy any of the positions of adverbs toward the end of a sentence. You are about to see, in fact, that *not* manifests many peculiarities in its positional behavior, and because of these, we will treat *not* as a form class unto itself. As a way of examining these peculiarities, let us attempt to make revisions in our grammar to account for the presence and the position of *not* in the sentences of 6.1.

Each sentence in 6.1 bears a close relation to the sentence in 6.2 with the same letter, the latter being in each case the affirmative counterpart of the former:

6.2a   The boys must bring beer.
 b   Nicholas has been listening to the chancellor.
 c   The rich are paying taxes.
 d   The informer was honored by the enemy.

We can thus assert that the deep structures of the sentences in 6.1 must resemble those in 6.2, but we must somehow add the morpheme *not* to the structure. Since *not* adds meaning to sentences but has no place in the PS rules so far discussed, its inclusion in sentences will require a revision of the PS rules. Our first inclination would be to revise the rules so that they can directly position *not* wherever it happens to occur in sentences. But where does it occur? In 6.1a it occurs between a modal and a verb. In 6.1b it occurs between *have-prs* and *be-en*. This would imply that it follows *have* and precedes *-en* in the deep structure. In 6.1c it occurs between *be-prs* and *pay-ing,* implying that it follows *be* and precedes *-ing* in the deep structure. And in 6.1d it occurs between *be-pst* and *honor-en,* after the *be* but before the *-en* which mark passive. Thus if we were to introduce *not* into deep structures in the very same position it occupies in the surface structures of 6.1, we would be forced to have the PS rules introduce it between the *have* and the *-en* that together mark PERF, or between the *be* and the *-ing* that together mark PROG. To account for 6.1d, we would have to revise the PASSIVE transformation to optionally introduce *not* between the *be* and the *-en* which enter the auxiliary. These facts exemplify again the kind of descriptive difficulty we face if we try to rely just on PS rules to account for syntactic structure. Alone, they cannot do the job; they need help from transformations. But we have a better reason than avoiding the above complexities to introduce *not* elsewhere in deep structures and to have a transformation account for its surface position. If negative sentences do indeed share the deep structure of their affirmative counterparts, except for the presence of *not,* then the grammar would do well to generate the exact same deep-structure tree for negatives as for affirmatives, and position *not* in such a way that its presence will not obscure the similarity. To this end, I propose 6.3 as the deep structure of 6.1a.

6.3

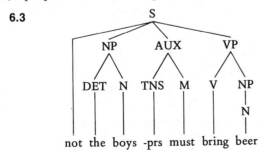

The entire constituent structure represented in 6.3, with the exception of the branch to *not,* is identical to the tree that our grammar generates for the affirmative sentence *The boys must bring beer.* By assigning this much of the structure of the affirmative sentence to the negative sentence as well, we adequately and accurately account for the similarities between the affirmative and negative sentences. The structure in 6.3 adequately accounts for another fact as well. Even though the word *not* appears in the surface structure buried in the auxiliary, it is nonetheless obvious that the idea of negation which it communicates is attributed to the entire sentence. By making *not* an immediate constituent of S and positioning it in front of the entire structure, we represent this fact. Thus the deep structure proposed in 6.3 fulfills yet another of the tasks deep structures are assigned: to represent meaningful relations only implicit in a surface sequence.

Having seen why a structure like the one in 6.3 is a desirable deep structure for 6.1a, we must now revise the PS rules so that they can generate 6.3, and we must also formulate a transformation to change a tree like the one in 6.3 into one which will account for the ordering of the morphemes in the surface structure. Here is a revision of PS rule i which will account for the appearance of *not* in the deep structure of negative sentences.

6.4 S → (not) + NP + AUX + VP + (ADVM) + (ADVP) + (ADVT) + (ADVR) . . .

Now what about the transformation which positions *not* in its proper place in surface sequences? We will call it NOT PLACEMENT, but before I present a formal statement of this transformation, let us see if we can determine with some accuracy just what tasks it must perform. If we assume that NOT PLACEMENT precedes AFFIX MOVEMENT, then its task is to change trees associated with the single-lettered sequences of 6.5 into those associated with the double-lettered sequences:

6.5a not the boys -prs must bring beer
aa the boys -prs must not bring beer
b not Nicholas -prs have-en be-ing listen to the chancellor
bb Nicholas -prs have not -en be-ing listen to the chancellor
c not the rich -prs be-ing pay taxes
cc the rich -prs be not -ing pay taxes

When AFFIX MOVEMENT is applied as needed to the double-lettered sequences, they become the surface structures of 6.1a, 6.1b, and 6.1c. Notice that in all the double-lettered sequences of 6.5, *not* appears immediately after the first stem in the auxiliary: after *must* in 6.5aa, after *have* in 6.5bb, and after *be* in 6.5cc. In 6.5bb, *not* actually invades the category PERF, appearing between the two morphemes which mark PERF, and in 6.5cc it invades the category PROG, appearing between the two morphemes which mark PROG. Thus we need to formulate the NOT PLACEMENT transformation in such a way that it will position *not* immediately after the first stem in the auxiliary. Here is the formal statement of the transformation:

6.6 NOT PLACEMENT (OBL)

SD: X " not " Y " $\begin{bmatrix} \text{TNS} + \text{M} \\ \text{TNS} + \text{have} \\ \text{TNS} + \text{be} \\ \text{TNS} \end{bmatrix}$ " Z

SC: 1   2   3   4   5 $\Rightarrow$
      1   3   4   2   5

COND: None

Examine the four lines of alternate choices in element number 4 of the SD. The first line accounts for the positioning of *not* after the modal *must* in 6.5aa. The second line accounts for the positioning of *not* after *have* in 6.5bb. And the third line accounts for the positioning of *not* after *be* in 6.5cc. The fourth line, which refers to TNS alone, stands ready to account for negative sentences without a stem in AUX. We shall examine such sentences later in the chapter. The analytical display for 6.1b is presented in 6.7 so that you can observe NOT PLACEMENT in action.

6.7 Nicholas has not been listening to the chancellor.

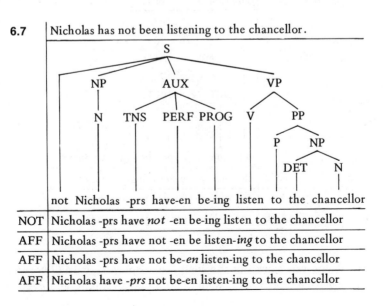

	not Nicholas -prs have-en be-ing listen to the chancellor
NOT	Nicholas -prs have *not* -en be-ing listen to the chancellor
AFF	Nicholas -prs have not -en be listen-*ing* to the chancellor
AFF	Nicholas -prs have not be-*en* listen-ing to the chancellor
AFF	Nicholas have -*prs* not be-en listen-ing to the chancellor

It is important to notice why NOT PLACEMENT must position *not* between the *have* and the *-en* of PERF. If *not* were positioned after *-en,* then AFFIX MOVEMENT would not be able to move *-en* to the right of *be,* and the grammar would generate the unacceptable sequence *Nicholas have-prs-en not be listen-ing to the chancellor.* Now it may seem unsystematic, if not brutal, to have a syntactic principle which for no apparent reason splits a meaningful syntactic category asunder (the *have* and the *-en* which together mark perfect). But in fact, this is exactly what happens in English sentences. Consider the ordinary spelled version of 6.1b again:

6.8   Nicholas *ha*s not be*en* listening to the chancellor.

There is no denying that the italicized letters *ha* in 6.8 indicating the presence of the stem *have* and the italicized letters *en* indicating the presence of the inflection *-en* are perceived by the user of English as a semantic unit even though they are separated by the morpheme *-prs* (spelled *s*), the morpheme *not,* and the morpheme *be.* These facts reinforce the need for, and the function of, the distinction between deep structure and surface structure. Our grammar shows that *have* and *-en* are a semantic unit by positioning them together in deep structure, but our grammar also shows how they attain the positions they occupy in 6.8 by the operation of NOT PLACEMENT and AFFIX MOVEMENT.

Examine 6.9 for the analytical display of 6.1c.

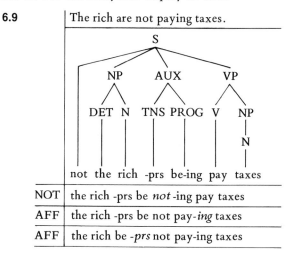

See if you can work out the analytical display for 6.1d *(The informer was not honored by the enemy).* While you are analyzing it, and even after you have completed the analysis, you should consider the question of why PASSIVE must apply before NOT PLACEMENT. Could our grammar, as presently formulated, generate 6.1d if the order of these two transformations were reversed?

CONTRACTED NEGATIVES

Can our grammar, even with the addition of NOT PLACEMENT, generate the sentences in 6.10?

6.10a The boys mustn't bring beer.
 b Nicholas hasn't been listening to the chancellor.
 c The rich aren't paying taxes.
 d The informer wasn't honored by the enemy.

Your first inclination should be to answer that our grammar can generate these sentences. They are identical in meaning to the sentences in 6.1. The contracted *n't* in each sentence is simply a spelling and pronunciation variant of the very same morpheme spelled *not* in the sentences of 6.1. Thus we should have no more reason to treat it differently from *not* than we would have to treat the various spellings of *-pst* differently from one another. But the syntax of *n't*, as it turns out, is different from the syntax of *not*, and thus we will have to distinguish the two transformationally. Consider the sentences in 6.11, which illustrate the difference:

6.11a Has Nicholas not been listening to the chancellor?
 aa *Has not Nicholas been listening to the chancellor?
 b *Has Nicholas n't been listening to the chancellor?
 bb Hasn't Nicholas been listening to the chancellor?

All four sentences are negative questions. The first two contain *not*, the second two, *n't*. The asterisks indicate that in a negative question containing *not*, *not* must remain after the subject NP when an auxiliary stem moves to a position in front of it. But in a negative question containing *n't*, *n't* moves along with the auxiliary stem to a position preceding the subject NP. When it comes time for us to cover the transformational syntax of English questions, we shall not be able to explain these facts unless the grammar has some way of distinguishing *not* and *n't*. For this reason, I propose a transformation, called CONTRACTION, which changes the free morpheme *not* into a suffix *-n't*. Thus we shall later be able to say that the transformation which creates question sequences like those in 6.11 will move the suffix *-n't* to a position preceding the subject NP, but that it does not move the free morpheme *not*. Here is the formal statement of the CONTRACTION transformation:

6.12 CONTRACTION (OPT)

SD: X " $\begin{Bmatrix} \text{TNS} + \text{M} \\ \text{TNS} + \text{have} \\ \text{TNS} + \text{be} \\ \text{TNS} \end{Bmatrix}$ " not " Y

SC: 1   2   3   4 ⇒
      1   2 -n't   4

COND: Blocked with certain modals (for example, *may*)

Look at the analytical display in 6.13 showing how CONTRACTION works with other transformations to generate 6.10d.

6.13 | The informer wasn't honored by the enemy.

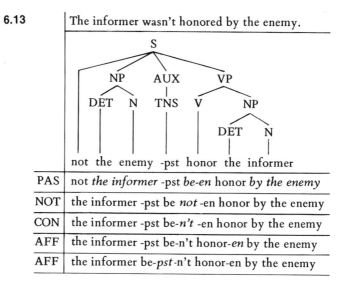

	not the enemy -pst honor the informer
PAS	not *the informer* -pst *be-en* honor *by the enemy*
NOT	the informer -pst be *not* -en honor by the enemy
CON	the informer -pst be-*n't* -en honor by the enemy
AFF	the informer -pst be-n't honor-*en* by the enemy
AFF	the informer be-*pst*-n't honor-en by the enemy

DO

Examine the negative sentences in 6.14. Before you ask yourself whether our grammar can generate them, ask yourself what their affirmative counterparts are:

6.14a The weather did not improve yesterday.
  b Crime doesn't pay.
  c Presidents do not lend burglars money.

You may be inclined to answer that 6.15 is the affirmative of 6.14a:

6.15 The weather did improve yesterday.

While 6.15 is an acceptable English sentence, it is more than just the affirmative counterpart of 6.14a. A sentence like 6.15 would ordinarily be pronounced with extra loudness on the word *did,* indicating that the speaker wishes to emphasize the fact that the weather improved. Thus the simple, unemphatic, affirmative counterparts of the sentences in 6.14 do not contain the words *do, does,* or *did:*

> **6.16a** The weather improved yesterday.
> **b** Crime pays.
> **c** Presidents lend burglars money.

The sentences in 6.14 are negatives of the sentences in 6.16. This means that the deep structures of the negative sentences in 6.14 would be exactly like the deep structures of the affirmative sentences in 6.16 except that the former trees will contain a leftmost branch to *not.* Thus 6.17 would be the deep structure of 6.14a.

6.17

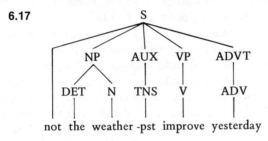

Now let us ask again, What is it about the surface sequence of morphemes in 6.14a that is not accounted for in the deep structure in 6.17 and that cannot be accounted for by any of the transformations so far discussed? It is of course the presence of the word *did.* In 6.14b, it is the presence of the word *does,* and in 6.14c, the presence of the word *do.* Actually in all three cases, it is the presence of *do,* since *did* is the past of *do* and thus manifests the sequence of morphemes *do-pst.* Similarly, both the spellings *does* and *do* manifest the sequence of morphemes *do-prs.* Our descriptive problem, then, is to account for *do* in each of the surface sequences in 6.14. Two observations about these sentences are relevant: (1) The presence of *do* seems not to add any extra meaning to the sequence—each sentence is simply the negative counterpart of an affirmative sentence in 6.16. (2) The AUX of each sentence contains only the category TNS. Since no meaning seems to be conveyed by the morpheme *do,* we have no reason to revise the PS rules to incorporate it into the deep structure. And since it seems to appear only in the surface structures of negatives having nothing but TNS in their AUX, we have a systematic basis for a transformational explanation. A good way to approach the problem is to have our grammar generate a surface structure from the deep structure in 6.17, and observe closely when problems develop. When NOT PLACEMENT is applied to 6.17 it produces the sequence in 6.18:

6.18 the weather -pst not improve yesterday

Ordinarily at this point in an analysis, we would simply notice how many affixes there are in the sequence and apply the requisite number of AFFIX MOVEMENT transformations. But notice what happens when we try to apply AFFIX MOVEMENT to the sequence in 6.18. (You may want to refer to the SD of AFFIX MOVEMENT in the Appendix.) AFFIX MOVEMENT can move a suffix to the right of an immediately following M, *have, be,* or V. But in 6.18 none of these immediately follows -*pst.* Thus AFFIX MOVEMENT is unable to move -*pst* to the right of *improve.* Actually we would not want it to be able to do so. If it did, it would generate the unacceptable surface sequence **The weather not improved yesterday.* But as the sequence stands in 6.18 it is also unacceptable: it contains an inflectional suffix with no stem to attach to. If you examine the sequence in 6.14a again, you will notice of course that the suffix -*pst* indeed precedes *not* but it does have a stem: *do.* We thus need a transformation for introducing a stem to carry a tense suffix which is "stranded" when NOT PLACEMENT cuts it off from a following stem and thus blocks the application of AFFIX MOVEMENT. Here is the formal statement of such a rule, which we call DO SUPPORT:

6.19 DO SUPPORT (OBL)
SD: X " TNS " Y
SC: 1   2   3 ⇒
      1 do 2   3
COND: 1 is not M, *have, be,* V

Notice that DO SUPPORT applies only to tense suffixes since *not* always precedes the -*en* of PERF and the -*ing* of PROG—or the -*en* of PASS for that matter. And DO SUPPORT applies only when TNS is the only deep structure AUX category: otherwise *not* would have been placed after the first auxiliary stem (a modal, *have,* or *be*), and AFFIX MOVEMENT would already have shifted the TNS suffix to the right of such a stem—in which case the condition on DO SUPPORT will have been violated and the transformation will not apply. Thus DO SUPPORT is a kind of "rescue" transformation, providing a stem for a tense suffix which has been cut off from all contact with an appropriate stem and which has thus been prohibited from affixing to such a stem.

Examine 6.20, which shows the analytical display for 6.14b.

6.20

Crime doesn't pay.

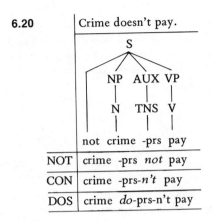

NOT	crime -prs *not* pay
CON	crime -prs-*n't* pay
DOS	crime *do*-prs-n't pay

See if you can draw the display for 6.14c *(Presidents do not lend burglars money)*. I shall have more to say about DO SUPPORT later in the chapter.

IMPERATIVES

Examine the sentences in 6.21 and evaluate them in light of our phrase-structure rules for generating deep structures and in light of those transformations already treated.

6.21a Open the door.
   b Discuss this problem with the ambassador.
   c Mail the president a letter today.

Anyone who knows English will recognize these sentences as commands (**imperatives**). As readers of this book, you should also notice that IN-DIRECT OBJECT MOVEMENT helped generate 6.21c. But what surface structural characteristics held in common in all three sentences cannot be accounted for with our grammar as expounded up to now? All the sentences begin with a verb, no sentence having any trace of a surface subject. We could possibly account for this by making the NP in PS rule i optional. But if we did, we would ignore the fact that the sentences in 6.21 all have a quite specific understood subject: *you*. The sentences in 6.22 provide evidence to support this contention.

6.22a Open the door, will you.
   b *Open the door, will he.
   c *Open the door, will they.
   d *Open the door, do you.
   e *Open the door, may you.

These sentences give clear indication of the shape of the deep structure of imperative sentences. In English, tag sentences such as *will you* and *will he* must contain a pronoun which matches the person and number of the subject of the tagged sentence. Notice this constraint operating in 6.23, where the tags are questions:

6.23a John is swimming, isn't he?
b They can ski, can't they?

This constraint on the pronoun explains the oddity of 6.22b and 6.22c: *will he* and *will they* are unnatural tags because *you* is indeed the understood subject of *open*. The sentences in 6.22 provide evidence for yet another constraint on tag sentences in English: they must contain the tense inflection and first auxiliary stem (if there is one) of the tagged sentence. The naturalness of 6.22a in contrast to 6.22d and 6.22e thus leads us to assert that the modal *will* is understood in the auxiliary of imperative sentences. Taking all these observations into consideration, let us propose the tree in 6.24 as the deep structure of 6.21a.

6.24

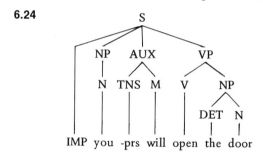

The structure in 6.24 does what an adequate deep structure must do. First, it explicitly represents elements of meaning implicit in the surface structure: IMP represents the fact that *Open the door* is a command, and the understood *you* and *will* appear. Second, the structure in 6.24 makes it possible to relate explicitly the deep structure of *Open the door* to the deep structures of other sentences, for example, to the simple statement *You will open the door* or the question *Will you open the door?* The deep structures of these last two sentences are exactly like 6.24 except that IMP does not appear in either one and, in the deep structure of the question, a morpheme indicating that the sentence is a question appears in the position which IMP occupies in 6.24. Notice that a minor revision in the PS rules is necessary to allow the branch from S to IMP in 6.24. We accomplish this by making IMP an optional constituent of S preceding NP in PS rule i. This revision is incorporated into the PS rules printed in the Appendix.

Now let us compare the deep structure proposed in 6.24 with the surface string in 6.21a so that we can determine the tasks the IMPERA- TIVE transformation must perform. The linear ordering of the mor- phemes in 6.24 is as follows:

> **6.25** IMP you -prs will open the door

The linear ordering of the morphemes in the surface sequence in 6.21a is as follows:

> **6.26** open -prs the door

How do the two linear sequences differ? First, 6.25 has three morphemes not present in 6.26. Second, -prs is ordered before *open* in 6.25 but after it in 6.26. The AFFIX MOVEMENT transformation accounts for the change in the position of -prs. We thus need to have the IMPERATIVE transformation delete the three morphemes of 6.25 which do not ap- pear in 6.26. Here is a formal statement of the transformation which will perform this task not only for the sentence under discussion but also for the whole range of imperative sentences in English:

> **6.27** IMPERATIVE (OBL)
> SD: IMP " you " TNS " will " X
> SC: 1   2   3   4   5 $\Rightarrow$
>   0   0   3   0   5
> COND: A verb in 5 cannot be a state

I am oversimplifying somewhat when I claim that *will* is the only modal to appear in the deep structure of imperative sentences, for *Open the door, could you* seems an acceptable command. And I am oversimplifying too when I claim that the underlying *you* and *will* must be deleted, for *You open the door* and even *You will open the door* (the latter with extra loud pronunciation of *will*) seem to be acceptable commands. I choose for the moment to ignore these variations so that our grammar can re- main reasonably uncomplicated and thus help illustrate how the set of transformations in the basic grammar work as a coherent whole. Later, when we consider the full range of possible syntactic speculation, you may want to revise the IMPERATIVE transformation to account for these and other subtleties.

Examine the analytical display in 6.28, which illustrates how the IMPERATIVE transformation operates in conjunction with the rest of the grammar to generate 6.21b.

6.28

Discuss this problem with the ambassador.

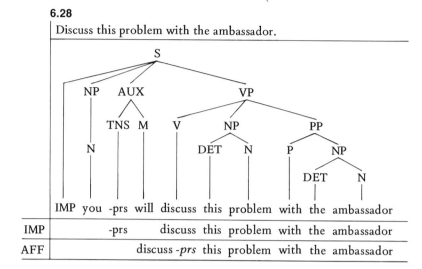

IMP		-prs	discuss this problem with the ambassador
AFF			discuss *-prs* this problem with the ambassador

The SD of the IMPERATIVE transformation applies straightforwardly to the deep structure in 6.28 deleting items 1, 2, and 4. The condition on the IMPERATIVE transformation accounts for the fact that imperative sentences like those in 6.29 are not likely to occur in English:

6.29a *Own the house.
b *Understand mathematics.

You may be able to think of situations where these sentences and others like them would indeed sound natural; I wish only to note that there seems to be a constraint against commanding someone to be in a state over which he has no immediate control, or relative to which he is powerless to act.

See if you can work out the analytical display for 6.21c *(Mail the president a letter today)*.

YES/NO QUESTIONS

Consider the sentences in 6.30, and ask yourself if our grammar can generate them:

6.30a Can the boys bring cokes?
b Has John taken the tapes?
c Weren't some students robbed by gypsies?

All three sentences are of course questions. They are a kind of question which calls on the addressee to respond yes or no, thus indicating whether a proposition is so or not so. In such questions, part of the auxiliary is positioned at the beginning of the sentence—in front of the NP which the PS rules generate at the beginning of a deep structure. Since users of English perceive a close relation between the sentences in 6.30 and the sentences in 6.31, their statement counterparts, we wish to have the deep structures of 6.30 resemble those of 6.31 as nearly as possible.

6.31a The boys can bring cokes.
b John has taken the tapes.
c Some students weren't robbed by gypsies.

But the deep structures of the sentences in 6.30, while explaining the sameness of questions and statements, must also explain the differences. Thus we propose 6.32 as the deep structure of 6.30a.

6.32

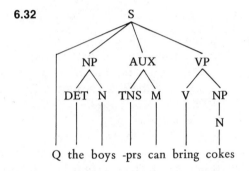

Notice that the tree in 6.32 except for the branch to Q can be generated by our PS rules as presently formulated, and that without the Q, it is the deep structure of 6.31a. If we revise PS rule i and allow it to generate a Q as the leftmost immediate constituent of S, then the PS rules will provide trees like the one in 6.32 as deep structures for questions like those in 6.30. These deep structures explain how users of English can answer such questions because the deep structure of the answer is contained in the deep structure of the question. The abstract morpheme Q can be glossed as a request for verification. That is, in questions like those in 6.30, the questioner presents a sentence to an addressee with a request for verification. In languages like Chinese, even the surface structures of questions manifest the same morpheme sequence as statements, but with a morpheme appended which means 'Is it true?' In English I propose that such a morpheme is present in the deep structure, but that a transformation normally deletes it, leaving a signal in the surface sequence of its deep-structure presence: the signal is of course the inversion of part of the auxiliary with the subject. Here is the formal statement of two transformations which act on deep structures like the one in 6.32 and convert them into surface sequences like 6.30a:

6.33 INVERSION (OBL)

SD: Q " NP " $\begin{cases} \text{TNS} + \text{M} \\ \text{TNS} + \text{have} \\ \text{TNS} + \text{be} \\ \text{TNS} \end{cases}$ (-n't) " X

SC: 1 2   3   4 ⇒
    1 3 2   4

COND: Cannot apply if 2 is a question word or whole S is a noun clause

6.34 Q DELETION (OBL)

SD: Q " X

SC: 1 2 ⇒
    0 2

COND: Cannot apply if whole S is a noun clause

INVERSION repositions the tense inflection and the first auxiliary stem —if there is one—immediately in front of the initial deep-structure NP. Notice that it also repositions *-n't*, if it is present in the tree which the transformation changes. This aspect of the rule accounts for the surface position of *-n't* in 6.30c. INVERSION must thus be ordered *after* CON-TRACTION. I will discuss the conditions on INVERSION in later sections. Q DELETION follows INVERSION and deletes the Q because there is ordinarily no trace of Q in surface structures. I will discuss the condition on Q DELETION in the next chapter. In 6.35 is the analytical display for 6.30a showing how INVERSION and Q DELETION help generate its surface sequence from the deep structure in 6.32.

6.35

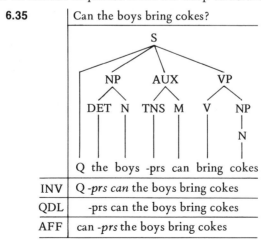

	Can the boys bring cokes?
	Q the boys -prs can bring cokes
INV	Q *-prs can* the boys bring cokes
QDL	-prs can the boys bring cokes
AFF	can *-prs* the boys bring cokes

We shall see in the next section that there is another type of question in English besides the yes/no question and that to generate the other type we make use of INVERSION and another transformation yet to be formulated.

The analytical display for 6.30b appears in 6.36.

6.36 | Has John taken the tapes?

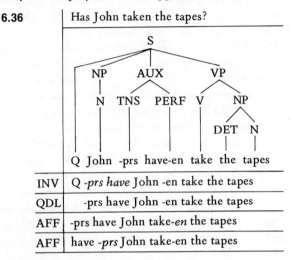

INV	Q *-prs have* John -en take the tapes
QDL	-prs have John -en take the tapes
AFF	-prs have John take-*en* the tapes
AFF	have *-prs* John take-en the tapes

Examine 6.35 and 6.36 carefully, and then try to work out the display for 6.30c *(Weren't some students robbed by gypsies?)* You will find that several transformations apply in generating it.

QUESTION-WORD QUESTIONS

Now consider the questions in 6.37. How do they differ from yes/no questions? Can our grammar generate them?

6.37a What has the musician composed?
   b Who can paint the house for us?
   c Why are they planting a garden in February?

One cannot appropriately answer any of these questions by saying yes or no, but rather must respond with a word or phrase which seems somehow to correspond to the initial word of each sentence, the word beginning with *wh.* One might respond to 6.37a with the NP *a symphony,* to 6.37b with *John,* and to 6.37c with the PP *through stupidity.* If complete sentence answers containing these words or phrases were given to the questions in 6.37, they would be sequenced as follows:

6.38a   The musician has composed a symphony.
  b   John can paint the house for us.
  c   They are planting a garden in February through stupidity.

Comparing the answers in 6.38 with the questions in 6.37 points out those characteristics of the questions in 6.37 which our grammar cannot presently account for. Let us focus on 6.37a to discuss them. First, it seems that the word *what* in 6.37a is logically the direct object of the verb *composed.* The fact that the NP *a symphony,* which corresponds to *what* in the answer, occupies a position after the verb is evidence of this. We thus have reason to claim that, in the deep structure of 6.37a, the word *what* should appear as an NP immediately following the V in the VP. No change in the PS rules is needed to generate *what* in the VP. It is a noun and will be generated, just as any other noun, in an NP after V. Notice that the PS rules in the Appendix include *what* along with *who* and *whom* as nouns which may be inserted by rule xvii. Our next problem is to account for the movement of *what* from its deep-structure position after the verb to a position at the beginning of the surface question sequence. Before I formulate a transformation to accomplish this movement, let me mention a third difference between 6.37a and 6.38a for which the grammar must account. Notice that *has* precedes *the musician* in 6.37a but follows it in 6.38a. We can account for this inversion of *has* and *the musician* by including Q in the deep structure and applying INVERSION exactly as in yes/no questions. In 6.39 you will find the proposed deep structure for 6.37a.

6.39

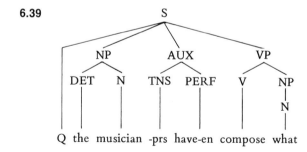

The Q at the beginning of the structure signifies, as in yes/no questions, that the sentence is a request for information. It also serves as a necessary element in the SD of the INVERSION transformation—without the Q, INVERSION would not be able to invert *-prs have* with *the musician.* The presence of *what* (a question word) serves to distinguish this type of question from yes/no questions: *what* indicates that the request for information is not a request to verify the truth of the entire sentence but rather that it is a request for the addressee to supply the questioner with a specific constituent of the sentence, one which can occupy the position filled by the question word in the deep structure. Let me now present the transformation accounting for the movement of *what* (and of course other question words) to the front of the sentence.

6.40 QUESTION-WORD MOVEMENT (OBL)
SD: Q " X " {who(m), what, how, where, when, why} " Y
SC: 1   2   3   4 ⇒
     3   2   4
COND: None

In 6.41 you will see the analytical display for 6.37a, which shows how INVERSION and QUESTION-WORD MOVEMENT work in conjunction with AFFIX MOVEMENT to generate the surface structure from the deep structure in 6.39.

6.41

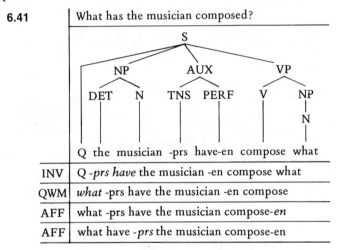

	What has the musician composed?
	Q the musician -prs have-en compose what
INV	Q *-prs have* the musician -en compose what
QWM	*what* -prs have the musician -en compose
AFF	what -prs have the musician compose-*en*
AFF	what have *-prs* the musician compose-en

Before we turn to the problem of analysis let us examine the question from 6.37b and the full sentence answer to it from 6.38b:

6.37b Who can paint the house for us?
6.38b John can paint the house for us.

Notice that *can,* the first stem in the auxiliary, occupies the very same position in 6.37b as it does in 6.38b. This means that the INVERSION transformation has not applied in generating 6.37b. If you examine the formal statement of the INVERSION transformation in the Appendix, you will notice that the condition listed there forbids application of the transformation when the initial NP contains a question word. This accounts for the general fact of English syntax, exemplified by 6.37b, that when a question-word question calls on the addressee to supply the subject of the sentence, no inversion takes place. Furthermore, no overt movement of the question word seems to take place either. *Who* in

6.37b occupies the same position as *John* in 6.38b. But recall that the deep structure of 6.37b contains Q (to indicate that the sequence is a request for information). Thus to generate the surface structure of 6.37b, the grammar must somehow delete the Q. If we allow question-word movement to apply to 6.37b, this deletion will be achieved, as shown in 6.42.

6.42

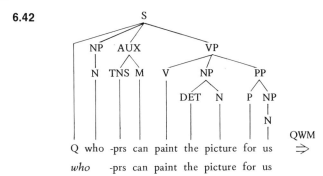

We have thus seen that, while most question-word questions require the application of both INVERSION and QUESTION-WORD MOVEMENT, others require only the application of QUESTION-WORD MOVEMENT. Examine 6.43 for the analytical display of 6.37c *(Why are they planting a garden in February?)*.

6.43

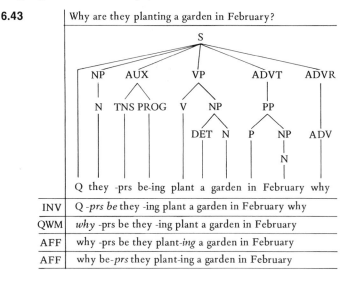

Additional question-word questions are presented for analysis in the exercise at the end of this chapter.

DO IN QUESTIONS

Examine the sentences in 6.44. What kind of sentences are they? Can our grammar generate them?

6.44a Did you enjoy the movie?
   b How do Italians cook spaghetti?
   c Doesn't the temperature vary in the tropics?
   d What did the bank send Bill?

6.44a and 6.44c are yes/no questions and 6.44b and 6.44d are question-word questions. And our grammar can generate them, but only by applying DO SUPPORT. Remember that we found DO SUPPORT to be necessary when NOT PLACEMENT positioned *not* between a tense suffix and a following stem, thus blocking the application of AFFIX MOVEMENT and in effect stranding the tense affix. DO SUPPORT simply inserted the stem *do* to carry the suffix in the surface structure. The sentences in 6.44 illustrate a similar situation but with a different cause. If the deep-structure auxiliary of a question contains only a tense affix and INVERSION applies, the affix is moved to a position in front of the initial sentence NP. When it comes time for AFFIX MOVEMENT to apply, it cannot because the tense suffix is not followed by one of the stem types called for in the SD of AFFIX MOVEMENT: M, *have, be,* or V. Thus the tense suffix is stranded, just as in negative sentences. When DO SUPPORT applies, it finds that AFFIX MOVEMENT has been unable to attach the tense suffix to an appropriate stem and so introduces *do* in front of the affix. In 6.45 and 6.46 I present the analytical displays of 6.44a and 6.44b so that you can observe the operation of DO SUPPORT in questions. You can learn more about the role of DO SUPPORT in questions by analyzing 6.44c and 6.44d.

6.45

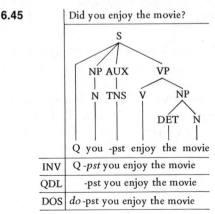

	Did you enjoy the movie?
INV	Q *-pst* you enjoy the movie
QDL	-pst you enjoy the movie
DOS	*do* -pst you enjoy the movie

6.46 | How do Italians cook spaghetti?

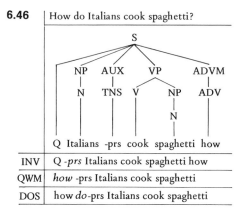

```
                          S
          ┌──────┬────────┬────────┐
         NP     AUX      VP      ADVM
          │      │       ╱╲        │
          N     TNS     V   NP    ADV
          │      │      │    │     │
          │      │      │    N     │
          │      │      │    │     │
          Q  Italians  -prs cook spaghetti how
```

INV	Q -*prs* Italians cook spaghetti how
QWM	*how* -prs Italians cook spaghetti
DOS	how *do*-prs Italians cook spaghetti

EXERCISES

Provide analytical displays for each of the following sentences:

1. Should Canada sell China some wheat openly?
2. Tell the candidate the results at the briefing.
3. Why wasn't Edward happy with the paycheck?
4. This car must not have been serviced by the manufacturer before shipment.
5. Do not deliver secrets to spies.
6. Are students trusted by the administration?
7. What did you listen to on the weekend?
8. Don't tell him the answer.
9. Do you agree with the president?
10. Who was handed a note by the terrorists yesterday?
11. Don't be sad about the news.

FOR FURTHER READING

Chomsky (1957) treats all the matters of this chapter in some detail. Our presentation, however, conforms most closely to those of Katz and Postal (1964) and Chomsky (1965). Another version of a transformational treatment of imperatives, negatives, and questions may be found in Burt (1971). Quirk et al. (1972) treat all the matters of this chapter in detail. A much broader perspective on English questions may be obtained from Malone (1967) or Chafe (1970).

Chapter 7

Transformational Syntax of English Complex Sentences

DEEP STRUCTURES FOR NOUN CLAUSES

Consider the sentences in 7.1 and evaluate them in light of the PS rules we have been using and in light of the transformations discussed in chapters 5 and 6.

7.1a That Joe will fail the test is clear.
aa It is clear that Joe will fail the test.
b Freud showed that boys like girls.
b' That boys like girls was shown by Freud.
bb It was shown by Freud that boys like girls.

Can the PS rules as presented in chapter 4 provide meaningful deep structures for these sentences? And can transformations already discussed generate the given sequences of morphemes? The answer to each question is no. All of the sequences in 7.1 are complex sentences, which means that the constituent structure generated by the PS rules must contain an S inside an S. There must thus be an S to the right of an arrow somewhere in the PS rules. But the rules presented in chapter 4 do not allow for this possibility. To revise the PS rules, we must examine the sentences in 7.1 and determine which words belong to the sentence within a sentence (the **dependent clause**) and which words belong to the containing sentence (the **main clause**). We then must determine just where in the main clause the PS rules should generate the dependent clause S. Let us begin by comparing 7.1a and 7.1b with 7.2a and 7.2b:

7.1a *That Joe will fail the test* is clear.
b Freud showed *that boys like girls.*
7.2a *The answer* is clear.
b Freud showed *the way.*

If a user of English posed the question *What is clear?* the italicized portions of either 7.1a or 7.2a might be given as an answer. Or if he posed the question *What did Freud show?* the italicized portions of either 7.1b or 7.2b might be given as an answer. This is evidence that the italicized portions of 7.1a and 7.2a represent the same constituent category and that the italicized portions of 7.1b and 7.2b represent the same constituent category. Since *the answer* and *the way* are noun phrases, we must conclude that the sequences *that Joe will fail the test* and *that boys like girls* are likewise noun phrases—at least relative to the unitalicized words (the main clauses which contain these sequences). But when we examine the internal structure of each of the latter two sequences, we also find that they contain sentences. We list these sentences in 7.3:

> **7.3a** Joe will fail the test.
> **b** Boys like girls.

Notice the word *that,* which in 7.1a and 7.1b is clearly part of the main-clause noun phrase, is not part of the sentence within that noun phrase. In fact, the word *that* seems to do little more than help indicate that the clause following it is a dependent clause functioning as a noun phrase in the main clause. Since the word *that* thus seems to contribute little to the meaning of the sentence, we will not include it in deep structures, but will later devise a transformation to insert it while generating surface structures. Therefore the PS rules do not need to be revised to account for it. Thus we have seen that the deep structures which we hope to have the PS rules generate for 7.1a and 7.1b must at least make clear that the dependent clauses function as noun phrases in the main clauses but that they remain sentences. In 7.4 I present provisional deep structures for 7.1a and 7.1b which adequately represent the fact that the dependent clauses are NPs in the main clause but that they remain sentences.

7.4a

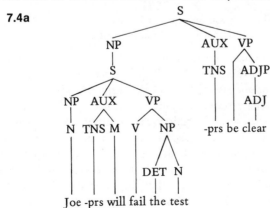

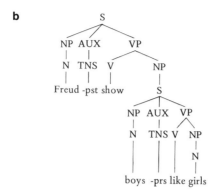

The label NP above the dependent S expresses the relation of the dependent clause to the structure of the main clause. The label S itself categorizes the elements it labels according to their internal relations. In order to have the PS rules generate deep-structure trees like the ones in 7.4 we need to make two revisions in the grammar. First we would revise PS rule vi—NP → (DET) + N—so that it could generate an S inside a noun phrase in addition to the two options it presently allows, a noun or a determiner and a noun. Second, we allow the PS rules to apply *recursively* in generating deep structures. All rules needed to generate the main clause apply in sequence. Then, if a dependent clause S has been generated as part of the main clause, the rules start over again and generate the dependent S. Let us consider **recursiveness** an integral part of our grammar from this point on. But before we actually reformulate PS rule vi to allow an S within a noun phrase, we will consider the sequences in 7.1aa and 7.1bb and determine just how they bear on the exact nature of the revision we hope to make. First let us compare 7.1a and 7.1aa:

7.1a　　That Joe will fail the test is clear.
　aa　　It is clear that Joe will fail the test.

Both of these sentences mean essentially the same thing. The adjective *clear* is predicated of the clause *Joe will fail the test* in both sentences, even though the dependent clause follows the adjective *clear* in 7.1aa. Now, whenever two surface sequences mean essentially the same thing, we want their deep structures to reflect the similarity. Were it not for the presence of the word *it* in 7.1aa, we could simply claim that both 7.1a and 7.1aa come from the deep structure in 7.4a. But in order to account for the presence of the word *it* when it does occur in surface sequences like the one in 7.1aa, let us claim that the deep structure contains this word. We will thus revise the provisional deep structure of 7.4a and claim instead that the deep structure of 7.1a and 7.1aa is that presented in 7.5.

7.5

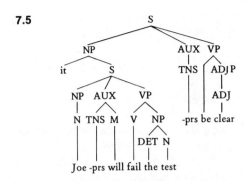

I will discuss in the next section the transformations needed to generate the surface orderings of 7.1a and 7.1aa from the deep structure in 7.5. I wish in the meantime to make a similar claim about the deep structure of 7.1b and 7.1bb. First examine the sequence in 7.1b' *(That boys like girls was shown by Freud)*. Notice that it is the passive of 7.1b, and thus has the same deep structure as 7.1b. But now examine 7.1bb and compare it with 7.1b':

7.1b'   That boys like girls was shown by Freud.
bb   It was shown by Freud that boys like girls.

Both are passive sentences. In fact, 7.1bb is identical in meaning to 7.1b' and is related to it exactly as 7.1aa is related to 7.1a. Therefore 7.1bb must have the same deep structure as 7.1b', which we have seen to have the same deep structure as 7.1b. So let us put *it* in the deep structure of all three sentences, 7.1b, 7.1b', and 7.1bb (and thus systematically account for the presence of *it* in surface sequences like 7.1bb). And let us revise the provisional deep structure in 7.4b, claiming instead that 7.6 presents the deep structure of 7.1b, 7.1b', and 7.1bb.

7.6

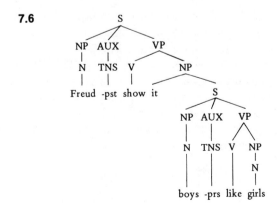

In order for the PS rules to generate deep structures like the ones in 7.5 and 7.6 we need to revise PS rule vi as follows:

7.7 $NP \rightarrow \begin{Bmatrix} (DET) + N \\ it + S \end{Bmatrix}$

This revision is incorporated into the complete set of PS rules given in the Appendix.

I have made the following claims in this section: (1) All of the sentences in 7.1 contain sequences which function as noun phrases but which are nonetheless sentences themselves. (For this reason we will call them **noun clauses**.) (2) The word *that* when introducing noun clauses does not appear in deep structures. (3) The word *it,* which appears in certain of the sequences in 7.1, is generated by the PS rules in the deep structure of every noun phrase containing a noun clause.

NOUN CLAUSE TRANSFORMATIONS

In 7.8a is the morpheme sequence contained in the deep structure in 7.5. In 7.8b you will find the surface morpheme sequence of 7.1a, which the grammar generates from the deep structure in 7.5. And in 7.8c you will find the surface sequence of 7.1aa, which also is generated from the deep structure in 7.5. Compare the two surface sequences with the deep-structure sequence and try to determine the changes which transformations must bring about to generate each surface structure from the deep structure.

> **7.8a** (7.5)   it Joe -prs will fail the test -prs be clear
>   **b** (7.1a)   that Joe will-prs fail the test be-prs clear
>   **c** (7.1aa)   it be-prs clear that Joe will-prs fail the test

We may assume that the AFFIX MOVEMENT transformation will account for the changes in position of the two *-prs* suffixes in both 7.8b and 7.8c. However, we presently have no transformation to account for the appearance of the word *that* in both 7.8b and 7.8c. Nor do we have a transformation to account for the disappearance of the word *it* in 7.8b. And we need a third transformation to account for the movement of the noun clause to the end of the main clause in 7.8c. In 7.9 is an ordered set of three transformations which will account for these changes not only in the example sentences but also in a large number of similar sentences in English.

7.9a NOMINALIZATION (OBL)
SD: X " [$_{NP}$ it [$_S$ " Y]$_S$]$_{NP}$ " Z
SC: 1   2   3   4   ⇒
     1   2 that 3   4
COND: Cannot apply if 3 begins with Q or question word

b EXTRAPOSITION (OPT)
SD: X " [$_{NP}$ it " S]$_{NP}$ " Y
SC: 1   2   3   4   ⇒
     1   2   4 3
COND: None

c IT DELETION (OBL)
SD: X " [$_{NP}$ it " S]$_{NP}$ " Y
SC: 1   2   3   4   ⇒
     1   0   3   4
COND: None

Notice that the structural descriptions of all three transformations are the same: they all operate on noun phrases containing a noun clause preceded by *it*. NOMINALIZATION creates a leftmost branch within the noun clause to the word *that*. EXTRAPOSITION moves the noun clause out of the NP containing it to a position at the far right of the main clause, leaving the morpheme *it* behind as a kind of record of the logical deep-structure relation of the extraposed noun clause to the remainder of the sentence. IT DELETION deletes an *it* that is still accompanied by a noun clause when the time comes for IT DELETION to apply. Notice that the ordering of EXTRAPOSITION and IT DELETION is significant, and that the two transformations are mutually exclusive. EXTRAPOSITION is optional, but if it is applied, IT DELETION cannot then be applied because the output tree of EXTRAPOSITION has no S following an *it* in a noun phrase, and thus the SD of IT DELETION is not satisfied. If, on the other hand, EXTRAPOSITION is optionally skipped, then the noun phrase composed of *it* + S is still intact when it comes time for IT DELETION to apply, and IT DELETION obligatorily deletes the *it*. In 7.10a I present the analytical display for 7.1a and in 7.10b the display for 7.1aa. Since both sentences have the same deep structure, I present it only once (in 7.10). Examine the displays closely and note how NOMINALIZATION and IT DELETION operate in generating 7.1a and how NOMINALIZATION and EXTRAPOSITION operate in generating 7.1aa. (I will comment in the next section on the ordering of transformations in the analytical displays. See especially page 152 for an explanation of why AFFIX MOVEMENT comes first in 7.10.)

7.10

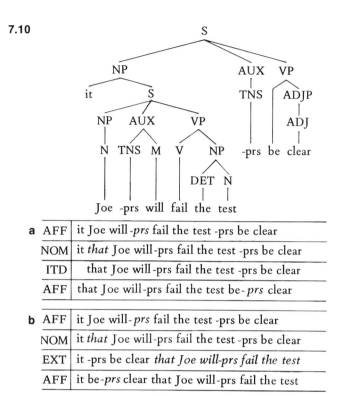

a	AFF	it Joe will -*prs* fail the test -prs be clear
	NOM	it *that* Joe will-prs fail the test -prs be clear
	ITD	that Joe will-prs fail the test -prs be clear
	AFF	that Joe will-prs fail the test be-*prs* clear

b	AFF	it Joe will-*prs* fail the test -prs be clear
	NOM	it *that* Joe will-prs fail the test -prs be clear
	EXT	it -prs be clear *that Joe will-prs fail the test*
	AFF	it be-*prs* clear that Joe will-prs fail the test

See if you can work out analytical displays for 7.1b, 7.1b', and 7.1bb.

ORDERING OF NOUN CLAUSE TRANSFORMATIONS

In the previous section I discussed three transformations for generating surface sequences containing noun clauses. I stated that the transformations were ordered among themselves as follows: (1) NOMINALIZATION, (2) EXTRAPOSITION, (3) IT DELETION. And I mentioned a few reasons for the given order. I wish now to elaborate briefly on these reasons. NOMINALIZATION must precede EXTRAPOSITION to avoid needlessly complicating the SD of NOMINALIZATION. Recall that EXTRAPOSITION takes a noun clause out of a noun phrase and creates a rightmost branch to it in the main clause. If NOMINALIZATION followed EXTRAPOSITION, we would need to have the SD of NOMINALIZATION refer both to an S following the word *it* in a noun phrase and to an S which is the rightmost immediate constituent of another S. Thus, by ordering NOMINALIZATION first, we can more

simply make reference only to the former structure. We in turn order
EXTRAPOSITION before IT DELETION because the claim that the
user of English has a choice about where he wants to position the noun
clause, with the fate of *it* contingent on this choice, seems intuitively
more satisfactory than the alternate claim that the user's basic choice is
about whether to include *it* or not, with the position of the clause contingent on this choice. Furthermore, the ordering presented for these three
transformations achieves considerable simplicity by providing all three
noun clause transformations with the same structural description.

But what about the ordering of the whole set of three noun clause
transformations relative to other transformations so far discussed in this
book? Let us consider the ordering of EXTRAPOSITION relative to
PASSIVE. Should EXTRAPOSITION be listed before or after PAS-
SIVE? Consider the sentences in 7.11 and ask yourself whether the
ordering of PASSIVE and EXTRAPOSITION has any bearing on the
grammar's ability to generate them:

7.11a Some philosophers claim that men love truth.
   b That men love truth is claimed by some philosophers.
   c It is claimed by some philosophers that men love truth.

The PASSIVE transformation has applied to 7.11b, and both PASSIVE
and EXTRAPOSITION have applied to 7.11c. But is the order of application EXTRAPOSITION then PASSIVE or PASSIVE then EXTRA-
POSITION?

Let us consider the consequences of both orderings, but first look at
7.12 for the deep structure which all three sentences in 7.11 hold in
common.

7.12

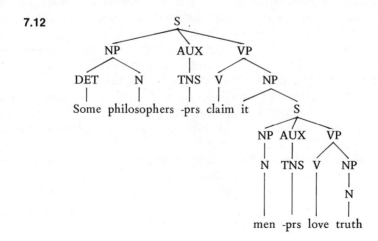

If EXTRAPOSITION preceded PASSIVE, there would be no need to apply EXTRAPOSITION when its turn came because the noun clause is already at the far right of the main clause in 7.12. Then, when PASSIVE's turn came, and it moved the NP containing *it* + S to the front of the main clause, there would be no way (because EXTRAPOSITION's turn is past) to account for 7.11c—where *it* is at the front but where the noun clause has indeed been extraposed to the end. However, if EXTRAPOSITION is listed, and can therefore be applied, after PASSIVE, then EXTRAPOSITION can easily move an S out of an *it* + S noun phrase after PASSIVE has moved such a noun phrase to the front of a main clause, and thus account for 7.11c. For this reason, we will list EXTRAPOSITION and the other noun clause transformations after PASSIVE.

It is difficult to find reasons for ordering the noun clause transformations either before or after other transformations on our list. I will more or less arbitrarily choose to order them before all the other transformations which we have already considered, apart from PASSIVE (and therefore, of course, apart from INDIRECT OBJECT MOVEMENT, which we saw in chapter 5 must precede PASSIVE). Notice that on the complete list of transformations in the Appendix the noun clause transformations are listed immediately after PASSIVE, but before NOT PLACEMENT, CONTRACTION, IMPERATIVE, INVERSION, QUESTION-WORD MOVEMENT, Q DELETION, AFFIX MOVEMENT, and DO SUPPORT.

Questions of ordering, and arguments about them, can become very complex. And spending additional time discussing them will not further my aim of shedding maximal light on English syntax. You do need to remember, however, that an ordered list of transformations is not only simpler in the scientific theoretical sense but is also easier to learn and to apply to the analysis of English sentences.

Linguists have also found evidence supporting the claim that the list of transformations is not absolutely ordered but, in some measure at least, *cyclically* ordered. This means that when the grammar is generating a complex sentence, the entire list of ordered transformations applies first to the dependent clause and then to the main clause. This is why in 7.10 I listed the AFFIX MOVEMENT transformation which applied to the dependent clause before the several transformations which applied to the main clause. If a sentence contains more than one dependent clause, then the **cyclic principle,** as it is called, requires that transformations apply to the *most dependent* clause (the S lowest in the tree), then to the next most dependent, and so on until the main clause is transformed and the complete surface structure generated. Actually, only some transformations need to apply in a cycle, but to make our analyses easier, we will adopt the practice of applying the whole set of transformations cyclically.

Examine the display in 7.13, which analyzes the sentence *It is important that lawyers admit that the theft was wrong.* Notice how the AFFIX MOVEMENT transformation applying to the most dependent clause *(the theft was wrong)* operates first, then the three transformations for the next most dependent clause, and finally the three transformations for the main clause.

7.13

It is important that lawyers admit that the theft was wrong.

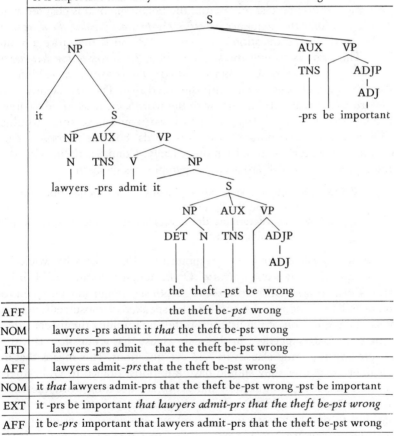

AFF	the theft be-*pst* wrong
NOM	lawyers -prs admit it *that* the theft be-pst wrong
ITD	lawyers -prs admit that the theft be-pst wrong
AFF	lawyers admit-*prs* that the theft be-pst wrong
NOM	it *that* lawyers admit-prs that the theft be-pst wrong -pst be important
EXT	it -prs be important *that lawyers admit-prs that the theft be-pst wrong*
AFF	it be-*prs* important that lawyers admit-prs that the theft be-pst wrong

See if you can work out analytical displays for the first two sentences in the exercises at the end of this chapter. Each sentence has a main clause and one dependent noun clause.

NOUN CLAUSE QUESTIONS

Examine the sentences in 7.14. Ask yourself if there is anything about the sentences which the grammar cannot account for.

7.14a The public doesn't know whether the president aided the deception.

b We can't determine why Jeb shredded the documents.

If you apply the same test we used at the beginning of this chapter, you will discover that the sequence *whether the president aided the deception* in 7.14a answers the question . . . *know what?* and is therefore a noun clause. The same is true of the sequence *why Jeb shredded the documents* in 7.14b. But unlike other noun clauses so far considered, neither of these two noun clauses begins with the word *that.* The first begins with the word *whether,* and the second with the word *why.* If we tried to draw the deep structures of 7.14a and 7.14b, we would have some trouble deciding how to incorporate these two words. For this purpose let us examine the sentences in 7.14 more closely. Compare them with the sentences in 7.15, which are accurate paraphrases of them.

7.15a The public doesn't know the answer to this question: did the president aid the deception?

b We can't determine the answer to this question: why did Jeb shred the documents?

A user of English might in fact respond to 7.14a, just as he would to a direct question, by saying *He did.* Or he might respond to 7.14b by saying *Through fear.* Ordinarily these responses would not be given to sentences like those in 7.14 because the speaker of those sentences is not asking a question of the listener; rather he is telling the listener that he, or some party specified in the main clause, has a question. But the fact remains: the noun clauses in 7.14 are questions. This means that in their deep structures they should have a leftmost branch to Q. Furthermore, 7.14a is a yes/no question and 7.14b is a question-word question. But notice that INVERSION, which obligatorily applies to yes/no questions and to question-word questions about any constituent except the initial deep-structure NP, has not applied to either of the noun clause questions in 7.14. You will notice that we have formulated INVERSION to anticipate this fact of English syntax: if you examine the INVERSION transformation in the Appendix, you will notice that it has a condition stating that the transformation cannot apply if the whole S is a noun clause. The position of the word *why* at the beginning of the noun clause in 7.14b is accounted for by the operation of QUESTION-WORD MOVEMENT on the deep structure of the noun clause, where *why* will be diagramed as an adverb of reason. This leaves the word *whether* unaccounted for. It is in no sense an adverb. We could account for it by having NOMINALIZATION introduce it as an alternate of *that*. But it only occurs in dependent clause questions, where *that* never occurs. So it is mutually exclusive with *that*. A very reasonable explanation of the word *whether* is that it is a surface pronunciation of the morpheme Q, and that Q is deleted only in main clause yes/no questions but not in dependent clause yes/no questions. We can thus account for *whether,* and have, in fact, already done so, by attaching a condition to Q DELE-TION which prohibits application of this transformation if the clause containing the Q is itself a noun clause. You may want to examine the condition in the Appendix.

We have thus seen that noun clauses can be either yes/no questions or question-word questions. If a noun clause is a yes/no question, neither INVERSION nor Q DELETION applies in generating the surface struc-ture. (The Q remains in the analytical sequence to the very last line and thus accounts for the word *whether* in the surface sequence—the word

7.16

The public doesn't know whether the president aided the deception.

AFF		Q the president aid-*pst* the deception
ITD	not the public -prs know	Q the president aid-pst the deception
NOT	the public -prs *not* know Q the president aid -pst the deception
CON	the public -prs-*n't* know Q the president aid -pst the deception
DOS	the public *do*-prs-n't know Q the president aid -pst the deception

whether itself never appears anywhere in an analytical display.) If a noun clause is a question-word question, INVERSION does not apply but QUESTION-WORD MOVEMENT does in generating the surface structure. In 7.16 on the preceding page is the complete analytical display for 7.14a. After examining it, you may want to work out the display for 7.14b.

DEEP STRUCTURES FOR RELATIVE CLAUSES

Consider the sentences in 7.17 and evaluate them in light of the PS rules we have been using and in light of the transformations so far discussed.

7.17a Joe bought the bench *which Albert made.*
aa Helen paid the boy *who sells newspapers.*
b We know the people *sick of violence.*
bb Howard boarded the bus *waiting at the terminal.*
c We know the *sick* people.
cc Howard boarded the *waiting* bus.

Can the PS rules presented in chapter 4 provide meaningful deep structures for these sentences? And can transformations already discussed generate the given sequences of morphemes? The answer to each question is no. The PS rules as presently formulated cannot generate the italicized portions of each sentence. Until we can have them do so, it is useless to ask if new transformations are needed to account for the sentences. Notice that 7.17a and 7.17aa are complex sentences, and the italicized sequences are clauses. In 7.17b and 7.17bb, the italicized sequences are phrases (portions of clauses). And in 7.17c and 7.17cc the italicized portions are single words. You might wonder why in fact these three types of italicized sequences are grouped together for consideration. Can you, in fact, determine any common characteristics of the italicized elements in all six sentences? (To answer this question, you may want to search your knowledge of traditional grammatical terminology, or you may want to use the linguist's tool of substitution—is there a word which will substitute for all the italicized elements?) In traditional grammatical terms you may answer that the italicized word or words in each sentence in 7.17 modify some noun. The linguist's manner of saying essentially the same thing is to note that in a question-word question seeking to elicit the italicized elements in 7.17, the question word which substitutes in every case is *which*. Here are questions to which the respective sentences in 7.17 are appropriate replies:

7.18a   Which bench did Joe buy?
  aa   Which boy did Helen pay?
   b   Which people do you know?
  bb   Which bus did Howard board?
   c   Which people do you know?
  cc   Which bus did Howard board?

One of the tasks of the PS rules is to show how clauses, phrases, and single words like those italicized in 7.17 share the ability to answer questions with *which*. In doing so, the PS rules will also show exactly what it means to claim that a clause, phrase, or word modifies a noun. Recall that our grammar accounts for both the sameness of function by assigning same deep structures and the difference in word ordering by attributing such differences to the work of transformations. The same tactic applies here. We need to revise the PS rules so that they make room for noun modifiers, but in a unified way. Any diversity in the surface sequencing of noun modifiers will be attributed to the operation of transformations.

Reexamine the italicized sequences in 7.17. Ask yourself, with the help of the questions in 7.18 if necessary, which noun the italicized sequence modifies. Do the modifying elements precede or follow the modified noun? In the first four sequences, the modifying elements follow the noun. In the last two they precede. In 7.19 I present the modified noun from each sentence in 7.17 along with the modifying word or words, still in italics. The lettering corresponds to that in 7.17.

7.19a   the bench *which Albert made*
  aa   the boy *who sells newspapers*
   b   the people *sick of violence*
  bb   the bus *waiting at the terminal*
   c   the *sick* people
  cc   the *waiting* bus

The fact that some noun modifiers follow and others precede the noun is something we must account for. If we want a unified deep-structure representation of noun modifiers, we must choose one of the surface positional possibilities and have a transformation account for the other. Compare 7.20a and 7.20b with 7.17c and 7.17cc respectively.

7.20a   We know the people who are sick.
   b   Howard boarded the bus which was waiting.
7.17c   We know the sick people.
  cc   Howard boarded the waiting bus.

The meaning of 7.20a is virtually the same as that of 7.17c, and that of

7.20b the same as 7.17cc. Furthermore, 7.21a and 7.21b correspond in a similar way to 7.17b and 7.17bb respectively.

7.21a   We know the people who are sick of violence.
   b   Howard boarded the bus which was waiting at the terminal.

We are thus able to paraphrase both single-word modifiers preceding a noun and phrasal modifiers following a noun with full-clause modifiers. But there is no way to paraphrase all full-clause modifiers with either phrasal modifiers or single-word modifiers. We cannot, for example, paraphrase 7.17aa *(Helen paid the boy who sells newspapers)* as **Helen paid the boy sells newspapers.* Since all nominal modifiers can be paraphrased as complete clauses following a noun, we can claim that all nominal modifiers derive from complete clauses in deep structure and that a transformation deletes portions of a clause to produce phrasal and single-word modifiers. Another transformation moves a single-word remnant of a partially deleted underlying clause to a position preceding the modified noun. But what is the exact shape of the relevant deep structures? Where is the clause to be branched into the structure of the main clause? Let us focus on 7.17a to find an answer to this question. Consider the sentences in 7.22, the first of which is a question and the second two of which are possible answers to the question. (Note that the last is 7.17a.)

7.22a   What did Joe buy?
   b   Joe bought *the bench.*
   c   Joe bought *the bench which Albert made.*

Both of the italicized sequences in 7.22 are appropriate answers to the question in 7.22a. Thus both sequences substitute for the question word *what.* This indicates that they share a constituent designation. But *the bench* in 7.22b is clearly a noun phrase. We thus should label *the bench which Albert made* as a noun phrase as well. There is further evidence that the latter sequence taken as a whole should be labeled NP. Recall that INVERSION moves a portion of an AUX to a position preceding the initial sentence NP. In 7.23a is a statement, and in 7.23b a question which corresponds structurally to the statement.

7.23a   The bench which Albert made has arrived.
   b   Has the bench which Albert made arrived?

Notice that in 7.23b INVERSION has moved *-prs have* around the entire sequence *the bench which Albert made.* Thus our grammar will be able to generate a sentence like this only if it assigns an NP label to the entire sequence. But there is no doubt that the sequence *the bench* is itself a noun phrase and should be designated as such. And we have already noted that *which Albert made* is a clause. Here then is the deep-structure configuration I propose for *the bench which Albert made,* the NP on the left labeling *the bench* and the S on the right labeling *which Albert made:*

7.24

NP
NP   S

To have the PS rules generate configurations like that in 7.24 we need to add the following possibility to rule vi:

7.25 $NP \rightarrow NP + S$

When this is included with the other possibilities in rule vi, the rule will look like 7.26 (and is so printed in the Appendix).

7.26
$$NP \rightarrow \begin{cases} (DET) + N \\ NP + S \\ it + S \end{cases}$$

One problem remains regarding the shape of deep structures of noun modifiers. I have called the sequence *which Albert made* a clause and have just revised the PS rules to generate it as an S following an NP in another NP. But if *which Albert made* is an S then its deep structure must conform to the PS rules. But the PS rules are not able to account for the word *which* at the beginning of this dependent clause. It is not a question word, so QUESTION-WORD MOVEMENT will not account for its position at the front of the clause. Do we need a new PS rule to allow for a branch to *which* at the beginning of an S? Such a rule would be especially complex because it would have to be constrained to apply only to dependent clauses modifying nouns. But it seems we do not need such a rule. Here is why. If a user of English heard the sentence *Joe bought the bench which Albert made* and were then asked the question *Who made the bench?* he would answer *Albert.* This means that the assertion *Albert made the bench* was contained in the complex sentence, *Joe bought the bench which Albert made.* When the listener heard the word *which,* he thought of the bench. And furthermore he related the NP *the bench* to the verb *make* as its direct object. Now if *which* in fact means *the bench,* it is quite appropriate to have the deep structure, which is meaning oriented, make this explicit. And if *the bench* is indeed the direct object of *make,* it is likewise appropriate to have the deep structure indicate this as well. I thus propose the following as the deep structure of 7.17a, *Joe bought the bench which Albert made:*

7.27

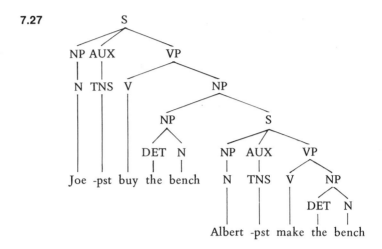

And here is the deep structure for 7.17b, *We know the people sick of violence* (and, incidentally, of 7.21a, *We know the people who are sick of violence*):

7.28

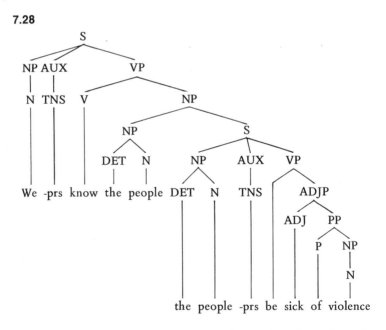

And here is the deep structure of 7.17c, *We know the sick people* (and, incidentally, of 7.20a, *We know the people who are sick*):

7.29

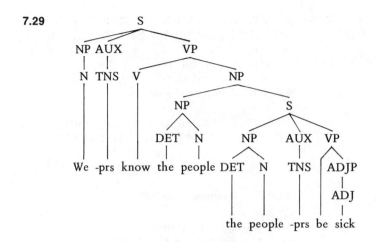

In this section I have made the following claims: (1) that the deep structures of clausal, phrasal, and single-word noun modifiers contain a complete dependent clause S—hereafter referred to as a **relative clause,** (2) that this S is in a noun phrase whose immediate constituents are another NP and the S itself, and (3) that the relative clause S contains an NP exactly like the modified NP. Examine the trees in 7.27, 7.28, and 7.29 once again and note how they illustrate these three claims.

RELATIVE CLAUSE TRANSFORMATIONS

If you compare the deep-structure trees in 7.27, 7.28, and 7.29 with the surface sequences in 7.17a, 7.17b, and 7.17c respectively, you will be able to determine the tasks transformations must perform to generate the latter sequences from the former structures. In every case, the identical NP in the dependent clause must be replaced by either *who* or *which,* hereafter called **relative pronouns.** In the case of 7.17b and 7.17c, the relative pronoun and a variant of *be* including its tense inflection must be deleted, and in the case of 7.17c the single-word remnant of the entire clause, *sick,* must then be transported to a position immediately preceding the N in the modified NP. In 7.30 is an ordered set of three transformations which will account for these changes not only in the example sentences but also in a large number of similar sentences in English.

7.30a RELATIVE PRONOUN INSERTION (OBL)
SD: X " [$_{NP}$ NP " [$_S$ Y " NP " Z]$_S$]$_{NP}$ " W
SC: 1   2   3   4   5   6 $\Rightarrow$
    1   2$\begin{Bmatrix} who \\ which \end{Bmatrix}$3   5   6
COND: 2 must be the same as 4

b RELATIVE CLAUSE REDUCTION (OPT)
SD: X " [$_{NP}$ NP " [$_S$ $\begin{Bmatrix} who \\ which \end{Bmatrix}$ be TNS " Z]$_S$]$_{NP}$ " W
SC: 1   2   3   4   5 $\Rightarrow$
    1   2   0   4   5
COND: 4 cannot be an NP

c MODIFIER SHIFT (OBL)
SD: X " [$_{NP}$ (DET) " N " $\begin{Bmatrix} ADJ \\ V\text{-ing} \end{Bmatrix}$]$_{NP}$ " Y
SC: 1   2   3   4   5 $\Rightarrow$
    1   2   4 3   5
COND: 3 cannot be *someone* or *something*

Let us examine each of these transformations. RELATIVE PRO-NOUN INSERTION changes the NP inside the relative clause (number 4 in the SD) into either *who* or *which,* then positions these words at the beginning of the clause (in front of number 3 in the SD). If the identical NP (number 4) is already the first element in the clause, the variable Y (number 3) is null and that part of the rule which moves *who* or *which* in front of 3 is simply not relevant. In short, RELATIVE PRONOUN INSERTION replaces the identical NP with a relative pronoun and positions the pronoun at the front of the relative clause if it is not already there. Notice that the rule fudges a bit on explicitness. It in no way specifies when *who* and when *which* is to be chosen. To have it do so would require the use of features, which I discuss in chapter 9. In applying the grammar to the analysis of sentences, you will have to rely on your own knowledge of English grammar in deciding whether to insert *who* or *which.* (*Who* replaces human nouns and *which* nonhuman ones.) This brings up a related issue. Examine the following sets of sentences:

7.31a Joe bought the bench which Albert made.
aa Joe bought the bench that Albert made.
b Helen paid the boy who sells newspapers.
bb Helen paid the boy that sells newspapers.

The single-lettered sentences are reprints of 7.17a and 7.17aa. The double-lettered sentences are equivalent in meaning to the single-lettered sentences preceding them but use *that* as a relative pronoun.

It should be clear that this word, while spelled the same as the word introduced by the NOMINALIZATION transformation, is a different morpheme. The word *that* which introduces noun clauses stands in place of no other word and is in fact almost devoid of meaning. But *that* in 7.31aa stands in place of *the bench,* and in 7.31bb stands in place of *the boy.* To help you avoid confusion when you later practice analyzing some rather complex English sentences, I shall carefully avoid using the relative pronoun *that* and will use only *who* or *which* as relative pronouns. This will help you to distinguish noun clauses and relative clauses more easily.

Now let us examine RELATIVE CLAUSE REDUCTION. Notice that it is necessarily ordered after RELATIVE PRONOUN INSERTION since its SD makes explicit reference to *who* or *which,* words that would not be present unless RELATIVE PRONOUN INSERTION had applied. The SD of RELATIVE CLAUSE REDUCTION requires a sequence beginning with *who* or *which* and immediately followed by *be* TNS. The rule deletes *who be* TNS or *which be* TNS, as the case may be. Notice that the rule is optional. This explains the presence in English of pairs of sentences like those in 7.32, both of which come from the deep structure in 7.28 and both of which have had RELATIVE PRONOUN INSERTION apply. But in the case of 7.32a RELATIVE CLAUSE REDUCTION was optionally skipped; in 7.32b the choice was to apply it.

    7.32a We know some people who are sick of violence.

       b We know some people sick of violence.

Now look at MODIFIER SHIFT. It is necessarily ordered after both RELATIVE PRONOUN INSERTION and RELATIVE CLAUSE REDUCTION since only by the previous application of these two transformations can a structure evolve which satisfies the SD of MODIFIER SHIFT. The SD looks for a noun (which may or may not be preceded by a determiner) followed by a verb with *-ing* affixed or an adjective. The structural change positions either type of word immediately in front of the modified noun.

In 7.33 I present complete analytical displays for 7.17a, 7.17b, and 7.17c so that you can closely examine the operation of the three relative clause transformations. They too apply cyclically. I choose to order them after the noun clause transformations but before NOT PLACEMENT and the other simple sentence transformations following it. (Notice that I have so listed them in the Appendix.)

In 7.34 is another analytical display. Examine it carefully noticing how the transformations apply cyclically and how MODIFIER SHIFT applies to a verb-*ing* when it is the only remnant of an underlying relative clause.

7.33a | Joe bought the bench which Albert made.

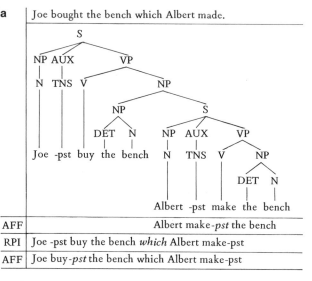

AFF	Albert make-*pst* the bench
RPI	Joe -pst buy the bench *which* Albert make-pst
AFF	Joe buy-*pst* the bench which Albert make-pst

b | We know the people sick of violence.

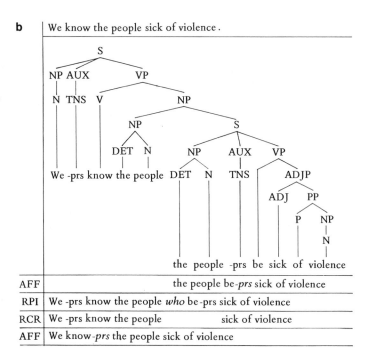

AFF	the people be-*prs* sick of violence
RPI	We -prs know the people *who* be-prs sick of violence
RCR	We -prs know the people sick of violence
AFF	We know-*prs* the people sick of violence

c | We know the sick people.

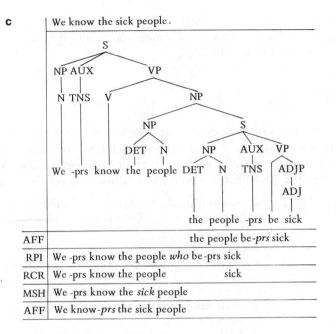

AFF	the people be-*prs* sick
RPI	We -prs know the people *who* be -prs sick
RCR	We -prs know the people sick
MSH	We -prs know the *sick* people
AFF	We know-*prs* the sick people

7.34

The working student has suffered at the university.

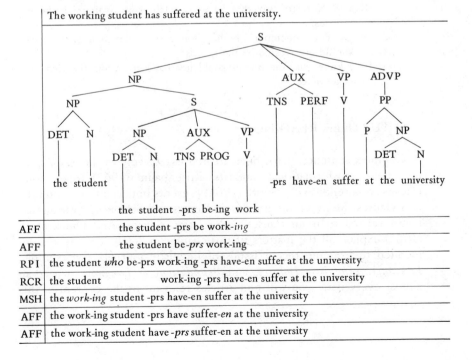

AFF	the student -prs be work-*ing*
AFF	the student be-*prs* work-ing
RPI	the student *who* be-prs work-ing -prs have-en suffer at the university
RCR	the student work-ing -prs have-en suffer at the university
MSH	the *work-ing* student -prs have-en suffer at the university
AFF	the work-ing student -prs have suffer-*en* at the university
AFF	the work-ing student have -*prs* suffer-en at the university

See if you can work out analytical displays for sentences 3 and 4 in the exercises. Each sentence has a main clause and two dependent relative clauses in its deep structure.

EXERCISES

Provide analytical displays for each of the following sentences. The first two contain only noun clauses as dependent clauses, and the next two only relative clauses. The remaining exercise sentences, numbered 5 through 10, all contain both noun clauses and relative clauses.

1. It is obvious that John has been telling the prosecutors lies.
2. Why did Bob tell the president that he shouldn't be nervous about the disclosures?
3. Don't listen to the advice which the letter on the table contains.
4. The girl who bribed the young counselor was commended by the community.
5. Explain it to him that honest candidates must lose.
6. It can't be denied by the press that rich politicians are abusing the masses.
7. Why did the man who thought that Republicans were corrupt vote for Richard?
8. Did Northrop say that an essay written by Swift might be humorous?
9. Do you remember whether it is certain that men carrying files should be arrested by the guards?
10. I know that the doctor could not have given him the virus in a clean office.

FOR FURTHER READING

Complex sentences have been treated extensively in the writings of generative-transformational linguists. Rosenbaum (1967) treats noun clauses comprehensively. Smith (1964) presents important ideas on relative clauses. Many of the articles in Reibel and Schane (1969) discuss issues related to noun clauses and relative clauses. And Quirk et al. (1972) explain all the matters of this chapter in detail. You are recommended to examine recent issues of linguistic journals, for example, *Language, Linguistic Inquiry,* and *Foundations of Language,* where in almost every issue you will find articles relevant to the content of this chapter.

Chapter 8

Expanding the Grammar: Practice in Syntactic Research

SYNTACTIC RESEARCH

The last four chapters have developed a basic transformational grammar for English: a set of phrase-structure rules for generating deep structures and a set of transformations for generating surface structures from these deep structures. As complex and comprehensive as this grammar may have seemed as you labored to learn it, the basic grammar only begins the task of describing the principles defining sentence structure in English. You need only glance at any randomly selected paragraph in English to learn that our grammar cannot in fact generate most of the sentences contained there. Consider the many syntactic phenomena just in this paragraph that our grammar fails to account for. How, for instance, is the word *four* in the first sentence to be generated? What about the expression *for generating deep structures,* which seems to come from an underlying clause? What about the word *and,* also in the first sentence? I have said nothing about compound structures so far in this book. What about the comparative expression *as complex and comprehensive as,* which begins the second sentence of this paragraph? Our grammar cannot generate this expression or any comparative expression. How do we treat the word *only,* which appears in both the second and third sentences of the paragraph? And there are several other such facts just in this paragraph. If we begin to look in earnest through a corpus of English, we can easily amass hundreds of problems calling for expansion of our basic grammar. Some will call for revision of the PS rules. The majority will call for the addition of transformations to our list.

A textbook such as this, while not being able to treat the whole of English syntax comprehensively, can treat the highlights comprehensively, as it has done in the last several chapters. More important, a book like this can give you the means to find out for yourselves how issues not explicitly covered can be analyzed and intelligently related to those issues that have been treated. This is the essence of syntactic research. The last several chapters have also aimed at providing a conceptual framework within which you can sketch additional details of English syntax when the need arises to do so. This chapter has two purposes: (1) to expose you in varying degrees of detail to many additional syntactic facts of English and (2) to help you learn to relate an ever increasing array of facts about English to the facts treated in this book—to help you practice syntactic research.

I shall first illustrate the methods of syntactic research by treating three problems comprehensively: agentless passives, particles, and deleted relative pronouns. Then I shall treat three additional problems in some detail, but leaving the final resolution of the issues raised to you: conjoining, adverbial clauses, and pronouns. Finally, in the exercises, I lay out the data for yet other syntactic problems and call on you to resolve them as best you can, using the methods practiced in the body of the chapter. The matters treated in this chapter are not incorporated in the basic grammar in the Appendix. It is now your job to keep a record of whatever revisions we make as we work through this chapter.

AGENTLESS PASSIVES

A syntactic researcher may get his data from an almost unlimited variety of sources. He may, like the structural linguist, formally elicit a corpus and set about explaining as best he can everything in the corpus. Generative-transformational linguists tend to consider their total linguistic experience a kind of elicitation procedure. They attune themselves to evaluating virtually all of what they hear and read in light of what they know about linguistic structures. Many of them carry notebooks to help remember interesting expressions they hear or read. In a sense then, to the linguist, the world is his laboratory. But if he is to be more than a dilettante, he must follow up on matters of linguistic interest which catch his fancy, and rigorously incorporate them into his grammar.

Let us consider the basic grammar developed in the last four chapters as our theory of how English sentences are structured syntactically. Given this assumption, suppose we hear or read a sentence like 8.1.

8.1 The plan was approved.

We know it to be an English sentence. Thus our grammar should be able to generate it. If our grammar cannot generate it, then the grammar is inadequate as a theory of English sentence formation and must be revised. Can the basic grammar generate 8.1? Because it has the auxiliary *was* followed by a stem with *-en,* we know that the sentence is passive. But unlike the passive sentences treated earlier, there is no prepositional phrase with *by.* Thus the nearest thing to an appropriate deep structure that our PS rules can generate for this sentence is that given in 8.2.

8.2

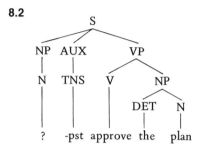

This attempt at drawing a deep structure assumes that the sentence in 8.1 is related to a sentence like 8.3.

8.3 John approved the plan.

The deep structure of 8.3 would resemble the tree in 8.2, except that instead of the question mark the word *John* would appear. Having thus generally identified the nature of the problem, we should, as linguists, seek additional instances of sentences which seem to be passive but do not specify, in a surface-structure prepositional phrase, the doer of the action (the agent) and which thus apparently come from seemingly anomalous deep structures like the one in 8.2. It is easy enough to think of many examples. Here are just a few in 8.4. Read them and then see if you can think of others.

8.4a The bomb was thrown.
  b The forgery has been detected.
  c The lobbyist was given a refund.

Since it is clear that sentences like 8.1 are quite common in English, we must indeed revise the grammar to account for them. Several questions are relevant: (1) What should the deep structures of such sentences look like? (2) Do the PS rules need revision to generate such deep structures? (3) Given the shape of the deep structures, do we need any new transformations to generate the surface sequences?

Most users of English, when they hear 8.1, feel that they have not only been told that the plan achieved an approved status but also that *someone* approved it. The speaker of the sentence simply chose not to name the person who approved it or perhaps did not know specifically who did the approving. The same is true of the sentences in 8.4: the bomb did not throw itself, but *someone* threw it; *someone* has detected the forgery; *someone* gave the refund to the lobbyist. This consensus that a word like *someone* is understood, coupled with the inability of the PS rules to generate deep structures with question marks (as in 8.2), is good enough reason to claim that the deep structures of sentences like those in 8.1 and 8.4 indeed contain the word *someone* instead of a question mark. Thus, with *someone* included as the initial noun phrase, a deep structure like 8.2 fulfills its task of making explicit elements of meaning that are implicit in a surface structure. And so we have answered the first question at the end of the previous paragraph. What about the second question. *Do* the PS rules need revision to generate the proposed deep structure? No. If we assume the word *someone* to be a member of the list of English nouns, it can be generated in a deep-structure tree just as any other noun. What about the third question. Do we need a new transformation to generate the surface structure? Let us see. In 8.5 is the deep structure proposed for 8.1.

8.5

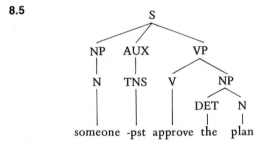

From this deep structure we want to generate the surface sequence *The plan was approved.* Let us see if the transformations listed in the basic grammar can do the job. The PASSIVE transformation takes 8.5 and changes it into 8.6.

8.6

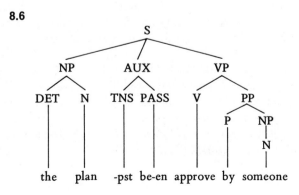

With the application of two AFFIX MOVEMENT transformations, the grammar can generate the morpheme sequence manifested in 8.7 from the structure in 8.6:

> **8.7** The plan was approved by someone.

But there is no way for the grammar to generate 8.1 (*The plan was approved*). To do so, it must be able to delete the phrase *by someone* from the structure in 8.6. So the answer to the third question at the end of the previous paragraph is yes. A new transformation is needed—to delete the prepositional phrase *by someone* generated by application of the PASSIVE transformation. But since sentences like 8.7 are perfectly acceptable English sentences, this new transformation must be optional. Here is a formal statement of such a transformation:

> **8.8** BY SOMEONE DELETION (OPT)
> SD: X " $[_{PASS}$ be-en $]_{PASS}$ " Y " $[_{PP}$ by someone $]_{PP}$ " Z
> SC: 1 2 3 4 5 $\Rightarrow$
> 1 2 3 0 5
> COND: None

And so we have answered the third question by formulating a transformation which can delete *by someone* from passive sentences in English. But our task as syntactic researchers is not quite complete even when we have formulated a transformation adequate to the data at hand. Since we have committed ourselves to a grammar with an ordered list of transformations, we need to decide for each new transformation just where it belongs on the list. This decision is often difficult and time-consuming. We must test the grammar's ability to generate sentences with the new transformation in various places on the list. Suppose, for instance, we try to list BY SOMEONE DELETION first. If we do so, can the grammar, even with BY SOMEONE DELETION on the list, generate *The plan was approved?* It cannot. Why not? If BY SOMEONE DELETION is first, it precedes PASSIVE. Thus when it examines the deep structure and looks for the prepositional phrase *by someone,* as its structural description requires it to do, it will not find it because such a phrase is not present in deep structure. Rather, it is created by operation of the PASSIVE transformation. If BY SOMEONE DELETION is going to be able to perform the task for which it was invented, it must be listed after PASSIVE in the grammar. Thus, to complete a rigorous account of agentless passives, we would reprint the list of transformations which appears in the Appendix, listing BY SOMEONE DELETION immediately after PASSIVE and before NOMINALIZATION.

PARTICLES

How would you, as a syntactic researcher, react to the sentences in 8.9? Is there anything about them that should lead you to start speculating about revisions in the grammar?

> **8.9a** Bob handed the tapes over.
> **b** Bob handed over the tapes.

Note first that the two sentences in 8.9 mean the same thing. But in spite of this, 8.9b should lead us to ask whether the sequence *over the tapes* might have a constituent grouping similar to 8.10, where *over the door* is a prepositional phrase:

> **8.10** The sign hung over the door.

Apparently it does not have a similar constituent grouping. Whereas we might ask *Where did the sign hang?* and get the answer *Over the door* indicating that these three words group together in constituent structure, we cannot ask *Where did Bob hand?* and get the answer *Over the tapes*. This indicates that *over* does not group with *the tapes* as a constituent. However we can ask *What did Bob hand over?* and get the answer *The tapes*. This is evidence that *over* groups rather with the verb in the constituent structures of both 8.9a and 8.9b. Thus there seems to be at least one word in English—*over*—which, though spelled like a certain preposition, is not a preposition and which manifests a constituent grouping with a verb rather than with a noun phrase. Furthermore, this constituent grouping with a verb seems unaffected even when *over* is separated from the verb by a noun phrase as in 8.9a. Can you think of other words spelled like prepositions which behave like *over* behaves in 8.9? Here are some others in the sentences in 8.11. The single-lettered sentences are like 8.9a and the double-lettered ones like 8.9b:

> **8.11a** Henry broke negotiations off.
> **aa** Henry broke off negotiations.
> **b** The committee drew a compromise up.
> **bb** The committee drew up a compromise.
> **c** The Pentagon sent a story out.
> **cc** The Pentagon sent out a story.
> **d** Lowell brought a solution about.
> **dd** Lowell brought about a solution.

Expressions like *hand over, break off, draw up,* and *send out* are often called **phrasal verbs.** There are hundreds of them in English. Can you think of any others? Here are some in 8.12:

8.12   call up, cut down, cut out, fill out, mark down, pass out, take away, take back, try on, turn off, turn over, write down

How can we account for phrasal verbs in our grammar? The same three questions raised in the previous section are relevant: (1) What should the deep structure of sentences with phrasal verbs look like? (2) Do the PS rules need revision to generate such deep structures? (3) Given the shape of such deep structures, do we need any new transformations to generate the relevant surface sequences?

Words like *over, off, up, out,* and *about* in 8.9 and 8.11 clearly group with a verb rather than with a noun phrase in constituent structure, often even changing the meaning of the verb somewhat. (Note the different meanings of *turn* in *He turned the light* and *He turned on the light.*) For these reasons I wish to claim (1) that these words belong to a form class so far unlabeled and unaccounted for in this book (let us call them **particles** and label them PCL) and (2) that the PS rules need revision to generate particles in close association with a verb in deep structure. The PS rules can incorporate these claims if revised as 8.13 suggests.

8.13   ii $\text{VP} \rightarrow \begin{Bmatrix} \text{V} + (\text{PCL}) + (\text{NP}) \ldots \\ \ldots \end{Bmatrix}$

xviii $\text{PCL} \rightarrow \{\text{on, off, up, out, about,} \ldots\}$

PS rule ii would allow a branch after V in a VP to the category symbol PCL, and a new PS rule would be added drawing branches from the form-class label PCL to the various members of this class. With these changes, the PS rules could generate a deep structure like the one in 8.14.

8.14

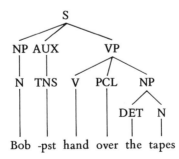

Except for the position of *-pst,* the ordering of the morphemes in 8.14 matches the surface sequence of 8.9b *(Bob handed over the tapes).* This means that, given the changes in the PS rules, the grammar is now capable of generating 8.9b—it just needs to apply **AFFIX MOVEMENT** to 8.14 to do so. But are the changes in the PS rules themselves adequate to account for 8.9a *(Bob handed the tapes over)*? Because it means the same thing as 8.9b *(Over* still groups logically with the verb *hand)*, I wish to claim that 8.9a has the same deep structure as 8.9b (the tree in 8.14). If 8.14 is the deep structure of 8.9a, we need a transformation to account for the movement of the particle to the position it occupies in 8.9a. Since the particle does not have to move, the transformation is optional. It is very easy to formulate. Before examining the version given in 8.15, try formalizing it yourself. Let us call this transformation **PARTICLE SEPA-RATION**. It moves a particle from between a verb and noun phrase to a position following the noun phrase.

    8.15 PARTICLE SEPARATION (OPT)
        SD: X " V " PCL " NP " Y
        SC: 1   2   3   4   5 $\Rightarrow$
               1   2   4 3 5

The analytical display in 8.16 shows how this transformation operates in generating 8.9a from the deep structure in 8.14 (PSP abbreviates PAR-TICLE SEPARATION).

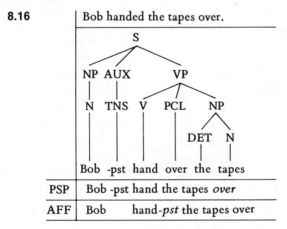

8.16	Bob handed the tapes over.
	Bob -pst hand over the tapes
PSP	Bob -pst hand the tapes *over*
AFF	Bob hand-*pst* the tapes over

We saw at the end of the last section that whenever a new transfor-mation is formulated, it must be ordered on the list of transformations before the researcher's task is complete. As it happens, there are no overriding reasons requiring **PARTICLE SEPARATION** to precede or follow any other transformation. It seems to be able to do its job no matter where it is placed on the list. But we still have to decide where to list it. Since it is optional like INDIRECT OBJECT MOVEMENT and PASSIVE, we might want to list it near them rather than among NOT PLACEMENT, CONTRACTION, IMPERATIVE, and the question transformations, which are obligatory. But recall that we found reasons, in chapter 7, requiring PASSIVE to precede EXTRAPOSITION and reasons, in chapter 5, requiring INDIRECT OBJECT MOVEMENT to precede PASSIVE. This is why both INDIRECT OBJECT MOVE-MENT and PASSIVE are listed before all the complex sentence transformations. But we have no reason to list PARTICLE SEPARATION before the complex sentence transformations and would prefer to keep it in the group of simple sentence transformations. So the only way we can place it close to INDIRECT OBJECT MOVEMENT and PASSIVE but keep it with the main group of simple sentence transformations is to list it after MODIFIER SHIFT and before NOT PLACEMENT. These are hardly compelling reasons, but they are at least not completely arbitrary.

There is yet another task of the syntactic researcher, a task we have so far taken quite for granted. Recall that many transformations in our grammar have conditions attached. Now notice that we made no mention of conditions when we formulated PARTICLE SEPARATION in 8.15. How does the syntactic researcher find out whether to list conditions with a rule and just what conditions to list? He must test the effectiveness of any newly formulated transformation against as large a body of sentences as he has time to examine. How might we go about doing this for PARTICLE SEPARATION? Suppose we begin by taking the list of phrasal verbs in 8.12 and try to compose pairs of sentences like the ones in 8.11 where PARTICLE SEPARATION has applied to one sentence in the pair but not to another. Here is a beginning in 8.17:

8.17a He called Bill up.
aa He called up Bill.
b They cut the tree down.
bb They cut down the tree.

Take the time now to create such a pair of sentences for each of the remaining phrasal verbs in 8.12. Please do not read on to the next paragraph until you have done so.

The odds are very good that you have come up with at least a few pairs of sentences like those in 8.18:

8.18a The doctor cut it out.
aa *The doctor cut out it.
b The applicants filled them out.
bb *The applicants filled out them.

    c   Some investigators marked it down.
    cc *Some investigators marked down it.

Because PARTICLE SEPARATION is optional, both sentences in each pair in 8.18 should be possible. The single-lettered sentences result from the option to apply the transformation and the double-lettered sentences from the option not to apply it. But the double-lettered sentences in 8.18, where the choice was not to apply PARTICLE SEPARATION, are apparently not appropriate English sentences. Thus the grammar should not generate them. To keep the grammar from generating them, we need to add a condition to PARTICLE SEPARATION to the effect that sometimes it is obligatory. Often, conditions on transformations are attributable to idiosyncrasies of particular words. Thus it is possible that the phrasal verbs *cut out, fill out,* and *mark down* always require application of PARTICLE SEPARATION. To test this, several pairs of sentences should be formulated for each verb to see if in every case PARTICLE SEPARATION is required. The sentences in 8.19 indicate that this is not the case; both members of the pair are quite appropriate. These sentences also give a clue to the real condition; they correspond almost exactly to the sentences in 8.18. The differences are the key to the condition.

    8.19a   The doctor cut the splinter out.
    aa   The doctor cut out the splinter.
    b   The applicants filled some forms out.
    bb   The applicants filled out some forms.
    c   Some investigators marked the total down.
    cc   Some investigators marked down the total.

What is the source of the condition? When must PARTICLE SEPARATION be applied, even though it is ordinarily optional? It must be applied when the noun phrase following the particle in the deep structure is a pronoun. And so the condition in 8.20 must be added to the rule formalized in 8.15:

    8.20 COND: Obligatory when 4 is a pronoun

DELETED RELATIVE PRONOUNS

In the previous two sections we have examined how the basic grammar can be revised to account for additional kinds of sentences in English. The approach might be outlined in five steps, each of which is an attempt to answer a question. (1) What should the deep structure of such sentences look like? (2) Do the PS rules need revision to generate such deep structures? (3) Given the shape of the deep structures, do we need new transformations to generate the surface sequences of the sentences? (4) Where are any new transformations ordered on the list of transformations? (5) Are there any conditions on the newly formulated transformations, and if so, what are they?

In this section, I present an array of sentences calling for revisions in the grammar. I then comment very briefly on the sentences giving some clues about the nature of the problem. Next I call on you to answer the five questions in the previous paragraph on your own. We will not reason through the solution together. However, five brief paragraphs answer each question so that you can compare your findings with mine. Here are the sentences that comprise the problem:

8.21a	He arrested the man who witnesses saw in the office.	
aa	He arrested the man	witnesses saw in the office.
b	He searched the office which witnesses saw a tape in.	
bb	He searched the office	witnesses saw a tape in.
c	He arrested witnesses who saw a tape in the office.	
cc	*He arrested witnesses	saw a tape in the office.

The arrangement and spacing of the sentences aims to help you focus on the nature of the problem. Assume that sentences with the same letter have the same deep structure. There seems to be a transformation which generates the double-lettered sentences from the same deep structure which underlies the single-lettered sentences, except that it must be formulated to prohibit the generation of 8.21cc from the deep structure of 8.21c. Try to revise the grammar to account for 8.21aa and 8.21bb. Ask and answer the five questions listed at the beginning of this section. Do not expect to answer the questions in a few minutes. It may take you a few hours. You will gain little from reading the remainder of this section unless you make at least some effort to answer the five questions on your own.

The answer to the first question is easy enough: I answered it while introducing the problem. The deep structures of 8.21aa and 8.21bb are the same as the deep structures of their single-lettered counterparts. The reason why they are the same should have occurred to you as you worked on the problem. In each case, the pair of sentences shares the same meaning. Put another way, the relative pronoun, which appears explicitly in the single-lettered sentences, is understood in the double-lettered sentences, except that for some reason it cannot be left out and understood in 8.21cc. The tree in 8.22, for example, is the deep structure of both 8.21a and 8.21aa.

8.22

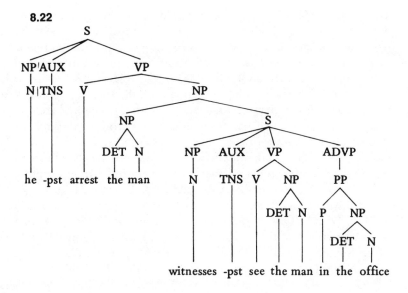

The PS rules are quite capable of generating 8.22 and so, in answer to the second question, no revisions are needed to account for 8.21aa and 8.21bb.

The answer to the third question is yes. We do need a new transformation to account for the surface sequences in 8.21aa and 8.21bb. The transformation must delete the relative pronoun in each sentence, but it must not allow deletion of the relative pronoun inserted into the tree of 8.21c. In 8.23 is a transformation which, with the help of transformations already in the grammar, will generate 8.21aa from the same deep structure as 8.21a, and 8.21bb from the same deep structure as 8.21b, but which will prohibit generation of 8.21cc from the deep structure of 8.21c.

8.23 RELATIVE PRONOUN DELETION (OPT)
SD: X " [NP" [$_S$ {who / which} " NP " Y]$_S$]$_{NP}$ " Z
SC: 1   2   3   4   5   6 ⇒
     1   2   0   4   5   6
COND: None

Notice that RELATIVE PRONOUN DELETION removes a relative pronoun only when a noun phrase immediately follows it in the tree. This explains the deletions manifested in 8.21aa and 8.21bb: in both cases a noun phrase immediately followed the relative pronoun. But notice that in 8.21c a noun phrase does not immediately follow the relative pronoun, and so the new transformation cannot apply. Our grammar thus accounts for the unacceptability of the sequence in 8.21cc. Recall that RELATIVE PRONOUN INSERTION places *who* or *which* first in the relative clause even if the noun phrase these replace is not already there. The relevant fact of English syntax thus accounted for is that a relative pronoun which has been inserted in front of the initial deep-structure noun phrase of the clause (as is the case in 8.21a and 8.21b) can be deleted (allowing sentences like 8.21aa and 8.21bb), but a relative pronoun which has replaced the initial deep-structure noun phrase (as is the case in 8.21c) cannot be deleted (prohibiting 8.21cc).

Now what about question four: where do we put RELATIVE PRONOUN DELETION on the list of transformations? Since *who* or *which* will never appear at the beginning of a relative clause unless RELATIVE PRONOUN INSERTION has put them there, RELATIVE PRONOUN DELETION must follow RELATIVE PRONOUN INSERTION. And since RELATIVE CLAUSE REDUCTION and MODIFIER SHIFT are a logical pair, the latter never applying except when the former has applied, we do not want to list RELATIVE PRONOUN DELETION between them. So let us list it immediately after RELATIVE PRONOUN INSERTION and before RELATIVE CLAUSE REDUCTION.

In answer to the fifth question, there is no reason to place conditions on the application of RELATIVE PRONOUN DELETION. Whenever its structural description is met, it may apply.

CONJOINING

So far, this book has virtually ignored sentences like the following, which are of course quite common in English:

8.24a   Bob and John lied.
  aa   The chairman and the young lawyer destroyed the documents.
  b   Richard was studying and writing.
  bb   The volunteers painted the house and plowed the garden.
  c   The negotiators were friendly and hopeful.
  cc   Those newsmen are skeptical about briefings and careful with sources.

    d   Relief will arrive now and later.

   dd   The guards are on the roof and in the hall.

All of the sentences in 8.24 contain expressions of one kind or another joined by the word *and*. In 8.24a two nouns are joined by *and;* in 8.24aa two noun phrases are so joined. In 8.24b two verbs are joined and in 8.24bb two verb phrases. In 8.24c and 8.24cc, *and* joins two adjectives and two adjective phrases respectively. And in 8.24d and 8.24dd, it joins two adverbs and two adverbial prepositional phrases. Now notice how each of the longer sentences in 8.25 seems to correspond in meaning to the similarly lettered sentence in 8.24:

   8.25a   Bob lied, and John lied.

     aa   The chairman destroyed the documents, and the young lawyer destroyed the documents.

      b   Richard was studying, and Richard was writing.

    bb   The volunteers painted the house, and the volunteers plowed the garden.

      c   The negotiators were friendly, and the negotiators were hopeful.

    cc   Those newsmen are skeptical about briefings, and those newsmen are careful with sources.

      d   Relief will arrive now, and relief will arrive later.

    dd   The guards are on the roof, and the guards are in the hall.

Let me first comment on the sentences in 8.25, which I shall call **compound sentences** because they are composed of two **conjoined clauses**. Since users of English perceive each sequence to be one sentence and not two, the PS rules need revision to allow an S to have branches directly from it to other S's. The rules need also to account for the word *and* when it appears between conjoined clauses. Furthermore, the revised PS rules need to allow a virtually unlimited number of successive branches to S + *and*'s because sentences like those in 8.25 can go on indefinitely (for example, *Bob lied, and John lied, and Herb lied, and Richard lied, and . . .*). Given appropriate revisions in the PS rules, we would need no new transformations to generate the surface sequences in 8.25. However, if the sentences in 8.24 do indeed convey the same messages as the sentences in 8.25 and must thus be generated from the same deep structures as corresponding sentences in 8.25, then we will indeed need a new transformation, or new transformations, to generate the surface sequences in 8.24. I am proposing, for instance, that both 8.24a and 8.25a have the deep structure in 8.26.

8.26

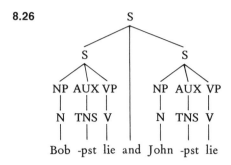

Bob -pst lie and John -pst lie

If 8.26 is indeed the deep structure of both 824a and 8.25a, only two applications of **AFFIX MOVEMENT** are needed to generate 8.25a. But a new transformation is needed to generate 8.24a. This new transformation has to fuse the two constituent sentences into one, keeping only one set of constituents where the structures match, but maintaining two sets where they differ. And the new transformation must reposition *and* between just those constituents that differ. That is, we need a transformation to change 8.26 into 8.27.

8.27

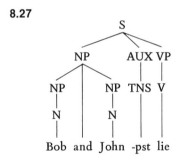

Bob and John -pst lie

Can you formalize such a transformation? Even better, could you formalize one transformation that can take the two trees joined by *and* which underlie each sentence in 8.25 and convert the trees into one tree associated with the morpheme sequence in the correspondingly lettered sentence in 8.24? Linguists call such a transformation CONJUNCTION REDUCTION. Where should this transformation be entered on the list of transformations? Are there any conditions on its application?

Comparison of the sentences in 8.24 with those in 8.25, plus the discussion and questions in the previous paragraph, indicates that the vast majority of conjoined structures in English surface sequences—conjoined nouns, verbs, adjectives, adverbs, noun phrases, verb phrases, and so forth are generated from conjoined clauses in deep structures. But are all conjoined surface constituents generated from underlying conjoined clauses? Examine the sentences in 8.28 carefully. (I forewarn you that they are ambiguous.)

8.28a Sam and Richard talked.
  b The bus and the car collided.
  c Henry and Anwar have met.
  d The president and the committee agree.
  e The students and the administration will speak.

It is possible to interpret the sentences in 8.28 the way we interpreted the sentences in 8.24—as equivalent in meaning to compound sentences:

8.29a Sam talked, and Richard talked.
  b The bus collided, and the car collided.
  c Henry met, and Anwar met.
  d The president agrees, and the committee agrees.
  e The students will speak, and the administration will speak.

Under this interpretation, a sentence like 8.29a does not convey the idea that Sam talked to Richard. Sam could be at the Senate talking to a colleague, and Richard might be in the White House talking to his lawyer. A sentence like 8.29d asserts that both the president and the committee agree, not with each other, but probably with third parties. The same is true of each sentence in 8.28 as paraphrased in 8.29. Now read the sentences in 8.28 again. They are not only susceptible to another interpretation—that paraphrased in 8.30—they are likely to be interpreted as in 8.30:

8.30a Sam talked with Richard/ Richard talked with Sam.
  b The bus collided with the car/ The car collided with the bus.
  c Henry met with Anwar/ Anwar met with Henry.
  d The president agrees with the committee/ The committee agrees with the president.
  e The students will speak with the administration/ The administration will speak with the students.

The paraphrases in 8.30 are intended to illustrate that a sentence like 8.28a conveys the idea that talking was going on *between* Sam and Richard. And 8.28b can refer to a collision *between* the bus and the car, 8.28c to a meeting *between* Henry and Anwar, 8.28d to an agreement *between* the president and the committee, and 8.28e to a conversation *between* the students and the administration. Since all the sequences in 8.28 are thus susceptible to two interpretations, we must assign two possible deep-structure sources to each clause. When the sequences have the interpretations paraphrased in 8.29, they come from conjoined clauses in deep structure to which CONJUNCTION REDUCTION has applied. What about the interpretations paraphrased in 8.30? To account for them we probably have to allow for conjoined noun phrases in deep structure and revise the PS rules accordingly. Thus the rules should generate a structure like 8.31 as the deep structure of 8.28a when it means the same as 8.30a.

8.31

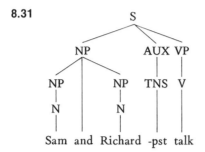

See if you can revise the PS rules to allow them to generate deep structures like the one in 8.31. Given the existence of such deep structures, do we need any new transformations to generate the surface structure of such a sentence?

There are countless other issues related to conjoined structures in English. But I simply do not have space to treat them. A few will be taken up in the exercises. I hope you have an inkling at least of how such issues relate to the view of syntax we have worked with.

ADVERBIAL CLAUSES

Read the sentences in 8.32, paying special attention to the italicized portions.

> **8.32a** William landed *there.*
> **aa** William landed *on the beach.*
> **aaa** William landed *where the cliffs meet the sea.*
> **b** The war ended *then.*
> **bb** The war ended *on a Tuesday.*
> **bbb** The war ended *when the bombing stopped.*
> **c** The executive has been uncooperative *deliberately.*
> **cc** The executive has been uncooperative *through fear.*
> **ccc** The executive has been uncooperative *because you lied.*

In each single-lettered sentence, the italicized word is an adverb. In each double-lettered sentence, the italicized words constitute an adverbial prepositional phrase. In the triple-lettered sentences, the italicized words include a clause. But notice that any one of the first three sentences might come in answer to the question *Where did William land?* And any one of the next three sentences might come in answer to the question *When did the war end?* And any one of the last three sentences might come in answer to the question *Why has the executive been uncooperative?* I used such facts in chapter 4 to show that both single words and prepositional phrases can be adverbs. Now you should see that entire sentences can also be adverbs. Can you revise the PS rules to allow a branch to include S as an alternate with ADV and PP under the various types of adverbials? Now examine the internal structure of the adverbial clauses in the triple-lettered sentences of 8.32. Are any revisions in the grammar needed to account for the surface sequences of the clauses? Specifically, how can we account for the words *where, when,* and *because* at the beginning of the adverbial clauses? Where should they be positioned in deep structure? Can the PS rules put them there? Are transformations needed to generate the surface sequences from the deep structures you would propose? Are there other words like *where, when,* and *because* which introduce adverbial clauses in English? How are they to be accounted for?

PRONOUNS

Throughout this book, I have treated the words in 8.33 as if they were in no way distinct from nouns. They have appeared in many sentences and I have always labeled them N in tree diagrams:

8.33	I	me
	you	you
	he	him
	she	her
	it	it
	we	us
	they	them

The words in 8.33, along with the words in 8.34, are **pronouns**. They are often called **personal pronouns** to distinguish them from other types of pronouns, such as relative pronouns.

8.34	my	mine	myself
	your	yours	yourself
	his	his	himself
	her	hers	herself
	its	its	itself
	our	ours	ourselves
	their	theirs	themselves

Often, a pronoun will have the same reference as a noun phrase else-where in the same sentence. If it does, linguists call it an **anaphoric pronoun**. (The Greek word *anaphora* means 'repetition'.) The italicized word in this sentence is an anaphoric pronoun because *it* has the same reference as (repeats) the initial noun phrase of this sentence. (The initial noun phrase of the last sentence was *The italicized word;* when you read *it,* that phrase reappeared in your consciousness.)

The italicized pronouns in 8.35 are anaphoric pronouns having the same reference as the italicized noun phrase elsewhere in the sentence.

8.35a *John* said that *he* destroyed the tapes.
 b That *they* discovered the truth surprised *the prosecutors.*

Notice that the noun phrase with the same reference as an anaphoric pronoun may *precede* it as in 8.35a or *follow* it as in 8.35b. But none of the words listed in 8.33 and 8.34 is ever necessarily an anaphoric pronoun. It is rare for words like *I, we, us,* and *you* to refer to another noun in a sentence. Rather they usually get their meaning from the context. The meaning (reference) of *I* is wholly dependent on who is speaking; *you* takes its meaning from who is listening. When pronouns take their meaning from the context of conversation rather than from a noun phrase elsewhere in a sentence, they are called **generic pronouns**. (The Latin word *genus* means 'species' or 'kind'—the term thus implies that the meaning of a generic pronoun is 'one of a kind': it means what it means for this sentence but just for this sentence.) Now the interesting thing about pronouns like *he* and *they* in the sentences of 8.35 is that they may be interpreted as *either* anaphoric or generic pronouns. You have already seen that *he* can refer to *John* in 8.35a, and *they* can refer to *the prosecutors* in 8.35b. But now read 8.35a again and picture the speaker of the sentence pointing to someone other than John as he says the sentence. In such a situation, *he* is a generic pronoun which takes its meaning from the context. (It refers to the person the speaker is pointing to—and the speaker does not even need to know the person's name.) You can imagine a similar situation for 8.35b. The speaker might be pointing to a picture of a Senate committee as he says the sentence, in which case both the reference of *they* and the meaning of the entire sentence changes drastically from the anaphoric interpretation. How is our grammar to distinguish between the anaphoric and the generic interpretation of a word like *he* in 8.35a? Where differences of meaning exist, deep structures should differ. Now if the anaphoric interpretation of *he* in 8.35a simply repeats *John,* we should claim that the noun phrase *John* is present twice in the deep structure. When *he* is interpreted generically, the word *he* is itself present in the deep structure. Thus 8.36 represents the deep

structure of 8.35a when *he* is taken to refer to *John*. And 8.37 represents
the deep structure of 8.35a when *he* is taken to refer to someone the
speaker is pointing to.

8.36

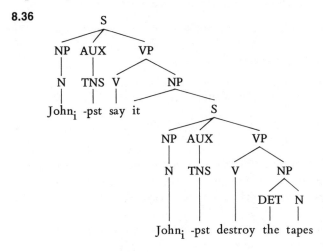

8.37

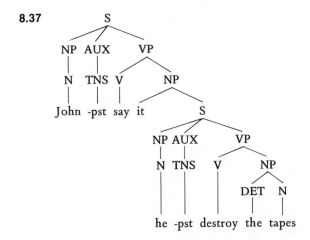

Since it is possible to have a sentence about two different people named
John, it was not enough to write *John* twice in 8.36. I used a subscript i to
indicate that two nouns so marked have the same reference.

Now if 8.36 is an appropriate deep structure for the anaphoric interpretation of 8.35a, how do we account for the fact that the word *John*
in the deep structure can be replaced by the anaphoric pronoun *he?* Indeed it must be replaced since the second *John* in the surface sequence

in 8.38 cannot be interpreted as having the same reference as the first
John:

8.38 John said that John destroyed the tapes.

It is not too difficult to formulate a transformation that will introduce
he in place of *John* in the dependent clause in 8.36. Here is a formaliza-
tion of such a transformation:

8.39 PRONOUN INSERTION (OBL)
SD: X " N_i " Y " N_i " Z
SC: $1 \quad 2 \quad 3 \quad 4 \quad 5 \Rightarrow$
$\qquad 1 \quad 2 \quad 3 \quad \text{he} \quad 5$
COND: ?

But such a formulation is obviously inadequate: (1) it fails to introduce
other possible pronouns like *she, it, they, her, him, them,* and (2) it fails
to show that anaphoric pronouns can precede the noun they refer to,
as in 8.35b. Let us bypass the first problem and try to formulate a rule
that tells us when one of two nouns with identity of reference in deep
structure can be changed to a pronoun. We will not bother to specify
which pronoun; we will just have the second line of the SC insert the
abbreviation PRO to show that a given noun may be replaced by whatever pronoun is appropriate. Thus we might reformulate 8.39 as follows:

8.40 PRONOUN INSERTION (OBL)
SD: X " N_i " Y " N_i " Z
SC: $1 \quad 2 \quad 3 \quad 4 \quad 5 \Rightarrow$
$\left\{\begin{array}{lllll} 1 & \text{PRO} & 3 & 4 & 5 \\ 1 & 2 & 3 & \text{PRO} & 5 \end{array}\right\}$
COND: ?

The formulation in 8.40 indicates that when two nouns in a deep structure share identity of reference either the first or the second must be
changed into a pronoun. This rule is still not adequate to the full range
of facts about anaphoric pronoun insertion in English. There is in fact
evidence of the need for two separate anaphoric pronoun insertion
transformations. One of them is optional, the other obligatory. One of
them also accounts for the use of what are called **reflexive pronouns**
(those in the third column in 8.34). See what you can find out about these
two transformations by examining the sentences in 8.41. Sentences with
the same letter designation may be assumed to have the same deep structure. An asterisk in front of a sentence indicates that the pronoun with
the subscript i *cannot* be interpreted as referring to the noun with the
subscript i.

8.41a   The lawyers whom he$_i$ hired told Richard$_i$ lies.
aa   The lawyers whom Richard$_i$ hired told him$_i$ lies.
b   *He$_i$ hired lawyers who told Richard$_i$ lies.
bb   Richard$_i$ hired lawyers who told him$_i$ lies.
c   That he$_i$ testified pleased John$_i$.
cc   That John$_i$ testified pleased him$_i$.
d   *It pleased him$_i$ that John$_i$ testified.
dd   It pleased John$_i$ that he$_i$ testified.
e   *He$_i$ deceived Richard$_i$.
ee   *Richard$_i$ deceived him$_i$.
eee   Richard deceived himself.

Ignore the last three sentences for the time being. Notice that in 8.41a to 8.41dd the second occurrence of identically referenced nouns can always be replaced with an anaphoric pronoun, but in two cases the first of the two cannot be replaced. Try to formulate two transformations, one which replaces the first noun and one which replaces the second noun with a pronoun. If you draw deep structures for the relevant sentences, you may notice something about the deep-structure configuration which tells you when you can and when you cannot replace the first of two identically referenced nouns with a pronoun. (What is it about the deep structures of 8.41a and 8.41c that is different from those of 8.41b and 8.41d?)

Now examine 8.41e to 8.41eee. The fact that *he* in 8.41e cannot refer to Richard is a corollary of the explanation of the asterisks on 8.41b and 8.41d. But what about 8.41ee? It is the only sentence in 8.41 where a word like *him* cannot replace the second of two identically referenced nouns in a deep structure. Rather, the word *himself* is called for. Can you explain the structural conditions when reflexive pronouns like *himself* must be used as anaphoric pronouns?

EXERCISES

1   When I discussed imperatives in chapter 6, I made mention of tag sentences and noted that most tag sentences are questions. In fact, a statement with a tag question attached is a very close paraphrase of a yes/no question. Let us assume that the sentences below come from the very same deep structures as the yes/no questions they paraphrase. Can you formulate a transformation to account for the creation of the tag question at the end of each surface sequence? Is the transformation optional or obligatory?

Where should it be placed on the list of transformations? Are there any conditions limiting its operation?

a. Congress can impeach a president, can't it?
b. Monticello was designed by Jefferson, was it not?
c. The Czar had entered the war through spite, hadn't he?
d. The bureaucrats aren't telling the truth, are they?
e. We shouldn't stand by helplessly, should we?
f. You believe in democracy, don't you?

2 The single-lettered sentences listed below in (1) and (2) are like sentences discussed in the body of this chapter. The surface sequences come from underlying conjoined clauses by operation of CONJUNCTION REDUCTION. The double- and triple-lettered sentences seem to come from the same deep structures as the single-lettered sentences they are listed with, but by operation of a transformation, or transformations, other than CONJUNCTION REDUCTION. The sentences in (1) are affirmative sentences, those in (2) are negative. The double-lettered sentences in (1) exemplify one kind of alternate to the application of CONJUNCTION REDUCTION, and the triple-lettered sentences exemplify another. Two alternate surface sequencings are likewise possible in the case of the negative sentences in (2). Can you formulate a transformation, or transformations, to generate the double- and triple-lettered sentences in (1) and (2)? Can one transformation do the job, or are two or even four separate ones needed? Will such transformations be optional or obligatory? What about ordering? What about conditions? Here are the sentences for your analysis:

(1)a Bob and John lied.
  aa Bob lied, and John did too.
 aaa Bob lied, and so did John.
   b Chomsky and Skinner have written provocative books.
  bb Chomsky has written provocative books, and Skinner has too.
 bbb Chomsky has written provocative books, and so has Skinner.
(2)a Presidents and senators should not lie.
  aa Presidents should not lie, and senators shouldn't either.
 aaa Presidents should not lie, and neither should senators.
   b Business and labor aren't helping the economy.
  bb Business isn't helping the economy, and labor isn't either.
 bbb Business isn't helping the economy, and neither is labor.

3   Examine the sentences listed below. The basic grammar in the Appendix can easily account for the first sentence of each pair, but what about the second sentence? The second sentence of each pair has an adverbial of one kind or another at the beginning of it. Can you formulate a transformation to move adverbials to the front of sentences? Can all types of adverbials be moved? If a sentence has more than one adverbial in its deep structure, are there constraints on which one can move to the front of the sentence? Can more than one adverbial move to the front of a sentence? Can adverbials move to other places in a sentence besides to the front? To answer all these questions, you will need to try out many more sequences than are listed here. These will simply start you thinking:

(1)a   We should proceed cautiously.
   b   Cautiously, we should proceed.
(2)a   We were arguing in the library.
   b   In the library, we were arguing.
(3)a   The students receive a refund tomorrow.
   b   Tomorrow, the students receive a refund.
(4)a   They have released the tapes because John lied.
   b   Because John lied, they have released the tapes.

4   The pairs of sentences listed below are like the pairs in the previous exercise except that the word *only* is added to each sentence. The word *only* is itself a problem calling for revision in the grammar. It seems to belong to a form class not mentioned earlier, a form class that seems to limit or in some way qualify an adverb. Can you revise the PS rules to make room for it as a constituent of adverbials? But even when you have done this, you have not yet fully accounted for the second sentence of each pair. If you answered the previous exercise, you will have accounted for the presence of an adverbial at the front of the second sentence of each pair. But you will not have accounted for something else in the following sentences. Read them and see if you can notice this other fact about the second member of each pair.

(1)a   We should proceed only cautiously.
   b   Only cautiously, should we proceed.
(2)a   We were arguing only in the library.
   b   Only in the library, were we arguing.

(3)a The students receive a refund only tomorrow.

  b Only tomorrow, do the students receive a refund.

(4)a They have released the tapes only because John lied.

  b Only because John lied, have they released the tapes.

Did you notice that when an adverbial introduced by *only* starts off a sentence, INVERSION applies? If such an adverbial remains at the end, INVERSION does not apply. Can you reformulate the SD of the INVERSION transformation to have it apply to sentences like those above in addition to questions? Do the sentences above tell you anything about where the adverb-movement transformation you formulated in the last exercise should be placed relative to INVERSION on the list of transformations? Can you think of words other than *only* which, when part of a sentence-initial adverb, require application of the INVERSION transformation?

5 All the single-lettered sentences listed below in (1) and (2) can be accounted for by the basic grammar in the Appendix. The single-lettered sentences in (1) contain a noun-clause object of a verb, and those in (2) a noun-clause subject of a predicate adjective. I treated such sentences at length in chapter 7. Some of the double- and triple-lettered sentences in (1) and (2) are marked with asterisks to show that they are not likely to occur in English. Those not marked with asterisks seem to convey the same message as the single-lettered sentences they are grouped with. Read all of the sentences in (1) and (2) and ask yourself how to incorporate into the basic grammar an explanation of those double- and triple-lettered sentences that *are* acceptable.

(1)a   They hope that I give evidence.

  aa   They hope for me to give evidence.

  aaa *They hope my giving evidence.

  b   They desire that the witnesses give evidence.

  bb   They desire the witnesses to give evidence.

  bbb *They desire the witnesses' giving evidence.

  c   They believe that John gives evidence.

  cc   They believe John to give evidence.

  ccc *They believe John's giving evidence. *('s = -poss)*

  d   They know that she gives evidence.

  dd   They know her to give evidence.

  ddd *They know her giving evidence.

(2)a   That I give evidence is necessary.

  aa   For me to give evidence is necessary.

  aaa My giving evidence is necessary.

b   That the witnesses give evidence is desirable.
bb   For the witnesses to give evidence is desirable.
bbb   The witnesses' giving evidence is desirable.
c   That John gives evidence is true.
cc   *For John to give evidence is true.
ccc   *John's giving evidence is true.
d   That she gives evidence is obvious.
dd   *For her to give evidence is obvious.
ddd   *Her giving evidence is obvious.

In chapter 7, I formulated NOMINALIZATION to insert *that* at the beginning of deep-structure noun clauses. Can you now revise NOMINALIZATION to allow it to insert *(for)* . . . *to,* as in some of the double-lettered sentences in (1) and (2), and -*poss* . . . -*ing,* as in some of the triple-lettered sentences? Can you formulate conditions which account for the asterisks in (1) and (2)? You may even want to question the validity of the asterisks. Make up sentences of your own like the ones in (1) and (2) so that you can learn more about the deep structures which NOMINALIZATION (including the two versions you have just formulated) can operate on. Does the configuration of the auxiliary in a deep-structure noun clause place limits on the version of NOMINALIZATION which can apply? These questions evoke some of the most complex issues in English syntax, so do not be frustrated if you cannot find ready answers.

Here is another problem related to the one above. Read the sentences in (3) carefully. What do they mean? Are there any words understood?

(3)a   The witnesses desire to give evidence.
b   John hopes to give evidence.

In each sentence in (3) there seems to be an understood subject of *to give.* Each sentence seems to be generated from the same deep structure as the sentence in (4) with the same letter:

(4)a   The witnesses desire that they (the witnesses) give evidence.
b   John hopes that he (John) gives evidence.

This seems to indicate that there is a transformation which can delete the subject of a deep-structure noun clause when that subject is the same as the subject of the main clause. But this can happen, apparently, only when the *(for)* . . . *to* version of NOMINALIZATION applies. Speculate on the shape of this transformation (linguists call it EQUI NP DELETION), its place on the list of transformations, and any conditions which limit its operation.

6   Pick any paragraph at random from a work of fiction by Ernest Hemingway and any paragraph from a work of fiction by William Faulkner. Copy a few sentences by each man on separate sheets of paper. Try to draw the deep structure of each sentence and to generate the surface structure by applying transformations in our grammar, both those in the basic grammar and any formulated in this chapter. It is likely that you can come close to accounting for the sentences by Hemingway. It is unlikely that you can even begin to account for the sentences by Faulkner. Ask yourself why? Your answer is a start in the study of syntactic aspects of each author's style. If you labor over the passage from Faulkner, you will uncover scores of facts calling for revisions in the grammar like those made both in the body of this chapter and in the exercises.

FOR FURTHER READING

For excellent discussion of all matters touched on in this chapter, consult Quirk et al. (1972). I have referred you to this work at the end of almost every chapter. It is the only fully comprehensive grammar of present-day English. Other comprehensive grammars of English, such as Jespersen's, treat historical facts in addition to current facts. You are especially recommended to consult the references in Quirk et al. for specific topics like phrasal verbs, conjoining, pronouns, and nominalizations.

Jespersen's seven volumes (1961) and the thirteen volumes of the *Oxford English Dictionary* are excellent sources of data for syntactic research. If, for instance, you are researching conjunction, you need only consult the entry for *and* in the *OED* to find hundreds of example sentences to analyze.

Articles in the anthologies edited by Jacobs and Rosenbaum (1970) and by Reibel and Schane (1969) treat many of the issues of this chapter in detail. Langacker (1972) presents, in addition to numerous foreign-language problems, many provocative problems in English syntax for resolution along lines taken in this chapter.

Chapter 9
English Semantics

SYNTAX AND SEMANTICS

Throughout this book, I have taken for granted a very important generalization about language: that any linguistic utterance is in essence a sequence of *sound* which is somehow associated with a *meaning.* For all the space I have taken and effort I have expended, I have said little explicitly about either meaning or sound. I have said in various places that the deep structure of a sentence must somehow make explicit ideas or relations that are implicit in the surface sequence. I have also noted that the surface structure must represent all the morphemes signaled in the spoken utterance and in the order in which they are said. But I have neither, on the one hand, shown exactly how a semantic interpretation is related to a deep structure, nor on the other, how the surface configuration of abstract morphemes is associated with certain complex sound waves produced by organs of speech in the human body. The former task is the province of **semantics** and the latter of **phonology.** In this chapter we will take a closer look at the way linguistics attempts to explain how meaning is associated with English syntactic structures. In the next chapter we will do the same for sound.

Recall some of the assertions made throughout this book while discussing either the formation of deep structures by the phrase-structure rules or their processing by transformations. I spoke, for instance, of the meanings of the modal verbs. I said that *can* means permission or ability, that *will* means certainty or command, that *must* means strong obligation or deduction, and so on. I said that *have-en* can mean that the action or state of a sentence has duration, or that *have-en* can relate a prior event or state to some current event or state as its cause or explanation. I also discussed meaning in other contexts. When discussing the passive transformation, I mentioned that the NP which is the leftmost immediate constituent of S in a deep structure is the doer of the action, and I implied that PASSIVE introduces the preposition *by* in order to take over that meaning. But our rules, up until now, nowhere incorporate any of these statements of meaning as formal principles. A fully explicit English grammar must do so.

Most of our treatment of English syntax in chapters 4 through 8 conforms to a model of grammar proposed by Noam Chomsky in *Aspects of the Theory of Syntax* (1965). In that book, Chomsky accepted and discussed an earlier claim that there is a separate body of rules whose job it is to formally make just such statements about deep-structure trees as I have alluded to in the previous paragraph. Various formal devices might be used to treat the cited examples, but essentially these would read as follows (for example):

9.1a Given a deep structure containing $[_M \text{will}]_M$, interpret the predication as *certain* . . .

b Given a deep structure containing $[_{PERF}\text{have-en}]_{PERF}$, interpret the predication as having *duration* . . .

c Interpret a deep structure NP which is the leftmost immediate constituent of S as an *agent* . . .

Notice that, for such formal statements to be made, a deep structure must have some distinctive structural element in it for each distinction in meaning or interpretation called for, the implication being that only on the basis of distinctions in a deep structure can distinctions in meaning be accounted for.

This brings us to a very significant aspect of deep structure, an aspect which Chomsky has dealt with in some detail, but which I have all but ignored because my purpose has been an in-depth treatment of syntax rather than semantics. Consider the following sequences of English words, all of which can be assigned a deep structure and processed by the transformations in the basic grammar, but which vary greatly in the kinds of semantic interpretation that may be associated with them.

9.2a　Cement shattered the glass.

aa　Fear shattered the glass.

b　Fire frightens animals.

bb　Fire frightens tulips.

c Antony married Cleopatra.
cc Fido married Cleopatra.
d Eloise ovulated.
dd George ovulated.
e Silas melted gold.
ee Silas melted water.
f Samson bent the nail.
ff Samson bent the sand.

When we compare the members of each set of sentences in 9.2, we find that our reaction to the single-lettered sentence is quite ordinary. However the double-lettered sentences seem somehow illogical or contradictory. Many linguists would say that the latter sentences are **semantically anomalous** or **semantically deviant**. The obvious observations are that fear cannot be said to shatter something—not literally—because only something concrete (rather than abstract) can shatter. Similarly, only animals or people can be frightened, not flowers; only humans marry; only females ovulate; only solids melt; only stiff but flexible concrete things bend. How can our grammar formally and systematically make the same kinds of observations about the double-lettered sentences as I have just made? (What does the job of semantic interpretation entail?) Is there anything in the deep structures of the double-lettered sentences, different from the deep structures of the single-lettered sentences, that such formal principles of semantic interpretation could be based on (such as a letter in the spelling of the anomalous words or something about constituent relationships)? Apparently not. It seems that such observations derive from the meanings of words, and we have done no more than include a spelling of words as the terminal elements in deep-structure trees.

Thus, before adequate semantic interpretation of sentences can be made possible, it is necessary to somehow make possible, at the very least, a semantic representation of the meanings of the words in deep structures. Linguists have attempted to do this by developing the concept of the **feature**. Let us examine the concept and see how it has been used to treat the kinds of phenomena in 9.2 and other phenomena as well.

FEATURES

My comments on the semantically anomalous sentences in 9.2 made use of terms of greater generality of meaning than the words that were the sources of the anomalies. For instance, in 9.2aa it is because *fear* is an abstract concept that the sentence is anomalous; it is not because *fear* signals an emotion or any particular emotion. Insertion of any abstract word—*love, hate, enjoyment, truth, uncertainty, beauty, clarity*—would result in the same kind of anomaly. In 9.2bb, the fact that *tulip* is a flower is not the source of the anomaly. Rather the source is the fact that *tulip* is not animate (that is, animal or human). Think back to the discussion of explanatory power in scientific investigations. We saw that *simplicity* was an important requirement for an effective explanation. In the present instance, this means that it is much simpler to say that *shatter* is one of a class of verbs requiring a concrete subject and that therefore 9.2aa is anomalous because *fear* is not a member of the class of concrete nouns, than it is to make a list, for every verb in the language, of all the nouns that produce such anomalies if used with that verb. Many nouns would of course appear over and over on the lists of many different verbs. But if we can explicitly associate terms such as concrete, animate, human with nouns in, say, their dictionary entries, we will have achieved two things: (1) the obviously necessary task of defining the words of a language and (2) the task of describing semantic anomalies by reference to such general terms rather than by redundant listings.

Let us begin to examine some formal conventions that we can use in conjunction with our grammar to make possible an account of semantic anomaly—and, of course, an·account of how ordinary, nonanomalous sentences are generated by the grammar.

Let us say that the meanings of words are built up out of building blocks of meaning called **features**. A language like English has very many features, but significantly fewer than the total number of words in the language. The meaning of a word is the sum total of the meanings of the features that make it up. Here are some possible features of English, which can be used to account for the anomalies in the double-lettered sentences in 9.2.

> **9.3a** ±concrete
> **b** ±animate
> **c** ±human
> **d** ±male
> **e** ±stiff
> **f** ±flexible
> **g** ±solid

It seems that a system of features which uses + and − values for one term is simpler in the scientific explanatory sense than a system with pairs of terms, such as abstract/concrete, animate/inanimate, human/nonhuman, male/female. Whether such a system is fully adequate to the task of describing the meanings of words has not been determined. Using the features in 9.3, we might represent (relevant parts at least of) the meanings of *man* and *woman* as follows:

9.4 man   woman
     +concrete +concrete
     +animate   +animate
     +human   +human
     +male   −male

If we add the feature ±young to the list in 9.3, we can show relations of meaning among *man, woman, boy,* and *girl:*

9.5 man   woman   boy   girl
     +concrete +concrete +concrete +concrete
     +animate   +animate   +animate   +animate
     +human   +human   +human   +human
     +male   −male   +male   −male
     −young   −young   +young   +young

The feature structure of *child* would be the same as boy and girl except that it would be **unmarked** for the feature ±male. I am, of course, oversimplifying in my discussion of these matters. But hopefully I have said enough for you to begin to realize that the use of features provides much potential for both explicating the meanings of individual words and for showing relations between the meanings of different words. Consider **synonyms,** for example. These are words with almost, but not quite, the same list of features (*child* and *boy* can serve as loose examples: all features are the same, except that *boy* is marked for a feature (±male) that *child* is not). Now consider **antonyms.** Interestingly, such pairs seem to tend to have all features in common, except that for one feature, and only one, the words are marked for opposite values (+ or −). The words *boy* and *girl* serve as examples.

Now, how can this treatment of word meanings (using features) help provide useful insight into the sources of the anomalies in 9.2? None of the problems of interpretation there seemed to have anything to do with the internal feature structure of any of the words. The problems of interpretation in 9.2 seemed rather to derive from using some noun in an inappropriate *context.* In 9.2aa, something about the features of *fear* conflicted with *shatter;* in 9.2bb, something about the features of *tulip* did not accord with those of *frighten,* and so with the rest of the double-lettered sentences in 9.2.

The kind of features I have been discussing, usually relevant to accounting for the meanings of nouns, are called **inherent features.** (The terminology implies that meaning *inheres* in nouns.) But what about verbs? Can we say that *shatter* is concrete in the same way that *ball* is concrete; that *frighten* is animate; that *bend* is stiff but flexible? No. Rather, it seems more appropriate to say that *shatter* expects a concrete subject, *frighten* expects an animate object, *bend* expects a stiff but flexible object, and so on. It seems indeed to be the case that, whereas most of the meaning of a noun is the noun's own, most of the meaning of a verb is **contextual**: we interpret a verb relative to the nouns or noun types that it expects in sentences. To think of the meaning of a noun— *man, bird, brick, fear*—whether in a sentence or in isolation, we do not need to think of any verbs or of any aspect of verb meanings. But with verbs, it is different. It is impossible to think of the meaning of *shatter,* or *frighten,* or *melt* without thinking of what shatters, who or what is frightened, or what melts. The meaning of *marry* cannot be conceived of—even outside of use in a sentence—except in terms of who is marrying whom.

It does seem, however, that at least part of the meaning of a verb is inherent. Consider *run, grow,* and *own* as examples. All three of these verbs can have a human subject: *John ran, John grew, John owned a house.* The verb *grow* will settle for any living thing as subject, and *run* for anything animate. These are contextual characteristics of the type mentioned in the previous paragraph. But it seems undeniable that there are other characteristics of these verbs which are not explained by reference to their contextual expectations: *run* seems to have an inherent feature, +action. We know this because we may use *run* in answer to a question like the one in 9.6:

9.6 What did John do? He ran.

However *grow* is marked −action because it does not ordinarily answer a question like the one in 9.6 *(What did John do? *He grew).* But *grow* seems to have another inherent feature, +process. We know this because we may use *grow* in answer to a question like the one in 9.7:

9.7 What happened to John? He grew.

The verb *own* differs from both *run* and *grow.* It seems to be marked both −action and −process because it does not ordinarily answer either type of question *(What did John do? *He owned the house; What happened to John? *He owned the house).* I wish however to emphasize that aside from very general inherent features of the type just mentioned, the vast majority of features of verbs—certainly those features that distinguish the meaning of any given verb from all others—are contextual and need to be formalized so as to make explicit reference to the inherent features of nouns: those features which the verb expects of any noun that accompanies it in a sentence without occasioning a semantic anomaly. These contextual features of verbs which make reference to the inherent features of nouns are called **selectional features.**

Here are formal representations of just those selectional features of the verbs in 9.2 that are needed to account for the anomalies which occur there. Each word has many other features, but the ones listed serve our purpose. (The anomalous sentences of 9.2 are reprinted here for ease of reference.)

9.8a	shatter	+concrete_____	(*Fear shattered the glass.)
b	frighten	_____+animate	(*Fire frightens tulips.)
c	marry	+human_____	(*Fido married Cleopatra.)
d	ovulate	−male_____	(*George ovulated.)
e	melt	_____+solid	(*Silas melted water.)
f	bend	_____+stiff	(*Samson bent the sand.)
		_____+flexible	

The line beside each feature represents the position of the verb relative to the position of some noun in a deep structure which is expected to have the inherent feature indicated. Thus the feature +concrete_____ expresses a constraint based on an inherent feature of a noun in front of the verb in any deep structure the verb might enter. A feature specification after the line expresses a constraint based on an inherent feature of a noun after the verb in some deep structure. Thus the anomalies of the double-lettered sentences in 9.2 are formally explained in each case as an incompatibility between the expectations of a verb as expressed in one of its selectional features and some inherent feature of a noun in the sentence. Here are all the sentences of 9.2 with the relevant features printed below the nouns and verbs in question. Note the compatibility between inherent features of nouns and selectional features of verbs in the single-lettered versions and the incompatibility in the double-lettered versions.

9.9a	Cement	shattered	the glass.
	+concrete	+concrete_____	
aa	*Fear	shattered	the glass.
	−concrete	+concrete_____	
b	Fire	frightens	animals.
		_____+animate	+animate
bb	*Fire	frightens	tulips.
		_____+animate	−animate
c	Antony	married	Cleopatra.
	+human	+human_____	

cc	*Fido	married	Cleopatra
	−human	+human___	
d	Eloise	ovulated.	
	−male	−male___	
dd	*George	ovulated.	
	+male	−male___	
e	Silas	melted	gold.
		___+solid	+solid
ee	*Silas	melted	water.
		___+solid	−solid
f	Samson	bent the	nail.
		___+stiff	+stiff
		___+flexible	+flexible
ff	*Samson	bent the	sand.
		___+stiff	−stiff
		___+flexible	−flexible

The addition of formalized features to the formal grammatical rules in the Appendix will make deep structures somewhat more complicated than they have been. They will look something like the diagram of *Silas melted gold* in 9.10. (I include in the diagram only features which I have discussed—several others would be required if a complete accounting of the semantics of the sentence were called for; the ellipsis dots indicate this.)

9.10

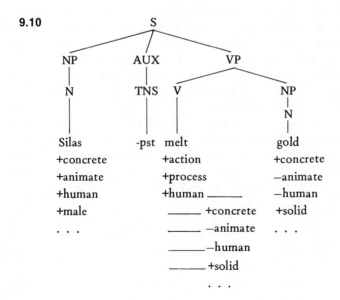

Silas — +concrete +animate +human +male . . .

-pst melt — +action +process +human___ ___+concrete ___−animate ___−human ___+solid . . .

gold — +concrete −animate −human +solid . . .

Having examined some of the devices necessary for an accounting of at least some crucial aspects of semantic interpretation, let me now mention how we can have the grammar generate, or assign the relevant features for, any and all English sentences—just as earlier in this book we saw that an adequate account of syntactic structure required formal devices such as tree diagrams to account for hierarchical constituent structure and formal mechanisms such as phrase-structure rules to assign an appropriate structure to any and all English sentences. Probably the best way to view this task is simply to claim that when PS rules xii to xvii select from the list of items of a given class (for example, N, V, ADJ), these items are stored (in the lexicon) with all necessary features as part of their lexical entry. This is, in essence, what linguists have proposed. Let us examine the implications of this proposal for the generation of the deep structure represented in 9.10. PS rules i to xi generate the constituent structure as given, except for the nouns and the verb. Then rule xii inserts the verb *melt*—with all the features stored with it in the lexicon. Next, rule xiii operates twice, inserting *Silas* and *gold* along with all the features stored with them in the lexicon.

Now just as there are conventions on the operation of PS rules (they are ordered; they are recursive; they may apply any number of times in succession), so there are conventions on (what we now need to call) **lexical-insertion rules**: such rules are constrained not to insert a noun into a deep structure if the noun contains any features that are incompatible with the expectations expressed by the selectional features in the verb (already in the structure). And so, anomalies are avoided.

But there is yet another kind of contextual feature in verbs. The phenomena that this new kind of feature accounts for are more properly syntactical than semantic but I treat them here because (1) I had to introduce the notion of features before I could treat them, (2) features are lexical (idiosyncratic) and therefore neither properly a matter just of semantics nor just of syntax, and (3) my treatment of them here will provide a useful transition to a discussion of important aspects of language structure that are quite relevant to semantic interpretation.

Recall PS rule ii. (You may want to look at it in the Appendix.) It allows several possible verb-phrase structures in English beginning with a verb. Here is the portion of the rule I will be discussing:

9.11   VP → V + (NP) + (PP) + (PP)

Now here are a set of sentences, all containing the verb *write,* which exemplify every possibility that 9.11 allows:

9.12a   VP → V
John wrote.

b   VP → V + NP
John wrote a letter.
c   VP → V + NP + PP
John wrote a letter to Bill.
d   VP → V + NP + PP + PP
John wrote a letter to Bill about the news.
e   VP → V + PP
John wrote to Bill.
f   VP → V + PP + PP
John wrote to Bill about the news.

The array of sentences in 9.12 does not present any difficulties that might call for any revisions of the grammar: we have a certain phrase-structure rule in our grammar, and I have presented a set of sentences showing that every possibility which the rule allows can indeed be realized in an English sentence. But now consider the following attempts to allow the PS rule to run its course with the verbs *own* and *listen:*

9.13a   VP → V
*John owned.
John listened.
b   VP → V + NP
John owned a house.
*John listened ?NP
c   VP → V + NP + PP
*John owned a house ?PP
*John listened ?NP ?PP
d   VP → V + NP + PP + PP
*John owned a house ?PP ?PP
*John listened ?NP ?PP ?PP
e   VP → V + PP
*John owned ?PP
John listened to a speech.
f   VP → V + PP + PP
*John owned ?PP ?PP
*John listened to a speech ?PP

The asterisks indicate that it is impossible to have a sentence where the given verb appears in the VP structure indicated by the rule. The notations ?NP and ?PP mean that no constituent of the given type could be found to complete the structure without causing a nonsensical sequence. Our grammar, as presently formulated, has no way of accounting for the asterisks in 9.13. We have no mechanism in the grammar to prevent it from generating whole sets of sentences like those in 9.10 for both *own* and *listen,* even sentences as absurd as *John owned the letter to Bill about the news.* Here is the fact to be dealt with: an individual verb has idiosyncratic (lexical) preferences about the kinds of deep-structure configurations in which it can be inserted—preferences expressible in terms of the categorical configuration of a deep structure and independent of anything having to do with the meanings (inherent features) of nouns that may occur with the verb in a structure. (Traditional grammatical terms like **transitive** and **intransitive** attempt to deal with this kind of preference.) Thus we need some explicit (formal) device that is part of the lexical representation of each verb and that will assure its insertion into an appropriate verb phrase and exclude its insertion into an inappropriate one. The device is another kind of feature. But whereas selectional features of verbs make reference to the inherent features of nouns, this new kind of feature will make reference to the *categories in a deep-structure tree.* Here is a formal representation of the features relevant to the structures in 9.12 and 9.13:

9.14a ±_____
  b ±_____ NP
  c ±_____ NP PP
  d ±_____ NP PP PP
  e ±_____ PP
  f ±_____ PP PP

As with selectional features, the line stands for the position of a verb relative to other elements in a structure. If a verb is marked plus (+) for the feature in 9.14a, it may occur as the only element in a verb phrase. A verb marked minus (−) for this feature cannot occur as the only element in a verb phrase. A verb marked plus (+) for the feature in 9.14b can occur with a noun phrase as the only other element in a verb phrase. A verb marked minus (−) for this feature cannot. And so on for all the features in 9.14. Now here are the relevant features of this type which form parts of the lexical representations of *write, own,* and *listen* and which show why *write* allows all the VP possibilities (as illustrated in 9.12) but *own* and *listen* allow only some of them (as illustrated in 9.13).

9.15

write	own	listen
+_____	−_____	+_____
+_____ NP	+_____ NP	−_____ NP
+_____ NP PP	−_____ NP PP	−_____ NP PP
+_____ NP PP PP	−_____ NP PP PP	−_____ NP PP PP
+_____ PP	−_____ PP	+_____ PP
+_____ PP PP	−_____ PP PP	−_____ PP PP

Since such features tend to classify verbs into subcategories (transitive, intransitive, and so forth) we can call them **subcategorizational features.** (Cumbersome as this term is, it is not quite as cumbersome as the term some linguists prefer—*strict subcategorizational features!*) Thus, if

we add a convention to PS rule xii (the rule that inserts verbs) to allow
insertion of a verb only into a verb-phrase structure for which the verb
has a plus (+) marking for the corresponding subcategorizational feature, we will have accounted for the appropriateness of the sentences
without asterisks in 9.12 and 9.13, and we will have prohibited the ones
with asterisks.

We have now, through the addition of features of various kinds, considerably enriched the notion of deep structure. Let me illustrate by
providing a diagram in 9.16 of the deep structure of *Silas melted gold.*
I list the subcategorizational features of *melt* before the selectional features because they do their job first: they control the insertion of the
verb itself into a structure; only after the verb is inserted do the selectional features operate, controlling the insertion of nouns. (Ellipsis dots
indicate that other features are probably called for, but that I have not
discussed them, or they are not necessary for our purpose.)

9.16

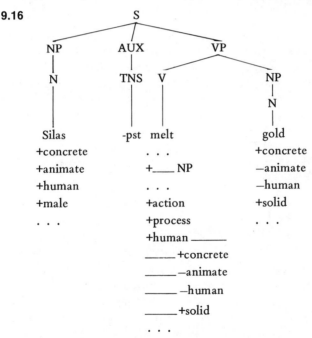

We have now surveyed some suggestions relevant to the semantic
interpretation of sentences that Noam Chomsky (1965) accepted and
discussed. Attempts to carry out a detailed description of English semantic and lexical structure along these lines have, in the years since
1965, uncovered some serious deficiencies in the proposals and led to
suggestions for substantial revision of the basic rules of grammar and

even of the interrelation of the various components of a linguistic description. In the next section we will examine some of these suggestions, discovering that attempts to subcategorize verbs and to state their selectional preferences by reference to the deep structures our grammar produces, meet with serious obstacles, obstacles that cannot be overcome without significant rethinking of grammatical theory. We will then briefly examine a proposal for restating the principles of deep-structure formation which can resolve the problems without undermining the progress made and the insights into English syntax so far achieved through our hard work in learning and using our language model. Hopefully some of the problems will already have occurred to you if you have been critically scrutinizing the various examples presented in this chapter.

CASE GRAMMAR

Let us take another look at the now familiar and seemingly simple sentence *Silas melted gold.* I presented in 9.16 a somewhat detailed version of the deep structure of this sentence, including in it all the relevant features that were associated with the lexical items and needed for an adequate account of how users of English are able to interpret semantically the message coded into its three words. Consider first the selectional features of *melt*. I listed the feature +human_____ with it because one does not expect bricks to melt gold, or flowers, or even raccoons to be able to do so for that matter. But now consider the following perfectly acceptable English sentences:

> **9.17a** Silas melted gold with the laser.
> **b** The laser melted gold.
> **c** Gold melted.

The obvious observation is that *melt* does not always require a +human subject. Did I err in including the selectional feature +human_____ in its deep structure in 9.16? It is hard to say. It is true that only humans (and possibly animals), though certainly no bricks and flowers, can perform the action of melting gold. So we do want the grammar to note the anomaly of sentences like *The tulip melted gold.* This was the reason I included the feature +human_____ in 9.16. But now we see that the feature would also prohibit 9.17b and 9.17c, which are perfectly natural. Hopefully you are thinking: "But the laser in 9.17b does not perform the action of melting the gold—some human must use it, or at least turn it on. And the gold in 9.17c most certainly does not perform any action; it melts, just as it melts in 9.17a and 9.17b!" Users of English will easily understand that the ordering of a noun phrase in front of the verb is not necessarily one of the really important facts for semantically interpreting sentences, as the sentences in 9.17 clearly indicate. Hence if selectional features are to be an adequate basis for the semantic interpretation of sentences, they must be based on (expressed in terms of) something more than position—or at least a richer notion of position than our deep-structure rules provide for. It is not therefore the noun phrase in front of the verb *melt* that must be +human but rather any NP naming the one who performs the act of melting something. Likewise, notice that the selectional features listed in 9.16 as applying to the noun phrase after the verb *(gold)* apply in 9.17c to the noun phrase in front of the verb *(gold)*. Thus, these restrictions too seem to apply not to a noun phrase in some position specifiable by our PS rules but to any noun phrase that undergoes a change of state (from solid to liquid) as a result of the melting taking place. Let us call a noun phrase naming the one who performs the action specified by a verb an **agent** and a noun phrase naming the entity undergoing a change of state as a result of the action specified by a verb a **patient**. Furthermore, there seem to be yet other selectional features of *melt* which our diagram in 9.16 did not take account of at all. For instance it seems that anything used in the act of melting by the agent in order to cause the patient to change from a solid state to a liquid state must have the inherent feature +hot. We wouldn't ordinarily come across sentences like these:

9.18a Silas melted gold with an ice cube.
b An ice cube melted gold.

We shall call a noun phrase naming the entity used to carry out the action specified by a verb an **instrument**. Thus, the expectations of the verb *melt* and (I could easily demonstrate) those of all verbs are much more complex than I first made them out to be—certainly too complex to be adequately stated in terms of the structures generated by our PS rules, which allow reference only to noun phrases before and after a verb.

For this reason, I wish now to examine a proposal that not only can resolve the problems just discussed, but can open the door to still other possibilities in the ongoing effort of linguists to adequately treat semantic issues. The proposal has resulted from a whole series of observations like the ones we have just examined about the semantic expectations of verbs. This different approach to the principles of deep structure is mainly the work of Charles Fillmore and is usually called **case grammar.**

Let us plunge right into the formalism and see what possibilities it provides. I propose to replace those portions of our PS rules i and ii reprinted here in 9.19.

9.19 i   S → NP + AUX + VP
     ii VP → V + (NP) + (PP) + (PP)

Assume that most of the other elements of our PS rules remain unchanged—even the parts of PS rules i and ii not reprinted here, but let us replace the portions in 9.19 with the rules in 9.20, where PAT abbreviates patient, AG, agent, and INS, instrument.

9.20 i   S → AUX + VP
     ii   VP → V + (PAT) + (INS) + (AG) . . .

iia $\begin{bmatrix} \text{PAT} \\ \text{INS} \\ \text{AG} \\ \text{. . .} \end{bmatrix} \rightarrow$ NP

Assuming that a complete array of PS rules—virtually the same as those we are familiar with except as specified in 9.20—is operating, let us see the kinds of deep structures (leaving out feature specifications) these new PS rules generate for the sentences in 9.17.

9.21a

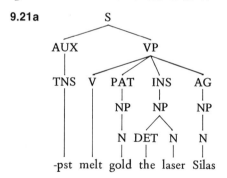

b

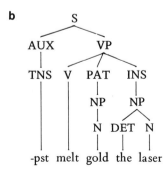

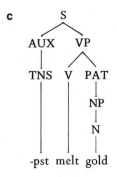

All the selectional inconsistencies noted earlier are resolved when stated in terms of deep structures like those in 9.21. Here are the selectional features of *melt* which show how this resolution is achieved:

9.22   melt
——[$_{PAT}$+solid]$_{PAT}$
——[$_{INS}$+hot]$_{INS}$
——[$_{AG}$+human]$_{AG}$

These features assert that any patient of *melt* must be +solid, any instrument must be +hot, and any agent, +human. The adoption of the rules in 9.20, which make such formal statements possible, need not entail the abandonment of the principles of syntax—especially the transformations—which we have developed throughout this book. Many of the PS rules are still quite relevant, and we can maintain virtually all of the transformations. We need only add a few transformations early in our list which will have the effect of changing deep structures of the type in 9.21 into structures, now' intermediate structures, like the ones our original PS rules generated. Thus all the transformations we have studied can still operate. Consider a transformation like the following for instance, which would be ordered before all the transformations listed in the Appendix:

9.23   SUBJECT SELECTION (OBL)
SD: X " AUX " V " Y " [$_z$ " NP "]$_z$
SC: 1   2   3   4   5   6   5 ⇒
        1 6   2   3   4
COND: Z = AG > INS > PAT . . .

This transformation identifies a category label like AG, INS, or PAT and requires that the NP the label categorizes move to a position in front of AUX, thus creating what is normally called the subject of a sentence. The tree-pruning convention then deletes the label itself. The condition in 9.23 is to be read as follows: let the variable Z be the agent, if an agent is present. If no agent is present, let Z be an instrument. If neither an agent nor an instrument is present, let Z be the patient. In 9.24 I show how the transformation in 9.23 operates on the deep structure given in 9.21b. (I again leave out the features, since they play no direct role in the process I am discussing.)

9.24

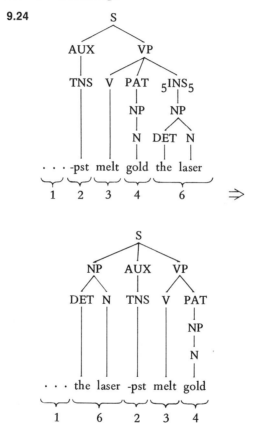

Notice how closely the output tree in 9.24 resembles the "deep-structure" tree that the PS rules in the Appendix would generate for the sentence. A transformation is still needed to delete the label PAT in the output tree of 9.24, thus producing a tree entirely ready to be processed by the set of transformations in the Appendix. My purpose here is not actually to develop a fully adequate set of transformations which can generate, from deep structures like those in 9.21, structures compatible with the list of transformations in the Appendix. Rather, my purpose is to show that it is possible to do so. That is, it is possible to hold to our accounting of the wide array of syntactic facts in chapters 5 through 8 but yet to revise our treatment of deep structure to account for the essentially semantic contextual preferences of verbs.

Category labels like PAT, INS, and AG are often called **semantic cases** or **semantic roles**. Such labels specify the relation of the noun phrase they classify to the verb in a sentence. We have seen that if a noun phrase is labeled AG, it performs the action specified by the verb. If it is labeled PAT, it undergoes a change of state as a result of the action specified by a verb. (PAT may also label a noun phrase existing in a state specified by a verb. For example, *house* is the patient of *own* in *John owns the house,* and *Harold* is the patient of *sleep* in *Harold slept.*) If a noun phrase is labeled INS, it is related to the verb as the thing used in carrying out the action specified by the verb. A transformation like SUBJECT SELECTION has the effect of translating a deep-structure role label into a surface-structure position. Thus we know that *Silas* is an agent in *Silas melted gold with the laser* because SUBJECT SELECTION specifies that agents, whenever present in deep structures, are made subjects of surface sentences. We know that *laser* is an instrument in *The laser melted gold* because the same transformation makes instruments subjects of surface sentences in the absence of a deep-structure agent. We know that *gold* is a patient in *Gold melted* because SUBJECT SELECTION makes patients into surface subjects in the absence of both an agent and an instrument in deep structure. But there are many more semantic roles besides agent, instrument, and patient, and the vast majority of the relational concepts which these other roles represent are not coded into surface word order. Most of these other relational concepts are represented in surface structure by prepositions. Before I list and exemplify some of these other roles, let us see by way of illustration how a preposition occasionally indicates the role of instrument. Consider 9.17a again *(Silas melted gold with the laser).* We know that *Silas* is an agent because SUBJECT SELECTION makes an agent the subject. We know that *gold* is a patient because it immediately follows the verb—is its surface direct object. (I have not formalized the transformation to do this, but the fact remains.) We also know that *laser* is an instrument. But how is this information communicated by the surface sequence? It is communicated by the word *with.* There is, then, a grammatical rule which at some point changes the deep-structure category label INS into the word *with*—but only when the instrument has not been made subject by SUBJECT SELECTION. There are many such rules which convert deep-structure semantic role labels into prepositions whenever the noun phrase so labeled has not been made either subject or direct object. In 9.25 to

9.27 are a number of sentences for consideration. See if you can determine the semantic role played by each noun phrase in each sentence, and then notice how prepositions in the surface sequence give information about the semantic roles of the various noun phrases.

9.25a The witness went to the hearing room.
  b The committee sent the subpoena to the president.
  c Many corporations give contributions to politicians.
9.26a These files come from the White House.
  b A message has arrived from the prosecutors.
  c That painting is from Paris.
9.27a The lawyer put the memorandum on the table.
  b John met Gordon in the park.
  c Tony hid the money at the airport.

Each of the above nine sentences contains a prepositional phrase. The noun phrases in all nine prepositional phrases convey information about *place.* In 9.25 the place is a **goal**; in 9.26 it is a **source**; in 9.27 it is a general **location.** Certain noun phrases, such as *the hearing room* in 9.25a, specify a place no matter how they are used in a sentence (although *the hearing room* does not automatically evoke the notion of a goal outside the context of a sentence like 9.25a). However, a noun phrase like *the president* in 9.25b in no way evokes the concept of place or of goal outside a sentence context like 9.25b. But notice that in the context of 9.25b we relate *the president* to the action of sending as the goal (the recipient) rather than the agent (the sender) or the patient (the thing sent). And we do so *because* the noun phrase *the president* is in a prepositional phrase introduced by *to.* Thus the sentences in 9.25 indicate that **goal** is a deep-structure semantic role and that—in some sentences at least—this relational concept is converted into the preposition *to* in surface structures. The sentences in 9.26 give indication of a semantic role, **source,** which can be converted into the surface preposition *from.* The sentences in 9.27 indicate a more general semantic place role, **location,** with a variety of prepositions conveying this relational concept in surface structures.

So far we have seen that noun phrases can play at least six semantic roles in sentences: agent, patient, instrument, goal, source, and location. The first three were relatively easy to define because their meanings related closely to fairly familiar notions like subject and direct object. The last three are fairly obvious because their meanings are quite concretely defined. But there seem to be at least some semantic roles whose meanings are somewhat elusive. The problem in finding terms to label them may derive from their possible evolution in English by a process of abstraction. Examine the prepositional phrases in the sentences in 9.28 to 9.30. Notice two things: (1) the roles played by the noun phrases in the prepositional phrases are more abstractly conceived than the essentially spatial roles played by the noun phrases in 9.25 to 9.27, but (2) the prepositions marking these abstract roles show a marked tendency to correspond to those marking concrete place roles in 9.25 to 9.27.

9.28a John told the news to the president.
b The government was a help to the burglars.
c The truth is known to the president.
9.29a The judge refused the request from fear.
b A guest became sick from the food.
c The patient was unconscious from shock.
9.30a They blamed the burglary on Howard.
b The burglars believe in the boss.
c Everyone was surprised at the disclosures.

9.28a shows a close affinity to the sentences in 9.25. It is easy to conceive of the president as the goal of the news. But he is a goal in a much more figurative way than any noun phrase in 9.25, and he is more than a goal. Information does not literally travel through space when someone is told something, so the notion *goal* if it were applied here would apply in an abstract, figurative way. Furthermore 9.28a tells us more about the president's relation to the verb in the sentence than that he received information. We are also told in effect that he retained the information, that his intellectual capacities have been exercised. This latter aspect of the semantic role manifested in 9.28a is especially clear in 9.28c, where the semantic relation of *the president* to the verb is solely as that entity whose intellectual capacities are exercised as a result of the action of the verb. For these reasons we should separate the role of goal from the role illustrated in 9.28. We may thus say that the prepositional phrases in 9.28 contain noun phrases which play the role of **experiencer**. Because *to* marks this role in surface structures we can think of it as abstractly related to the concrete spatial role, goal. The noun phrases introduced by *from* in 9.29 seem similarly to be abstract derivatives of the concrete role, source. We may call the role they play **reason**. And finally notice how the roles played by the nouns in the prepositional phrases in 9.30—in a *very* abstract way—relate to the more concrete place roles in 9.27. It is probably impossible to assign the same label to the three roles indicated by *on, in,* and *at* in 9.30. Perhaps *on* indicates a role we may label **victim**. I leave it to you to find labels for the roles indicated by *in* and *at;* for we have reached a point where your choice is perhaps as good as that of the professional linguist. This is because professional linguists have not yet developed a comprehensive treatment of the various semantic roles that English noun phrases play in deep structures. Nor have they developed a complete set of rules showing just how such deep roles are converted into prepositions in surface structures. So I leave you to seek out the writings on these matters and, as I said in the introduction, to consider even making your own contribution so that future textbooks can present fuller treatments of such matters.

EXERCISES

1   Reexamine the list of thirty sentences which we used for practice with the PS rules at the end of chapter 4. See if you can add inherent features to the nouns in their deep structures and both selectional and subcategorizational features to the verbs. Do not be afraid to invent features besides those discussed in this chapter when you think they are necessary for a full accounting of the relevant semantic facts.

2   Take the same thirty sentences referred to in exercise 1 and try to determine the semantic role played by each noun. You will probably find it necessary to come up with some additional role labels besides the ones used in our brief treatment of case grammar.

FOR FURTHER READING

Chomsky's ideas on the relation of syntax to semantics and on the use of features reflect the treatment of these matters by Katz and Fodor (1963) and by Katz and Postal (1964). Charles Fillmore (1968 and 1970) has written seminal articles on case grammar. A detailed introductory account of semantic roles in deep structures for English is contained in Langendoen (1970). Comprehensive book-length treatments of English semantics along lines of this chapter, but each with its own special emphasis, are Leech (1969), Katz (1972), Chafe (1970), and Anderson (1971). Fillmore and Langendoen (1971), Kiefer (1970), and Steinberg and Jakobovits (1971) have edited anthologies of articles on linguistic semantics. These readers cover a broad range of issues, many of which are so recent and so unsettled that I have chosen not to attempt to synthesize them in this chapter. For this reason, you are especially urged to consult the references here mentioned.

Chapter 10

English Phonology

ARTICULATORY PHONETICS

Earlier in this book, I treated English word structure in some detail, and then went on to treat sentence structure in considerable detail. A visitor from another planet, unfamiliar with human languages, might get the impression from this book that a human language like English is a purely abstract symbolic system with no necessary relation to any particular medium of perception—that it might just as easily be coded into visual symbols, tactile symbols, aural symbols, or even symbols which appeal to the sense of taste or smell. But the simple fact is that English and all human languages have a primary and necessary dependence on sound as their basic perceivable medium for transmitting messages coded according to principles of morphology and syntax. There is no human language that is not spoken. While many are also written, some are not. So only sound, which appeals to the sense of hearing, is a necessary communication medium. When we want to know whether someone can communicate in the system we call English, we do not ask, "Do you possess linguistic competence in English?" Nor do we ask, "Can you structure morphemes into syntactic sequences according to the principles of English?" Nor do we even ask, "Do you write English?" Rather, we ask, "Do you *speak* English?" An adequate account of the English language must say something about the sounds which somehow are able to convey the messages structured in accord with the principles of morphology, syntax, and semantics discussed earlier in this book.

218

I have not totally ignored the sounds of English in my earlier discussions. In chapter 1, I briefly outlined American structuralist approaches to English sounds. But in chapter 2, I sought to emphasize that, while sound is indeed meaningful in English, the meaningful units are not the sounds themselves but abstract categories called morphemes, which can group a variety of sounds into one unit of communication. In this chapter, I shall first discuss the sounds of English in a rudimentary way and then show how a rigorous accounting of the sound system of English (its **phonology**) can be coherently related to what I have said about its morphology and syntax.

When we speak of the sounds of a language, what do we mean? Can language sounds be produced by a musical instrument such as a trumpet or a drum? Can they be produced by banging a stick on a stone? No. They are a special class of sounds: they must be sounds which are producible by the human body. But is any sound producible by the human body a sound of language? If you clap your hands, or snap your fingers, or stomp your foot, are you producing a language sound? No. To be part of the phonology of a language, a sound must be producible by specific parts of the body. These are called the **organs of speech**. And while machines such as phonographs can imitate or reproduce the language sounds, this does not change the definition of such sounds. Machines can be built to produce a variety of sounds, but unless the sounds correspond to sounds the organs of speech can produce, they are not language sounds.

Figure 10.1, on page 220, is a diagram of a portion of the human anatomy with some of the organs of speech labeled. It is a side view of a human head, neck, and upper chest. Examine the diagram and the labels. After you have done so, we will examine the functions of the various labeled parts in the production of human language sounds.

All the organs of speech shown in figure 10.1 have primary bodily functions entirely independent of language. The lungs are for breathing; the teeth, lips, and tongue for eating. The nose filters air and makes it possible to breath with the mouth closed. The lips close the mouth. Even the vocal cords have a primary function other than their language function: when these two separable membranes in the throat are closed tightly, they can trap air in the lungs, which is necessary when a human performs a highly strenuous task such as lifting a heavy load. The various organs were apparently adapted by our distant ancestors to the additional function of producing language sounds because the additional function did not interfere substantially with their basic functions: we can, for instance, breath and talk at the same time—though it is difficult to eat and talk at the same time.

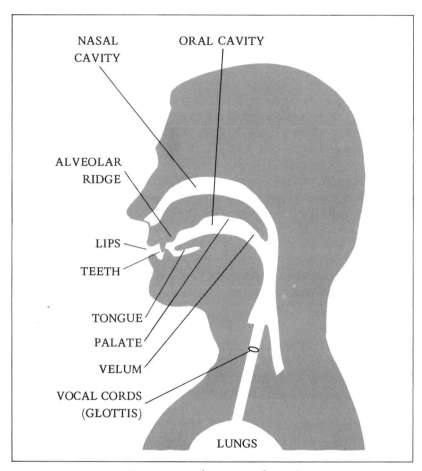

Figure 10.1: The organs of speech.

Speech sounds, like all sounds, are waves traveling through a medium —usually air. The lungs initiate the movement of air, much as an oar pushed in a stream of water produces a wave in the water. The other organs of speech affect the pattern of waves in the air stream, much as a rock can cause a wave in water to split and change direction or can even cause a new wave to travel back through the oncoming wave. It is such a pattern of sound waves traveling through air that is perceived by the ear of a listener as a given speech sound. Physicists and mathematicians have highly sophisticated means of measuring and describing patterns of sound waves in air. When they do so, they are practicing **acoustic** phonetics. Linguists are more interested in accounting for the behavior of the speaker and the perceptions of the listener than the precise nature of the wave patterns that constitute the sounds of English. We can make this our goal because the human ear is well attuned to distinguishing one pattern of waves from another—despite the sometimes amazing acoustic complexity of such patterns. Let us thus begin our treatment of English phonology by describing for each sound just what happens to the air stream as it travels from the lungs through the organs of speech. When the sounds of a language are described in this manner, we are practicing **articulatory phonetics.**

Numerous things can happen to a stream of air pumped from the lungs. The velum can close the nasal cavity, causing the air to travel only through the oral cavity. If the velum is lowered, the air stream may pass through both the oral and nasal cavities. If the velum is left lowered and the oral cavity is closed, the air may travel only through the nasal cavity. Each of these options produces significant variation in the pattern of waves in the air stream. Think again of the analogy of waves in water. Picture a wave approaching an island with a long channel on one side (like the nasal cavity) and a shorter channel on the other side (like the oral cavity). If first the one channel, then the other, and then both are left open for the wave to pass, the wave pattern that fills the stream at the far end of the island looks different in each of the three cases. This same principle operates within the oral cavity. Because the tongue is a highly flexible organ, it can change the shape of the oral cavity in almost limitless ways. Each change of shape causes a different pattern of sound waves to leave the mouth. But patterns of sound waves can be affected by things other than the shape of the spaces they travel through. If an air stream is squeezed through a very narrow passage, a quality perceived as friction is added to the wave pattern. If air is pushed from the lungs against a closure in the oral cavity, forcing an abrupt explosion of air, this too causes a special pattern of waves. If such squeezings of air or explosions of air occur at different places in the oral cavity, further differences occur in the pattern of waves that ultimately leaves the organs of speech. Every such difference can be perceived by a listener as a different speech sound.

Thus each sound of a language is a complex pattern of overlapping waves traveling through air. And different patterns are caused by different configurations of the various organs of speech as air travels from the lungs out through the nose or mouth or both. We have already noted that the tongue can make the oral cavity into an almost infinite variety of shapes. The tongue can also squeeze or explode air at almost any point in the oral cavity. Each subtle change in the place of the squeezing or the

	LABIAL	LABIODENTAL	DENTAL	ALVEOLAR	ALVEOPALATAL	PALATAL	VELAR	GLOTTAL
STOP	p b			t d	č j		k g	
FRICATIVE		f v	θ ð	s z	š ž			
LATERAL				l				
RETROFLEX				r				
NASAL	m			n			ŋ	
SEMIVOCALIC	w					y		h

Figure 10.2: English consonant symbols.

explosion causes a slightly different wave pattern. Thus the number of possibly different human language sounds is very large indeed. But the number of differentiations, from among the many potential ones, that any given language actually makes use of and incorporates into its phonological system is usually relatively small. Let us now take a look at only those configurations of the organs of speech used to differentiate sounds in the English phonological system.

We shall distinguish between two basic kinds of sounds in English: **consonants** and **vowels**. Consonants are produced when the air traveling from the lungs is stopped, or squeezed, or in any way rerouted from a path through the oral cavity over the center of the tongue. Vowels are produced when the air is allowed to travel through the oral cavity over the center of the tongue without being stopped or squeezed or in any way rerouted.

Figure 10.2 lays out a set of phonetic symbols for consonant sounds of English. The symbols are in a matrix where each one is defined along the side according to the kind of interference the air stream encounters on its way from the lungs, and along the top according to the place in the vocal tract where such interference with the air stream occurs. When two symbols occupy one box, the lower represents a concurrent vibration of the vocal cords. After you examine the chart and the terminology, I will comment more specifically on the symbols and the terms defining them.

Those symbols labeled fricative consonants in figure 10.2 represent a squeezing of the air stream through a tightly constricted space. This stricture and the friction that accompanies it may occur in English through interaction of the lower lip and the upper teeth, thus defining the symbols [f] and [v], the former voiceless and the latter voiced. (The brackets around a phonetic notation distinguish it from alphabetic notation.) If the fricative articulation occurs through interaction of the tip of the tongue and the teeth, we represent it with the symbols [θ] (voiceless) and [ð] (voiced). If the friction is caused by interaction of the front part of the tongue and the alveolar ridge, we represent it with the symbols [s] and [z] (respectively voiceless and voiced). If the stricture is a little farther back along the roof of the mouth, we represent it with the voiceless symbol [š] and the voiced symbol [ž]. You can feel the vibration of the vocal cords which defines the phonetic quality of voicing by lightly holding your larynx (Adam's apple) with your thumb and index finger and alternating between articulation of the sound [s] and the sound [z]. (Try to pronounce this sequence: [ssszzzssszzzssszzz . . .].) Notice two things as you do this: (1) the manner and place of articulation in the mouth remain constant, and (2) the sounds are entirely distinguished according to the presence or absence of the vibration you can feel in your throat.

Those symbols labeled stop consonants represent a complete stoppage of the air stream followed by an explosion of the air. This closure and explosion may occur in English at the lips, thus defining the symbols [p] and [b]. If the stop articulation occurs through interaction of the front of the tongue and the alveolar ridge, we represent it with the symbols [t] and [d]. If the closure and explosion is a little farther back along the roof of the mouth, we represent it with the symbols [č] and [ǰ]. A final set of stop consonant symbols is [k] and [g]. These represent a closure and explosion of air caused by interaction of the back of the tongue and the velum. Both members of each of the four sets of stop consonants are identical in manner of articulation (stop) and place of articulation (labial for [p] and [b], alveolar for [t] and [d], alveopalatal for [č] and [ǰ], and velar for [k] and [g]). The distinction between each member of the respective pairs derives from whether or not the vocal cords vibrate as the explosion of air takes place. The vocal cords do not vibrate when the first member of each pair is articulated. (Thus [p], [t], [č], and [k] are called voiceless stop consonants.) The vocal cords do vibrate when [b], [d], [ǰ], and [g] are articulated. (Thus they are called voiced stop consonants.)

All of the remaining consonant symbols in figure 10.2 are voiced.

The symbol [l] is called a lateral consonant because the air stream is diverted around the sides of the tongue; it is alveolar because the tip of the tongue is in contact with the alveolar ridge when [l] is articulated. We label [r] a retroflex consonant because the front portion of the tongue is tightly bent back (*retro* means 'back' and *flex* means 'bend' etymologically) when [r] is articulated. It is called an alveolar consonant because the tip of the tongue is close to (though usually not in contact with) the alveolar ridge during its articulation. The symbols [m], [n], and [ŋ] are labeled nasal consonants. During their articulations the oral cavity is completely closed off and the air stream is diverted through the nasal cavity. Closure of the oral cavity at the lips defines the symbol [m]. Closure at the alveolar ridge defines the symbol [n]. And closure at the velum defines [ŋ]. The symbols [w], [y], and [h] are called semivocalic consonants because they tend to conform to the generic definition of vowels: the air stream is not really interfered with as it passes over the tongue and out through the oral cavity. However there is a slight interference in each case. The lips are tightly rounded when [w] is articulated (for this reason we call it a labial consonant), the center of the tongue is very close to the roof of the mouth (the palate) when [y] is articulated (for this reason we call it a palatal consonant), and there is slight friction in the vocal cords (the glottis) when [h] is articulated (for this reason we call it a glottal consonant).

A useful way to familiarize yourself with the actual values of the consonant symbols is to pronounce English words in which they occur and notice as best you can what is happening in your vocal organs as you do so. In 10.1 I list the consonant symbols and, beside each one, several English words containing the sound it represents. The words are written in conventional English orthography with the letters underlined which more or less correspond to the symbol the words accompany. Read the words aloud, both to help yourself become familiar with the values of the phonetic symbols and to notice how English spelling is sometimes inconsistent in its representation of English sounds.

10.1

p	pair, spare, nip
b	bear, shabby, snob
t	tear, stop, rat
d	dare, Eddie, fad
č	chair, sketchy, fetch
ǰ	jeer, edgy, cage
k	kid, scare, tack
g	gear, soggy, tag
f	phone, taffy, laugh
v	vet, novel, have

θ	thigh, ether, cloth
ð	thy, either, clothe
s	seal, fussy, bus
z	zeal, fuzzy, bruise
š	share, pressure, bush
ž	pleasure, decision, beige
l	lore, sulk, ball
r	rate, merry, tore
m	more, Tommy, tame
n	nor, Tony, tone
ŋ	singer, thanks, long
w	wet, beware, twice
y	year, p_ure, _university
h	hair, inhale, rawhide

Figure 10.3 lays out a set of phonetic symbols for the vowel sounds of English. Examine it briefly and then go on to the explanation.

	FRONT	CENTRAL	BACK
HIGH	i I		u U
MID	e ε	ə	o ɔ
LOW	æ		ɑ

Figure 10.3: English vowel symbols.

The symbols in figure 10.3 are defined according to the shape of the tongue in the oral cavity as the air stream passes through it. More specifically, each symbol represents the location in the oral cavity of the highest part of the tongue. If, for instance, the front part of the tongue is highest, then one of the symbols under the heading **front** labels the vowel. If, the front of the tongue being higher than the center or back, it is as high as it can go without causing friction or stoppage of the air stream, then we label the vowel with the symbol [i]. If, with the front of the tongue still higher than the center or back, it is nonetheless considerably lower than [i]—in fact, just about as low as it can be without getting lower than the center or back—then we label the vowel with the symbol [æ]. The symbol [e] represents a vowel where the front of the tongue is higher than [æ] but lower than [i]. The word *eat* contains the sound [i]; *ate* contains [e]; *at* contains [æ]. Say the words *eat, ate,* and *at* aloud. Now say them again, but do not pronounce the [t] sound; just think it. Notice how, when you pronounce the sounds [i], [e], and [æ], the front of your tongue drops noticeably with each successive vowel.

The same principle holds for the vowels headed **back** in figure 10.3. We call a vowel a back vowel if the back of the tongue is higher than the front or center. It is a high back vowel if the back of the tongue is quite near the roof of the mouth. It is a low back vowel if the back of the tongue is as low as it can go without getting lower than the front or center. The word *ooze* contains the high back vowel [u]; *owes* contains the mid back vowel [o]; *Oz* contains the low back vowel [ɑ]. Say the words *ooze, owes,* and *Oz* aloud. Now say them again, but don't pronounce the [z] sound; just think it. Notice how, when you pronounce the sounds [u], [o], and [ɑ], the back of your tongue drops noticeably with each successive vowel.

The symbol [ɪ] represents a front vowel between [i] and [e]; the symbol [ɛ] represents a front vowel between [e] and [æ]. The symbol [ʊ] represents a back vowel between [u] and [o], and the symbol [ɔ] represents a back vowel between [o] and [ɑ]. The symbol [ə] under the heading **central** represents a vowel where the center of the tongue is higher than either the front or the back.

As with the consonant symbols, you can familiarize yourself with the actual values of the vowel symbols by pronouncing English words in which they occur and trying to notice the position of your tongue relative to its position for other vowel sounds. It is of course quite difficult to feel these differences the way one can feel the differences among consonant articulations. So the example words themselves must serve as the best clues to the value of a given vowel symbol. Thus until you sharpen your ear, you may have to think of the symbol [u] as "the vowel of *ooze*" and [o] as "the vowel of *owes*," and so forth. In 10.2 I list the vowel symbols and, beside each one, some words containing the vowel. Where possible, I list four example words, first with the vowel at the beginning of a syllable, second with the vowel between two consonants, third with the vowel at the end of a syllable, and fourth with the vowel before [r]. Read all the words in 10.2 aloud and listen carefully to the vowel sound so that you can fix the value of the given phonetic vowel symbol. I warn you that the symbol [ɔ] may cause you some problems. Many speakers of English use [ɔ] rarely or not at all. The words given as examples of [ɔ] may for many have the sound [ɑ]. The pronunciations with [ɔ] are common in northeastern states, especially around Baltimore, Philadelphia, and New York. If you think your [ɔ] words and [ɑ] words sound pretty much alike, then your teacher may have to help you to practice recognizing the distinction between these two vowel symbols. Here is the list of example words:

10.2	i	eat	beat	pea	beer
	ɪ	it	bit		
	e	ate	bate	bay	hair
	ɛ	ebb	bet		
	æ	at	bat	baa	Harry
	ə	up	but	the	burr
	u	ooze	boot	two	tour
	ʊ	oomph	book		
	o	owes	boat	toe	
	ɔ	awe	bought	saw	or
	ɑ	Oz	Bach	ha	bar

When the front vowels of English ([i], [ɪ], [e], [ɛ], and [æ]) are articulated, the lips are more or less spread, but in articulating the back vowels ([u], [ʊ], [o], [ɔ], and [ɑ]), the lips are more or less rounded. An accident of history has produced this situation in modern English, for there is no necessary relationship between lip rounding and back vowels, on the one hand, and the lack of rounding and front vowels, on the other. Many of the world's languages (for example, French) have rounded front vowels in addition to unrounded ones, and other languages (for example, Russian) have unrounded back vowels. Thus it is useful to be aware of the nature of the articulatory characteristic of rounding, even though it does not play an especially important role in the vowel system of modern English.

The vowels in certain English words manifest what is called a glide articulation. A glide begins with the tongue position of one vowel and moves to the tongue position of another. Figure 10.4 presents notations we can use for the three most common glides in English and graphically illustrates the nature of their articulations. For each case the first vowel symbol represents the initial tongue position and the second vowel symbol the terminal position. The arrow represents the movement of the high point of the tongue during the articulation. It is this movement that defines the essential nature of a glide.

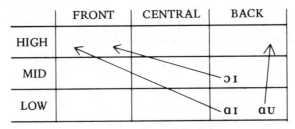

Figure 10.4: English glides.

In 10.3 I present example words for each glide. Four examples, arranged just as were those in 10.2, are given for each glide.

10.3 ɑɪ   eye   bite   tie   tire
       ɑʊ   out   bout   cow   tower
       ɔɪ   oil   coin   boy   lawyer

Note that only certain speakers of English pronounce an [r] immediately after a glide as implied by the fourth example in each set in 10.3 ([tɑɪr], [tɑʊr], and [lɔɪr]). Many pronounce these words with two syllables ([tɑɪyər], [tɑʊwər], and [lɔɪyər]).

Before we proceed to the more complex aspects of the phonological system of English, you are advised to sensitize your ear to phonological phenomena by attempting complete phonetic transcriptions of all the example words in 10.1, 10.2, and 10.3. After you have done this, take the transcriptions at random, conceal the spellings of the words transcribed, and then practice reading the transcriptions aloud to determine by the sound what word the transcription represents. These tasks will give you practice both in coding sounds into phonetic transcriptions and in pronouncing such transcriptions.

PHONEMES

While performing the tasks suggested at the end of the preceding section, you probably encountered a number of difficulties with, and even doubts about, the transcription system you were attempting to learn. For example, you probably had some problems transcribing vowels in front of [r]; these seem somehow different there than elsewhere. The vowel of *burr*, for instance, is not quite the same as the vowel of *up*—even though both *burr* and *up* are listed as examples for the symbol [ə]. The vowels of both words are indeed mid central vowels, but the tongue position for *burr* is higher than that for *up*. Some phoneticians use separate symbols to capture this distinction, transcribing *burr* [bɚr], and *up* [ʌp]. Another problem like this shows up in the example words given for [p] (*pair, spare,* and *nip*). The [p] in *spare* is indeed an uncomplicated voiceless bilabial stop. But in *pair* the explosion following the stop articulation is accompanied by an extra puff of air. Phoneticians call it **aspiration**. (You can observe it by holding a lighted match two or three inches from your mouth and saying *spare* a few times and then *pair*. Each time you say *spare,* the flame will flicker but not go out, but when you say *pair,* the aspiration accompanying [p] will extinguish the match.) Phoneticians sometimes represent aspiration with an apostrophe, and so would transcribe the [p] of *pair* as [p']. Let us turn to the pronunciation of *nip*. When pronounced casually, *nip* shows no explosion of air at all following the articulation of [p]; the air stream is stopped but not released—the lips close and stay closed. Such an unreleased [p] can be transcribed [pꟳ].

The variations in the actual articulations of [ə] and [p] described in the last paragraph are not special cases. Every symbol in the system you have learned alters its pronunciation to one degree or other in different contexts. I shall discuss a few more such alternations below. But before I do, let us examine the implications of this type of phenomenon for an account of English phonology. The scientific linguist's aim in accounting for English phonology is to state how English is pronounced and why. Like any scientist, he wishes not only to gather and accurately record data but also to discover and state patterns and relationships manifested by the data. Thus, while it is accurate to notice and record that the tongue position of the mid central vowel in *burr* is higher than that in *up,* it is not at all sufficient just to make the distinction and to ignore systematic relationships, like the following, between the two vowels: first, it is noteworthy that the two vowels are quite similar, both being mid central vowels; second, and perhaps more important, the two vowels are *systematic alternates;* that is, the higher variant occurs only in front of [r] and the lower variant elsewhere. A scientific explanation must take account of this kind of pattern. And the transcription system learned in the previous section did just that. Since [ɚ] always occurs before [r], and [ʌ] always occurs elsewhere, it is much simpler scientifically to state the alternation once and then use one symbol (I chose to use [ə]) to represent, not only the two articulations, but the systematic relationship between them. Thus the symbols in our system are not mechanical labels for entirely invariant configurations of the organs of speech. Rather, they are abstract classes, each encompassing a family of similar but systematically alternating articulations.

The [p'] of *pair,* the [p] of *spare,* and the [pꟳ] of *nip* represent another such family of sounds. We are able to group them together and use just one symbol to transcribe them because (1) they are similarly articulated, all being voiceless bilabial stops, and (2) the differences in their articulations are systematically determined, [pꟳ] occurring at the end of an utterance, [p'] initially before a vowel, and [p] elsewhere. Once the principles of alternation are stated, then one symbol [p] can serve to transcribe all three, its exact articulation determined by the context. When one symbol is used for a variety of similar but nonetheless distinct articulations, each of which is systematically determined, the symbol, and of course the systematic set of articulations it labels, is called a **phoneme**. American structural linguists followed the practice of distinguishing between phonemic notation and phonetic notation, writing phonemes between virgules, for example, /p/, and phones between brackets, for example, [p'], [pᵓ], and [p]. I do not make such a notational distinction throughout this chapter. I generally write all symbols representative of the sounds of English in brackets. It should be clear, however, that the symbols so far discussed and practiced are closer to phonemic notation than to a strictly mechanical phonetic notation.

Let us now look at some other examples of systematically determined sound alternation in English, hoping to gain insight into the nature of the phoneme. First notice that the symbols [t] and [k] as we have used them stand for a number of different sounds whose alternations are similar to the alternations represented by [p]. The example words given for [t] in 10.1 were *tear, stop,* and *rat;* those for [k] were *kid, scare,* and *tack.* Notice that the [t] and [k] in the first word of each set is aspirated and in the last word unreleased. Thus the three distinct articulations labeled [t] and the three labeled [k] alternate according to the same systematic principles determining the alternation among the three variants of [p].

Now consider the words in 10.4, taking special notice of the pronunciations of the underlined letters:

10.4a nor, Tony, tone
   b tenth, enthralling
   c inform, inflate, infant

Are all of the underlined letters pronounced exactly alike? No. The underlined nasals in 10.4a are *alveolar* nasals, but those in 10.4b are *dental* nasals, and those in 10.4c are *labiodental* nasals. Do these differences in the place of articulation require us to use three different symbols to transcribe the nasals in 10.4? According to what I have said so far in this section, the answer depends on (1) whether the articulations are similar and (2) whether the alternation among them is systematic. The articulations are similar: all are nasal consonants articulated toward the front of the mouth. And the alternation does seem to be systematic: the labiodental articulation in 10.4c seems to occur before labiodental consonants, the dental articulation in 10.4b before dental consonants, and the alveolar articulation in 10.4a elsewhere. Thus we can claim that English has a phoneme which we can transcribe with the symbol [n], but which stands for three distinct but systematically determined articulations.

American structural linguists used the term **allophone** to refer to each variant articulation classed together with others as members of the same phoneme class. Thus a class of sounds defined by phonetic similarity and systematic alternation is a phoneme, and the individual articulations belonging to the class are its allophones. English was said, for instance, to have an "n" phoneme, whose allophones were an alveolar nasal, a dental nasal, and a labiodental nasal. A structuralist might in fact have laid out a summary display of the facts discussed in this section as follows:

10.5	*phoneme*	*allophones*	*environment*	*example*
a	/ə/	[ɚ]	before /r/	burr
		[ʌ]	elsewhere	up
b	/p/	[p']	initially before a vowel	pair
		[p˺]	at end of an utterance	nip
		[p]	elsewhere	spare
c	/t/	[t']	initially before a vowel	tear
		[t˺]	at end of an utterance	rat
		[t]	elsewhere	stop
d	/k/	[k']	initially before a vowel	kid
		[k˺]	at end of an utterance	tack
		[k]	elsewhere	scare
e	/n/	[ɱ][1]	before labiodental consonant	infant
		[n̪][1]	before dental consonant	tenth
		[n]	elsewhere	nor

The display in 10.5 is just the beginning of a structuralist phonology of English. It is incomplete on two counts: (1) it does not treat all the phonemes of English, and (2) it does not list all the allophones even of those phonemes which are listed. I will not present here a complete structuralist English phonology. Rather my purpose has been to draw your attention to the kinds of facts on which phonemic analysis is based. Nonetheless, the consonant symbols listed in figure 10.2 represent a widely accepted inventory of English consonant phonemes, and the vowel symbols in figure 10.3 represent a widely accepted listing of English vowel phonemes. You can learn a great deal about the phonemes of English, and about some problems of basing phonology on them, by extending the display in 10.5. You can do so as follows: (1) For each of the phonemes listed in figures 10.2 and 10.3, think of as many words as you can in as many phonetic environments as you can—put the sound at the beginning, at the end, and in the middle of words, before and after as wide a variety of other sounds as you can think of. (2) Notice whether the pronunciation varies according to context and, if so, how it varies.

[1]The symbol [ɱ] represents a labiodental nasal; [n̪] represents a dental nasal.

(3) Then determine whether the variation can be stated according to the sound environment as was done in 10.5. If you make a serious attempt at such an analysis, you will most likely notice problems like those forming the basis of a brief critique of structuralist phonology at the beginning of the next section.

PHONOLOGICAL RULES

Confirmation of the phonemic status of the consonant and vowel symbols charted in figures 10.2 and 10.3 and listed with examples in 10.1 and 10.2 is often derived from the existence of what are called **minimal pairs**—pairs of words exactly alike except for one sound. Minimal pairs can be used as negative criteria to establish phoneme status: if two sounds are found to contrast in exactly the same phonetic environment, they cannot be the same phoneme. Thus the minimal pair *Tim* and *tin* confirms the distinction between the phonemes [m] and [n], the pair *some* and *sung* confirms the distinction between the phonemes [m] and [ŋ], and the pair *sin* and *sing* confirms the distinction between [n] and [ŋ]. The existence of three contrasting nasal stop phonemes in English is thus verified. And since no minimal pairs can be found where a labiodental nasal (as in *inform*) contrasts with an alveolar nasal, our grouping the two as allophones of one phoneme is similarly confirmed. The aim of a phonemic analysis is thus twofold: (1) to express the systematic alternations among similar sounds by grouping them as allophones of the same phoneme, and, perhaps even more important (2) to express the system of meaningful contrasts in a language as just those that hold among the phonemes listed in the analysis—to divide the sounds of a language into phonemes. An assumption of the second aim is that a given morpheme will always be pronounced with a fixed sequence of phonemes. Since [m] and [n] can signal different meanings, one must be sure to pronounce an allophone of [m] rather than [n] if one hopes to communicate the difference between two given morphemes containing them. (*Hem* and *hen,* for instance, are different morphemes whose different meanings in communication rest crucially on the distinction between their final phonemes.)

But now read the sentences in 10.6 aloud in a rapid and natural way.

> **10.6a** Henry is in Paris.
> **b** Henry is in Fairbanks.
> **c** Henry is in Thebes.
> **d** Henry is in Toledo.
> **e** Henry is in Kansas City.

Did you notice that the articulation of the nasal consonant in the morpheme *in* is different in each of the sentences in 10.6? In 10.7 I list phonetic transcriptions of *in* for each sentence of 10.6. The lettering corresponds to that in 10.6. Beside each transcription I describe the articulation of the nasal consonant of *in*.

10.7a ɪm bilabial nasal stop
   b ɪɱ labiodental nasal stop
   c ɪn̪ dental nasal stop
   d ɪn alveolar nasal stop
   e ɪŋ velar nasal stop

In the last paragraph, I claimed that the definition of the phoneme rests crucially on the assumption that a given morpheme will always be pronounced with a fixed sequence of phonemes. But the data in 10.6 demonstrate that this is clearly not the case with the morpheme *in*. In 10.6a it is pronounced with an allophone of the phoneme [m], in 10.6b to 10.6d with allophones of the phoneme [n], and in 10.6e with an allophone of the phoneme [ŋ]. The situation is further complicated when we consider how the morpheme *in* is pronounced in the sentences in 10.8. (In these sentences, *in* has extra loudness for emphasis.)

10.8a Henry is not near Paris; he is in Paris.
   b Henry is not near Fairbanks; he is in Fairbanks.
   c Henry is not near Thebes; he is in Thebes.
   d Henry is not near Toledo; he is in Toledo.
   e Henry is not near Kansas City; he is in Kansas City.

In all of the sentences of 10.8 the nasal consonant of *in* has an alveolar articulation: it does not conform its place of articulation to that of the following consonant as was the case in the sentences of 10.6. This fact coupled with the facts illustrated in 10.6 illustrate that the phonological system of English is even more complex than the assumptions underlying phonemic analysis take it to be. Apparently, users of English know more than a list of all the articulations of English grouped according to differences into phoneme classes. In the case of the morpheme *in* (and it is but an example of a wide variety of similar phenomena) the user of English knows that its final sound is indeed an alveolar nasal (at some level of abstraction), even though he often pronounces *in* with the entire gamut of nasal articulations, from labial to velar.

Generative-transformational linguists have treated at great length phenomena of the type illustrated in the previous paragraph. And this is no accident. The generative-transformational distinction between competence and performance and the resultant aim of constructing a theory of competence led to an attempt to describe what the user knows about pronouncing English, rather than just to describe relationships that can be observed in the pronunciations themselves. And the generative-transformational distinction in syntax between deep and surface structure linked by a system of transformations provided an analogy on which to base an account of phonological phenomena like the variation in pronunciation of *in*. It seems that there is in fact a kind of deep structure and surface structure in phonology and a set of phonological rules which systematically link the two levels much as transformations link deep and surface structure in syntax. Thus a generative phonologist would claim that on the more abstract level of morphological representation the user of English knows that the morpheme *in* does indeed end in an alveolar nasal. Evidence for such knowledge on the user's part was provided in 10.8, where *in* was pronounced in every case with an alveolar articulation. But the user of English also knows a phonological rule which requires that any nasal in an unstressed syllable conform its place of articulation in surface phonological structure to that of a following consonant, thus accounting for the pronunciations of *in* in 10.6. This phonological rule is sometimes referred to as NASAL ASSIMILATION. In the remainder of this section we will examine a series of additional phenomena calling for phonological rules and showing how these rules interact in interesting ways. We will also take a brief look at some of the formal symbolic devices generative phonologists make use of to express phonological rules explicitly and efficiently.

Read the sets of words in 10.9 aloud, and pay careful attention to any variant pronunciations of a given morpheme in each set.

    10.9a   ignite, ignition
       b   divide, divisive, division
       c   evade, evasive, evasion
       d   abuse, abusive

Here is an indication of the morphemes which occur in the above words:

    10.10a   ignite, ignite-ion
       b   divide, divide-ive, divide-ion
       c   evade, evade-ive, evade-ion
       d   abuse, abuse-ive

Notice that the first morpheme is the same for all the words in each set, the second and third words simply adding derivational suffixes to the first morpheme. Now read the words in 10.9 again, taking specific note of how the pronunciation of the first morpheme in each set changes when derivational suffixes are added. As you read the words in 10.9, compare your pronunciations with their phonetic transcriptions presented in 10.11.

10.11a   ɪgnɑɪt, ɪgnɪš-ən
   b   dɪvɑɪd, dɪvɪs-ɪv, dɪvɪž-ən
   c   ɪved, ɪves-ɪv, ɪvež-ən
   d   əbyuz, əbyus-ɪv

All four sets of words in 10.9 illustrate that one morpheme can come to be pronounced with a diversity of phonemic sequences. The transcriptions in 10.11a show that the morpheme *ignite* can appear with two quite different vowels in its second syllable—[ɑɪ] and [ɪ]—and two quite different final consonants—[t] and [š]. 10.11b shows that the morpheme *divide* can appear with two different vowels in its second syllable—[ɑɪ] and [ɪ] —and three different final consonants—[d], [s], and [ž]. The morpheme *evade* in 10.11c appears with the same three different final consonants as *divide* (which should lead you to suspect that general phonological principles may control such variations in pronunciation). And finally, 10.11d shows that the morpheme *abuse* can appear with two different final consonants, [z] and [s].

In 10.12 I present informal statements of four phonological rules of English which, when used on one underlying phonological representation of *ignite, divide, evade,* and *abuse,* can account for the wide variety of surface articulations these morphemes manifest. By assigning each morpheme just one underlying phonological representation, we account for the user's ability to recognize it and its meaning in all of the words of each set in 10.9. By positing phonological rules which systematically account for the variant pronunciations and by assuming the rules to be part of the user's competence, we account for the fact that the morphemes are in fact pronounced differently in different contexts.

   10.12a   LAXING
        Change the vowel [i] into the vowel [ɪ] in a syllable preceding a derivational suffix.

      b   SPIRANTIZATION
        Change [t] to [s], and change [d] to [z] at the end of a syllable preceding a derivational suffix beginning with a high front vowel.

      c   DEVOICING
        Change [z] to [s] in front of the derivational suffix *-ive*.

      d   PALATALIZATION
        When an [s] or [z] occurs at the end of a syllable and before a syllable which begins with [y], change the [s] to [š] and the [z] to [ž].

      e   VOWEL SHIFT
        Change the high front vowel [i] into the glide [ɑɪ].

In 10.13 I present applications of the phonological rules to all the words in 10.9. The words are listed in italics above their underlying phonological representations at the top of the display. Notice that the underlying representation of the base morpheme in each set of words is the same whether or not it is followed by a derivational suffix. Then notice how the phonological rules act in a variety of combinations systematically generating the entire array of variant surface pronunciations in 10.11, which appear again at the bottom of the display in 10.13. In the transcription beside the name of a rule, the underlined symbols indicate the effect of the rule. When no transcription appears in the space beside the name of a rule, the nearest articulation transcribed above the space is retained. Notice, for instance, that no rules act on the underlying phonological representations of the words *evade* and *abuse,* and thus their surface transcriptions are the same as their underlying transcriptions.

10.13

		ignite	*ignition*
		ɪgnit	ɪgnit-yən
		divide	*divisive*	*division*
		dɪvid	dɪvid-ɪv	dɪvid-yən
	evade	*evasive*	*evasion*
	ɪved	ɪved-ɪv	ɪved-yən
	abuse	*abusive*
	əbyuz	əbyuz-ɪv

LAXING		dɪvɪd-ɪv	ɪgnɪt-yən
			dɪvɪd-yən
SPIRANTIZATION		dɪvɪz-ɪv	ɪgnɪs-yən
		ɪvez-ɪv	dɪvɪz-yən
			ɪvez-yən
DEVOICING		dɪvɪs-ɪv	
		ɪves-ɪv	
		əbyus-ɪv	
PALATALIZATION			ɪgnɪš-yən
			dɪvɪž-yən
			ɪvež-yən
VOWEL SHIFT	ɪgnɑɪt		
	dɪvɑɪd		

	ɪgnɑɪt		ɪgnɪš-ən[1]
	dɪvɑɪd	dɪvɪs-ɪv	dɪvɪž-ən[1]
ɪved		ɪves-ɪv	ɪvež-ən[1]
əbyuz		əbyus-ɪv	

[1] A rule which I have not discussed accounts for the deletion of [y] after [š] and [ž] (Chomsky and Halle 1968, 231). I leave out explicit mention of it to keep the display as simple as possible.

The phonological rules listed in 10.12 and applied in 10.13 are not the most significant ones in English. Nor is even one of them stated with complete adequacy. There are, for example, other facets to the SPIRAN-TIZATION rule, one of which accounts for an underlying [k] in morphemes like *electric* and *plastic* which surfaces as an [s] before a derivational suffix with a high front vowel in words like *electricity* and *plasticity*. But I hope that the rules stated in 10.12 and the applications of them in 10.13 have given you a solid impression of the highly systematic way in which phonological rules generate surface articulations from underlying phonological representations of morphemes. You should especially notice how the pronunciation of surface sequences is commonly contingent on essentially grammatical information like whether a morpheme is followed by a derivational suffix or not. For many years, it was thought possible to treat the phonology of a language exhaustively in isolation from its morphology and syntax. Phonological rules like those in 10.12 provide strong evidence that this cannot be done. Generative-transformational linguists have in fact stated that the principles accounting for pronunciation (the phonological component of a linguistic theory) can operate accurately and efficiently only after the principles of syntax have fully specified the morphology and syntax of a surface structure. The principles of phonology then operate to specify exactly how an entire syntactic surface structure is pronounced.

We saw in chapter 5 that generative-transformational linguists were not satisfied to express grammatical transformations in the wording of ordinary sentences—although it was possible to do so. Greater explicitness and scientific simplicity was achieved by expressing them in formal symbolic notation; and you became quite familiar with such notation. Similar efforts have been made in phonology. Instead of informal statements such as those in 10.12, formal symbolic notations have been developed so that phonological systems can be stated explicitly and evaluated rigorously. These formulations generally make use of what are called **phonological features**. The feature approach to phonological representation originated independently of the need to express phonological rules. One impetus was the desire to integrate the insights of acoustic and articulatory phonetics. Another was the desire to account for the fact that users of a language tend to perceive only certain distinctions in the articulatory flow of language. Many gross characteristics of articulation are often totally ignored in decoding phonetically coded language sequences. Features attempt to express just those distinctive characteristics of the linguistic sound wave which the user is attuned to as he decodes the message the wave carries. In 10.14 I present a set of features which can be used to represent the distinctive sounds of English. Most of the features are defined by both articulatory and acoustic phenomena, though a few rest almost exclusively on acoustic definitions: on characteristics of the sound wave such as might be recorded by machines which can draw pictures of sound waves. The articulatory characteristics entailed by many of the feature labels, such as consonantal, vocalic, nasal, voiced, high, low, and back, are essentially the same as those already discussed. Note the brief descriptions of articulatory characteristics entailed by the other feature labels—those not discussed explicitly earlier.

10.14

±consonantal

±vocalic

±continuant — The air stream passes through the oral cavity with no stoppage.

±nasal

±anterior — There is an obstruction at or in front of the alveolar ridge.

±coronal — The front part of the tongue is involved in the articulation.

±voiced

±strident — There is greater noisiness, or turbulence; the air stream passes over a rougher surface. (This feature is better defined acoustically.)

±high

±low

±back

±tense — There is explicit muscular tension in the oral cavity, and a tendency for longer and more distinct articulation.

Figure 10.5 shows how we can use the features listed in 10.14 to represent the distinctions among the consonant symbols of English. Examine the chart to see how it manages both to express similarities among cer-

	p	b	t	d	k	g	č	j	f	v	θ	ð	s	z	š	ž	m	n	ŋ	r	l
consonantal	+	+	+	+	+	+	+	+	+	+	+	+	+	+	+	+	+	+	+	+	+
vocalic	−	−	−	−	−	−	−	−	−	−	−	−	−	−	−	−	−	−	−	+	+
continuant	−	−	−	−	−	−	−	−	+	+	+	+	+	+	+	+	−	−	−	+	+
nasal	−	−	−	−	−	−	−	−	−	−	−	−	−	−	−	−	+	+	+	−	−
anterior	+	+	+	+	−	−	−	−	+	+	+	+	+	+	−	−	+	+	−	−	+
coronal	−	−	+	+	−	−	+	+	−	−	+	+	+	+	+	+	−	+	−	+	+
voiced	−	+	−	+	−	+	−	+	−	+	−	+	−	+	−	+	+	+	+	+	+
strident	−	−	−	−	−	−	+	+	+	+	−	−	+	+	+	+	−	−	−	−	−

Figure 10.5: Some phonological features of English consonants.

tain subsets of consonants, but yet provides a distinct combination of plus and minus feature values for each one of the consonants.

In figure 10.6 the features for English semivowels are charted. Notice that semivowels are distinguished from consonants (and vowels) by having a minus marking for both the feature consonantal and the feature vocalic.

	w	y	h
consonantal	−	−	−
vocalic	−	−	−
high	+	+	−
back	+	−	−

Figure 10.6: Some phonological features of English semivowels.

Figure 10.7 charts the features for English vowels. Examine the chart, noting how it expresses similarities among subsets of vowels (for example, the class of mid vowels is defined by minus marking for both the feature high and the feature low) but yet provides a distinct combination of plus and minus feature values for each one of the vowels.

	i	ɪ	e	ɛ	æ	u	ʊ	o	ə	ɔ	ɑ
consonantal	−	−	−	−	−	−	−	−	−	−	−
vocalic	+	+	+	+	+	+	+	+	+	+	+
high	+	+	−	−	−	+	+	−	−	−	−
low	−	−	−	+	+	−	−	−	−	+	+
back	−	−	−	−	−	+	+	+	+	+	+
tense	+	−	+	−	−	+	−	+	−	+	−

Figure 10.7: Some phonological features of English vowels.

The formal notation presented in 10.15 illustrates how features can be used to express the phonological rule of PALATALIZATION with greater explicitness and efficiency than the wording in 10.12.

10.15

$$+\text{anterior} \rightarrow -\text{anterior} \ \Big/ \ \overline{\begin{array}{c}+\text{strident}\\+\text{coronal}\end{array}} + \begin{array}{c}-\text{vocalic}\\+\text{high}\\-\text{back}\end{array}$$

The rule in 10.15 reads as follows: change the feature +anterior to −anterior when it is part of a sound that also has the features +strident and +coronal and is followed across a syllable boundary by a sound with the features −vocalic, +high, and −back. (The arrow means "changes to" and the diagonal line means "in the following context." The horizontal line above +strident and +coronal shows the place of +anterior in the structure to which the rule applies: it is part of a sound, together with +strident and +coronal, which precedes another sound having the features −vocalic, +high, and −back. The large plus sign indicates a syllable boundary.)

A formal notation like the one in 10.15 is preferable to a statement in words, such as was given in 10.12, for a number of reasons. First, features can generalize the type of sound to which the rule applies. Instead of stating that PALATALIZATION applies to [s] and [z], the formal rule defines its input as sounds marked +anterior, +strident, and +coronal—*both* [s] and [z] but *only* [s] and [z] are so marked. Second, instead of stating that PALATALIZATION changes [s] to [š] and changes [z] to [ž], the rule in 10.15 simply changes +anterior to −anterior, leaving all other features unchanged. *Both* [s] and [z] are marked +anterior, +strident, and +coronal, but *only* these two sounds are so marked, so just by changing +anterior to −anterior, 10.15 changes [s] to [š] and [z] to [ž], leaving markings for the feature ±voiced unchanged.

When I first introduced the formal notational system for syntactic transformations in chapter 5 and claimed that it was simpler than statements in ordinary prose, you may have felt some skepticism, for the notation was certainly not simple to learn. But when I went on in later chapters to organize a large body of syntactic facts around the notational system, it became clear how much simpler the notational system really was than prose formulations of the transformations would have been. You may now have similar doubts about the formalized phonological notation in 10.15. But just as in syntax, the system proves itself when applied to the full range of highly complex facts comprising the phonology of English. It is, however, well beyond the scope of this book to develop these rules any further, for such a treatment would double the size of the book. But, having read this chapter, you should be able to read and understand fuller treatments of the generative phonology of English mentioned in the suggestions for further reading at the end of this chapter.

EXERCISES

1   Two very useful exercises were written into the body of the chapter. If you did not do them, you may have found the reading of later portions of the chapter less fruitful. The first such exer-

cise was to transcribe phonetically the example words listed in
10.1, 10.2, and 10.3, and having done so, to scramble your
transcriptions and then practice reading them aloud. The second
suggestion was to expand the display of phonemic analysis given
in 10.5 to gain additional insight into the nature of the phoneme
and observe the principles determining systematic sound alternations in English. Another useful project, not mentioned in the
body of the chapter, is to try to build a matrix of minimal pairs
to verify for yourself the contrasts among English phonemes.
You should probably make one matrix for consonants and another for vowels. For the former, list the consonant symbols
across the top and also along the side of a large sheet of paper.
In the spaces on the paper where each phoneme's column inter-
sects other phonemes' rows write a minimal pair to verify the
contrast. Many of the pairs will be easy to find, others not so
easy. And minimal pairs may not exist at all to verify a few of the
contrasts. This task may seem mechanical, but it can lead you to
interesting insights into the system of contrastive relationships
that holds among the sounds of English. Here is a sample portion
of the consonant matrix:

	p	b	t	d	. . .
p		pin/bin	pan/tan	pan/dan	
b			bin/tin	bin/din	
t				tin/din	
d					
.					
.					

2   Apply the phonological rules in 10.12 and create a display, like
the one in 10.13, to account for the variant pronunciations of
morphemes in the bases of the following sets of words:

a. contrite, contrition
b. revise, revision
c. fuse, fusion
d. deride, derisive, derision
e. corrode, corrosive, corrosion

3   See if you can express the other phonological rules given in
10.12 in the same kind of formal feature notation as the PALA-
TALIZATION rule in 10.15. If you attempt a formal statement
of the SPIRANTIZATION rule, try to revise it as well, so that
it will do its part in accounting for the phonological alternations
manifested in the sets of words listed below. And after you re-

vise the SPIRANTIZATION rule, see if you can apply it together with the other rules and create a display like the one in 10.13 to account for the variant pronunciations of morphemes in the bases of the sets of words listed here:

a. plastic, plasticity
b. electric, electricity, electrician
c. logic, logician
d. music, musician

4   Copy the numbers 1 to 6 on a sheet of paper and beside each number list all the phonological symbols of English whose feature composition includes the feature or features listed with the number here:

(1) +consonantal
    −vocalic
(2) +consonantal
    +vocalic
(3) −consonantal
    +vocalic
(4) +continuant
(5) +strident
(6) +tense

FOR FURTHER READING

Comprehensive introductory treatments of articulatory phonetics and the phonemes of English are included by Gleason (1961) and Hockett (1958). Kurath (1964) presents a quite comprehensive treatment of the facts of English phonology essentially in the structuralist tradition. Trager and Smith (1963) present the classic structuralist analysis of the phonemes of English.

Harms (1968) and Schane (1973) introduce generative phonological theory. Liles (1971) in the last several chapters provides a readable introduction to English generative phonology. Chomsky and Halle (1968) give the most comprehensive phonology of English in their foundation work of generative phonological theory.

A Basic Transformational Grammar for English

A SET OF PHRASE STRUCTURE RULES FOR ENGLISH

i $\quad S \rightarrow (\begin{Bmatrix} Q \\ IMP \end{Bmatrix}) + (not) + NP + AUX + VP + (ADVM) + (ADVP) + (ADVT) + (ADVR) \ldots$

ii $\quad VP \rightarrow \begin{Bmatrix} V + (NP) + (PP) + (PP) \\ be + (\begin{Bmatrix} ADJP \\ NP \end{Bmatrix}) \end{Bmatrix}$

iii $\quad \begin{Bmatrix} ADVM \\ ADVP \\ ADVT \\ ADVR \end{Bmatrix} \rightarrow \begin{Bmatrix} PP \\ ADV \end{Bmatrix}$

iv $\quad ADJP \rightarrow ADJ + (PP)$

v $\quad PP \rightarrow P + NP$

vi $\quad NP \rightarrow \begin{Bmatrix} (DET) + N \\ NP + S \\ it + S \end{Bmatrix}$

vii $\quad AUX \rightarrow TNS + (M) + (PERF) + (PROG)$

viii $\quad TNS \rightarrow \begin{Bmatrix} \text{-prs} \\ \text{-pst} \end{Bmatrix}$

ix $\quad M \rightarrow \{can, may, will, shall, should, must, \ldots\}$

x $\quad PERF \rightarrow have\text{-}en$

xi	PROG → be-ing
xii	V → {build, work, write, . . .}
xiii	ADV → {enthusiastically, there, then, deliberately, . . . / how, where, when, why, . . .
xiv	ADJ → {diligent, fond, happy, . . .}
xv	P → {with, at, in, for, . . .}
xvi	DET → {a, the, this, that, . . .}
xvii	N → {woman, leader, car, William, play, . . . / who(m), what

A SET OF TRANSFORMATIONS FOR ENGLISH

1 INDIRECT OBJECT MOVEMENT (OPT)
SD: X " $[_{VP}$ V " NP $[_{PP}$ " $[_P$ to$]_P$ " NP$]_{PP}$ " Y$]_{VP}$ " Z
SC: 1   2   3   4   5   6   7 ⇒
    1   2 5 3   0   6   7
COND: Sometimes must apply; sometimes cannot

2 PASSIVE (OPT)
SD: X"NP"$[_{AUX}$Y"$]_{AUX}$ $[_{VP}$V"NP"Z"$]_{VP}$ W
SC: 1 2   3   4   5   6   7 ⇒
    1 5   3$[_{PASS}$be-en$]_{PASS}$ 4   6 $[_{PP}[_P$by$]_P$ 2$]_{PP}$ 7
COND: Sometimes blocked

3 NOMINALIZATION (OBL)
SD: X " $[_{NP}$ it $[_S$ " Y $]_S$ $]_{NP}$ " Z
SC: 1   2   3   4 ⇒
    1   2 that 3   4
COND: Cannot apply if 3 begins with Q or question word

4 EXTRAPOSITION (OPT)
SD: X " $[_{NP}$ it " S $]_{NP}$ " Y
SC: 1   2 3   4 ⇒
    1   2   4 3
COND: None

5 IT DELETION (OBL)
SD: X " $[_{NP}$ it " S $]_{NP}$ " Y
SC: 1   2 3   4 ⇒
    1   0 3   4
COND: None

6 RELATIVE PRONOUN INSERTION (OBL)

SD: $\quad$ X " $[_{NP}$ NP " $[_S$ Y " NP " Z $]_S$ $]_{NP}$ " W

SC: $\quad$ 1 $\qquad$ 2 $\qquad$ 3 $\quad$ 4 $\quad$ 5 $\qquad$ 6 $\Rightarrow$

$\qquad$ 1 $\qquad$ 2$\begin{Bmatrix} who \\ which \end{Bmatrix}$3 $\qquad$ 5 $\qquad$ 6

COND: $\quad$ 2 must be the same as 4

7 RELATIVE CLAUSE REDUCTION (OPT)

SD: $\quad$ X " $[_{NP}$ NP " $[_S$ $\begin{Bmatrix} who \\ which \end{Bmatrix}$ be TNS " Z$]_S$ $]_{NP}$ " W

SC: $\quad$ 1 $\qquad$ 2 $\qquad$ 3 $\qquad$ 4 $\qquad$ 5 $\Rightarrow$

$\qquad$ 1 $\qquad$ 2 $\qquad$ 0 $\qquad$ 4 $\qquad$ 5

COND: $\quad$ 4 cannot be an NP

8 MODIFIER SHIFT (OBL)

SD: $\quad$ X " $[_{NP}$ (DET) " N " $\begin{Bmatrix} ADJ \\ V\text{-ing} \end{Bmatrix}$ $]_{NP}$ " Y

SC: $\quad$ 1 $\qquad$ 2 $\quad$ 3 $\quad$ 4 $\qquad$ 5 $\Rightarrow$

$\qquad$ 1 $\qquad$ 2 $\quad$ 4 3 $\qquad$ 5

COND: $\quad$ 3 cannot be *someone* or *something*

9 NOT PLACEMENT (OBL)

SD: $\quad$ X " not " Y " $\begin{Bmatrix} TNS + M \\ TNS + have \\ TNS + be \\ TNS \end{Bmatrix}$ " Z

SC: $\quad$ 1 $\quad$ 2 $\quad$ 3 $\qquad$ 4 $\qquad$ 5 $\Rightarrow$

$\qquad$ 1 $\qquad$ 3 $\qquad$ 4 $\quad$ 2 $\quad$ 5

COND: None

10 CONTRACTION (OPT)

SD: $\quad$ X " $\begin{Bmatrix} TNS + M \\ TNS + have \\ TNS + be \\ TNS \end{Bmatrix}$ " not " Y

SC: $\quad$ 1 $\qquad$ 2 $\qquad$ 3 $\quad$ 4 $\Rightarrow$

$\qquad$ 1 $\qquad$ 2-n't $\qquad$ 4

COND: $\quad$ Blocked with certain modals (for example, *may*)

11 IMPERATIVE (OBL)

SD: $\quad$ IMP " you " TNS " will " X

SC: $\quad$ 1 $\quad$ 2 $\quad$ 3 $\quad$ 4 $\quad$ 5 $\Rightarrow$

$\qquad$ 0 $\quad$ 0 $\quad$ 3 $\quad$ 0 $\quad$ 5

COND: $\quad$ A verb in 5 cannot be a state

12 INVERSION (OBL)

SD: Q " NP " $\begin{cases} \text{TNS} + \text{M} \\ \text{TNS} + \text{have} \\ \text{TNS} + \text{be} \\ \text{TNS} \end{cases}$ (-n't) " X

SC: 1   2   3   4 ⇒
     1   3   2   4

COND: Cannot apply if 2 is a question word or whole S is a
       noun clause

13 QUESTION-WORD MOVEMENT (OBL)

SD: Q " X " {who(m), what, how, where, when, why} " Y

SC: 1   2   3   4 ⇒
     3   2   4

COND: None

14 Q DELETION (OBL)

SD: Q " X

SC: 1   2 ⇒
     0   2

COND: Cannot apply if whole S is a noun clause

15 AFFIX MOVEMENT (OBL)

SD: X " $\begin{cases} \text{-prs} \\ \text{-pst} \\ \text{-en} \\ \text{-ing} \end{cases}$ " $\begin{cases} \text{M} \\ \text{have} \\ \text{be} \\ \text{V} \end{cases}$ " Y

SC: 1   2   3   4 ⇒
     1   3   2   4

COND: None

16 DO SUPPORT (OBL)

SD: X " TNS " Y

SC: 1   2   3 ⇒
     1 do 2   3

COND: 1 is not M, *have, be,* V

Bibliography

ANDERSON, JOHN M. 1971. *The Grammar of Case.* Cambridge: Cambridge University Press.

BLOOMFIELD, LEONARD. 1933. *Language.* New York: Holt, Rinehart and Winston.

BOCHEŃSKI, J. M. 1965. *The Methods of Contemporary Thought.* Dordrecht, Netherlands: Reidel.

BURT, MARINA K. 1971. *From Deep to Surface Structure: An Introduction to Transformational Syntax.* New York: Harper and Row.

CHAFE, WALLACE L. 1970. *Meaning and the Structure of Language.* Chicago: University of Chicago Press.

CHOMSKY, NOAM. 1957. *Syntactic Structures.* The Hague: Mouton.

———. 1961. "Some Methodological Remarks on Generative Grammar." *Word* 17: 219–39.

———. 1965. *Aspects of the Theory of Syntax.* Cambridge, Mass.: M. I. T. Press.

CHOMSKY, NOAM, and HALLE, MORRIS. 1968. *The Sound Pattern of English.* New York: Harper and Row.

COOK, WALTER A., S.J. 1967. *An Introduction to Language Analysis.* Prepublication ed. Washington, D.C.: Georgetown University.

EHRMAN, MADELINE. 1966. *The Meanings of the Modals in Present-day American English.* The Hague: Mouton.

FILLMORE, CHARLES J. 1965. *Indirect Object Constructions in English and the Ordering of Transformations.* The Hague: Mouton.

———. 1968. "The Case for Case." *Universals in Linguistic Theory.* Edited by Emmon Bach and Robert T. Harms. New York: Holt, Rinehart and Winston.

———. 1970. "Types of Lexical Information." *Studies in Syntax and Semantics.* Edited by F. Kiefer. Dordrecht, Netherlands: Reidel.

FILLMORE, CHARLES J., and LANGENDOEN, D. TERENCE, eds. 1971. *Studies in Linguistic Semantics.* New York: Holt, Rinehart and Winston.

247

FODOR, JERRY A., and KATZ, JERROLD J., eds. 1966. *The Structure of Language: Readings in the Philosophy of Language.* Englewood Cliffs, N.J.: Prentice-Hall.

FRANCIS, W. NELSON. 1958. *The Structure of American English.* New York: Ronald Press Company.

FRIES, CHARLES C. 1952. *The Structure of English.* New York: Harcourt, Brace and World.

GLEASON, HENRY A. 1961. *An Introduction to Descriptive Linguistics.* Rev. ed. New York: Holt, Rinehart and Winston.

GRINDER, JOHN T., and ELGIN, SUZETTE HADEN. 1973. *Guide to Transformational Grammar: History Theory Practice.* New York: Holt, Rinehart and Winston.

HARMS, ROBERT T. 1968. *Introduction to Phonological Theory.* Englewood Cliffs, N.J.: Prentice-Hall.

HOCKETT, CHARLES F. 1958. *A Course in Modern Linguistics.* New York: Macmillan Company.

JACOBS, RODERICK A., and ROSENBAUM, PETER S., eds. 1970. *Readings in English Transformational Grammar.* Waltham, Mass.: Ginn and Company.

JESPERSEN, OTTO. 1961. *A Modern English Grammar on Historical Principles.* London: Allen and Unwin.

JOOS, MARTIN. 1957. *Readings in Linguistics I.* 4th ed. Chicago: University of Chicago Press.

———. 1964. *The English Verb: Form and Meanings.* Madison and Milwaukee: University of Wisconsin Press.

KATZ, JERROLD J. 1972. *Semantic Theory.* New York: Harper and Row.

KATZ, JERROLD J., and FODOR, JERRY A. 1963. "The Structure of a Semantic Theory." *Language* 39: 170–210.

KATZ, JERROLD J., and POSTAL, PAUL M. 1964. *An Integrated Theory of Linguistic Descriptions.* Cambridge, Mass.: M. I. T. Press.

KIEFER, F., ed. 1970. *Studies in Syntax and Semantics.* Dordrecht, Netherlands: Reidel.

KURATH, HANS. 1964. *A Phonology and Prosody of Modern English.* Ann Arbor: University of Michigan Press.

LAKOFF, GEORGE A., and ROSS, JOHN ROBERT. 1966. "A Criterion for Verb Phrase Constituency." *Mathematical Linguistics and Automatic Translation No. NSF–17.* Edited by Anthony Oettinger. Cambridge: Harvard Computation Laboratory.

LANGACKER, RONALD W. 1972. *Fundamentals of Linguistic Analysis.* New York: Harcourt Brace Jovanovich.

LANGENDOEN, D. TERENCE. 1970. *Essentials of English Grammar.* New York: Holt, Rinehart and Winston.

LEECH, GEOFFREY. 1969. *Towards a Semantic Description of English.* Bloomington: Indiana University Press.

LESTER, MARK. 1971. *Introductory Transformational Grammar of English.* New York: Holt, Rinehart and Winston.

LILES, BRUCE L. 1971. *An Introductory Transformational Grammar.* Englewood Cliffs, N.J.: Prentice-Hall.

LYONS, JOHN. 1969. *Introduction to Theoretical Linguistics.* Cambridge, Mass.: Cambridge University Press.

MALONE, JOSEPH L. 1967. "A Transformational Re-examination of English Questions." *Language* 43: 686–702.

MARCHAND, HANS. 1969. *The Categories and Types of Present-day English Word-formation.* 2d ed. Munich: Verlag C. H. Bech.

NIDA, EUGENE A. 1946. *Morphology: The Descriptive Analysis of Words.* Ann Arbor: University of Michigan Press.

Oxford English Dictionary (A corrected reissue of *A New English Dictionary on Historical Principles*). 1933. Oxford: Clarendon Press.

QUIRK, RANDOLPH; GREENBAUM, SIDNEY; LEECH, GEOFFREY; and SVARTVIK, JAN. 1972. *A Grammar of Contemporary English.* New York: Seminar Press.

REIBEL, DAVID A., and SCHANE, SANFORD A., eds. 1969. *Modern Studies in English: Readings in Transformational Grammar.* Englewood Cliffs, N.J.: Prentice-Hall.

ROSENBAUM, PETER S. 1967. *The Grammar of English Predicate Complement Constructions.* Cambridge, Mass.: M. I. T. Press.

ROSS, JOHN R. 1967. *Constraints on Variables in Syntax.* Ph.D. dissertation, M. I. T.

SAPIR, EDWARD. 1921. *Language: An Introduction to the Study of Speech.* New York: Harcourt, Brace and World.

———. 1950. *Selected Writings of Edward Sapir.* Edited by David G. Mandelbaum. Berkeley and Los Angeles: University of California Press.

SCHANE, SANFORD A. 1973. *Generative Phonology.* Englewood Cliffs, N.J.: Prentice-Hall.

SMITH, CARLOTA S. 1964. "Determiners and Relative Clauses in a Generative Grammar of English." *Language* 40: 37–52.

STAGEBERG, NORMAN C. 1970. *An Introductory English Grammar.* 2d ed. New York: Holt, Rinehart and Winston.

STEINBERG, DANNY D., and JAKOBOVITS, LEON A., eds. 1971. *Semantics: An Interdisciplinary Reader in Philosophy Linguistics and Psychology.* Cambridge: Cambridge University Press.

TOULMIN, STEPHEN. 1960. *The Philosophy of Science: An Introduction.* New York: Harper and Row.

TRAGER, GEORGE L., and SMITH, HENRY LEE. 1963. *An Outline of English Structure.* Washington, D.C.: American Council of Learned Societies.

Index

WXYZ

Printer and Binder: The Maple Press Company
81 82 83 84 12 11 10 9 8 7 6 5 4